THE EYE OF THE STORM

THE EYE OF THE STORM

THE VIEW FROM THE CENTRE
OF A POLITICAL SCANDAL

ROB WILSON

Biteback Publishing

First published in Great Britain in 2014 by
Biteback Publishing Ltd
Westminster Tower
3 Albert Embankment
London SE1 7SP
Copyright © Rob Wilson 2014

ISBN 978-1-84954-501-3

10 9 8 7 6 5 4 3 2 1

A CIP catalogue record for this book is available from the British Library.

Set in Adobe Garamond Pro by 525 Graphic Design

Printed and bound in Great Britain by
CPI Group (UK) Ltd, Croydon CR0 4YY

MIX
Paper from
responsible sources
FSC® C020471
FSC
www.fsc.org

CONTENTS

ACKNOWLEDGEMENTS

A number of people have helped with the writing of this book. Above all, I would like to thank sincerely those politicians who generously agreed to be interviewed and co-operate with my writing about their experiences. The events I describe were nearly always life-changing; in most instances the person lost their job and saw long-cherished career ambitions extinguished. Many of the matters at the heart of each chapter were embarrassing and the experiences were often personally very painful. In some cases, the emotions are clearly still raw.

Even for hardened politicians it cannot have been easy to dig up bad memories and talk with frankness about such difficult times. Some of those approached understandably refused to be interviewed. I hope that those who kindly gave me their time and shared their views and memories with me will feel that I have been fair, accurate and that the book serves a useful purpose.

I should also like to thank those around Westminster and in the media who have shown an interest in the book. Even brief and informal conversations have led me to sources or prompted me to ask questions about the various scandals and crises that I might otherwise have missed. Although the book is aimed equally at a politically-interested audience and the general public, I hope those within Westminster and the political media will find much of interest and much to reflect upon.

Once again, I would like to thank the team at Biteback Publishing for commissioning me to write a book, and for their support and patience. Olivia Beattie, Managing Editor at Biteback, has been a superb editor. Her constructive and thoughtful comments have made the book better than it might otherwise have been.

Writing books can get in the way of family time, particularly as much of this book was largely written on holiday! I would like to thank Jane, Joseph, Elizabeth, Fern and Megan for being patient with me. We still managed to visit the places we wanted to go to and do the things we wanted, albeit occasionally delayed. This book is dedicated to them as a thank you for letting me write it.

INTRODUCTION

"When you're not in that firestorm you just can't appreciate how stressful it is."

         – Conservative MP

'Parliament's darkest day' blazed the headline on the front page of *The Times* on 15 April 2009. The scandal over MPs' and peers' expenses was raging at its fiercest, with fresh outrages by apparently greedy and grasping MPs being revealed on a daily basis on the front pages of the newspapers. It was, as the current Speaker of the House of Commons would later describe it, a case of 'reputational carnage' affecting the entire political class.

For once, the goings-on of MPs in Parliament were at the front and centre of public consciousness and conversations. The British public appeared united in its disgust and outrage that whilst they suffered amidst the fallout of the financial crisis of 2008 and the worst recession in living memory, their so-called political representatives had been caught helping themselves to second homes, expensive televisions and even duck houses, moats and pornographic films from the public purse. The impact of the scandal has seared itself into public memory; some four years later, a poll found that politicians were trusted less than journalists, estate agents, and even bankers.

Few, if any, MPs or candidates could escape the fallout from the expenses scandal. But the politicians whose cases were at the very centre of the scandal suddenly found their reputations and careers in ruins. For those charged on the front pages of the newspapers, there seemed to be no way of getting a fair hearing against the wave of public anger, hostility and cynicism, even when they had a reasonable explanation. And it wasn't just their professional lives that were affected; it was their privacy and their families' lives too. What had started as a scoop by one newspaper had turned into a runaway triumph for many, emboldening the entire media and turning its appetite for political scandal, and particularly anything expenses-related, into a frenzy. Journalists were looking into seemingly all aspects of MPs' lives. Even the Parliamentary Standards Commissioner complained that he had *Daily Mail* photographers outside his house and felt under pressure. Whilst numerous MPs threw in the towel, a few buckled completely under the strain, with at least one suffering a mental collapse at the prospect of jail time and another attempting suicide.

The 2009 expenses scandal was, of course, not the beginning of political scandal and not the first political crisis in Britain. But nor has it marked the end of it. Despite a huge clear-out of MPs at the 2010 general election, their replacement with a younger generation, and solemn promises by the main party leaders to clean up politics, in the few years since the expenses scandal five senior members of the Cabinet have been forced to resign as a result of scandals, with one even going to jail. The political class as a whole was once again brought into disrepute when the close links between leading politicians and media barons were revealed during the scandal over phone hacking and similar unscrupulous behaviour by members of the press. And the usual stream of stories about MPs' personal conduct and their private lives has continued, with political blogs and social media now providing another, less-controlled space in which rumours can gather momentum and the fires of potential scandals be fuelled.

QUESTIONS

In an age where public cynicism towards politicians in Britain now appears to be firmly entrenched, it would seem that any politician could find him or herself in the line of fire, almost at any time. And when a politician finds themselves on the front pages and towards the top of broadcast bulletins – in the eye of the storm, so to speak – they would appear to have the odds stacked against their political survival. The person at the centre of the storm would be forgiven for assuming that the public, if not their colleagues and the 'Westminster village', would presume them guilty until proven innocent. When journalists start picking up another's 'scoop' and following it up, the odour of bad publicity starts to spread and it suggests that those 'in the know' believe there is more to come. If the media 'pack' starts to scent blood – and that an admission of guilt, a resignation or sacking may be in the offing – all hell can break loose for the politician at the centre of it.

Looking back at individual scandals or crises alongside each other prompts us to ask some interesting questions: just how do those politicians in the eye of the storm attempt to overcome the odds and emerge with their political careers and reputations intact? What strategies are used? Why do some succeed and some fail? And although most people in Britain would agree that vigorous press scrutiny of politicians is a good thing, what lessons could be learned and what mistakes should be avoided in the heat of the moment to stop otherwise worthwhile political careers being needlessly cut short? Given that there are so many scandals of varying degrees of seriousness in politics, is there a 'standard operating manual' or reserve of expertise on hand to support politicians in trouble, or do they find themselves isolated, forced to reinvent the wheel alone as the clamour grows for their downfall?

THE HUMAN SIDE OF POLITICAL SCANDALS

Alongside the strategic and tactical considerations, it must be remembered that periods of crisis and scandal form some of the most intense periods of political careers, and indeed the lives, of those at the centre of them. Whilst the attention of the media and the public often swiftly moves on, regardless of the outcome, the personal impacts can last for years. Indeed, the experience is often life-changing. It is at these times that the strongest friendships may be formed, consolidated or broken. Invariably, spouses, parents, children, neighbours and friends find themselves dragged in. Crises and scandals make for exciting and compelling stories with moments of high drama. But their impact on real, *human* lives can be devastating, and sometimes harrowing to recount, even years later.

This book is an attempt to tell the human story of what it was like, and to give readers a sense of what it *is* like, to be the person at the centre of a political scandal or crisis. It goes behind the face in the photograph and the name in the headlines. It tries to convey how things looked through the eyes of the person looking back at the bank of photographers and journalists outside their house, and into the eyes of colleagues, staff, frightened spouses and children. Likeable or loathsome as readers may find the book's subjects, it reveals the inside story of what really goes on when political careers are, to all appearances, hanging by a thread.

The book is based upon a series of interviews with people in politics who, in recent years, have found themselves at the centre of a political storm. The focus is predominantly on the years since the 2010 general election and the formation of the coalition government, and the book covers many of the most significant scandals to have hit Cabinet ministers over the course of the coalition since its formation. But with the issue of expenses still looming so heavily over British politics (expenses still remains to this day a 'third rail' issue for political careers, as will be discussed later), the book also recollects on one of the most prominent cases of the MPs' expenses scandal in 2009. For a broader perspective, the book will also look back on a scandal that emerged from the Blair–Brown in-fighting in the 2000s and the experiences of one Conservative Leader of the Opposition whose tenure seemed, from the outside, to be in a permanent state of crisis.

Each chapter tells the story from the perspective of the person at the centre of the storm. Although I have sought to paint a fair and accurate picture of what happened in each case, the chapters do not attempt to provide a completely objective assessment of the various scandals or to take accounts from everyone involved. At times of scandal and crisis in politics, the people at the centre often fail to get a fair hearing. When they do publish a full account from their viewpoint, it is often too late and the public and their peers have already made up their minds. By describing the events from beginning to end from the perspective of the person accused, this book seeks to redress the balance.

The presentation of each case may not be entirely neutral, but I hope readers will find that I have not been completely uncritical. I am not defending politicians as a 'class', nor did I set out to defend any of the subjects of the book. I have not tried to make a judgement on the rights and wrongs. With the opportunity to look back on events that often gathered momentum very quickly and amidst excited reporting and speculation, readers may wish to make their own reappraisal.

As will be clear by now, this book is not meant to be a definitive history of the scandals and crises of recent years in British politics. Nonetheless, I hope it will give a sense of the dynamics of political crises. It may inform thinking about how crises can be better handled: how political parties can support their own at times of trouble and how those in trouble can better help themselves, or at least avoid making unnecessary mistakes. What follows may also inform the ongoing debate about the activities of the press, and the relationship between the press and politicians.

Above all, my aim for this book is to provide readers with a better sense of the human beings that play out the game of politics. The approaches people take to political crises, how they view themselves and the situation they find themselves in, reveal a huge amount about the true character of politicians. It is a well-known truism that a person's character is most clearly revealed when the chips are down. I hope this book will give readers a sense of the real character of their politicians, as revealed during times of greatest stress.

CHAPTER OVERVIEW

The book's opening chapter tells the story of one of the most intense scandals to hit a member of the Conservative–Liberal Democrat coalition government, the aftershocks of which are still making the news as this book goes to print. In the space of little more than thirty days, Andrew Mitchell, the then newly-appointed Government Chief Whip charged with bringing discipline to the increasingly rebellious Conservative parliamentary party, was driven to personal despair and out of his job as the Government's enemies used allegations that he had used class-based insults during an argument with a police officer to launch wave after wave of attacks against him and the Government. Mitchell, a powerful, if sometimes abrasive figure with friends throughout the British and international political elites, found himself quickly helpless against the onslaught as the media piled in.

To his shock, Mitchell found himself very much thrust into the eye of the storm. Even if most of the allegations made against him have subsequently been discredited, and he is now viewed sympathetically across the political spectrum as the victim of a dangerous conspiracy, for a month in the autumn of 2012 he was Public Enemy No. 1. His experiences provide a vivid account of life at the centre of a major scandal in the British politics of today.

But the 'plebgate' affair involving Andrew Mitchell was not the first scandal to hit the coalition government, nor was he the first Cabinet minister of that government to be forced to resign. Following the early departure of David Laws, Chapters 2 and 3 detail the events leading up to the departures of two other political heavyweights, from the Conservatives and Liberal Democrats respectively: Liam Fox and Chris Huhne.

Fox, a reforming Defence Secretary at a time when the country was engaged in a courageous but risky military intervention in Libya (on top of its ongoing engagement in Afghanistan), found himself engulfed by allegations after stories about the activities of his best friend were allowed to snowball, bringing Fox into disrepute. Not for the first time, the growing scandal was played out against the backdrop of rumours and innuendo of a gay relationship between two men in politics who happened to be close friends. This element appears to be a particular source of fascination in political and media circles, further whetting appetites for drama. Perhaps out of disdain for such gossip, we will see how Fox's main problem was that he didn't treat the accusations against him seriously enough until it was too late.

Chris Huhne's fall from grace was far more protracted than either Fox's or Mitchell's, but the personal consequences were altogether far more drastic. Having sacrificed his marriage to stem the damaging publicity over an affair he was having, Huhne, as is well known, ended up in jail. In contrast to many of the other subjects of this book, Huhne was well aware of his guilt. What is fascinating about Huhne's case was his extraordinary ability to detach himself from the personal and emotional impact of the crisis he found himself in and to use his formidable powers of reasoning to plot his way out. Even though he ended up losing his liberty as well as his political career, Huhne projected such self-confidence throughout his time in the line of fire that his ultimate capitulation came as a genuine shock to politicians throughout Westminster, the media and probably many of the public. Through the sheer force of willpower and apparently unbreakable self-esteem, Huhne almost got away with it.

Chapters 4 and 5 deal in depth with a scandal that grew to embroil the entire coalition government, leading to a public inquiry that saw the Prime Minister and three of his predecessors, the Deputy Prime Minister and Chancellor, and several other Cabinet ministers present and past, summoned to give evidence before a judge. In December 2010, the issue of News Corporation's proposed takeover of the whole of BSkyB led to the biggest scandal to hit the coalition since the early resignation of David Laws over his expenses claims. Vince Cable, known to be a reluctant member of the Conservative–Lib Dem coalition, found himself at the very eye of the storm for several days after explosive comments he had made in a private conversation were published and broadcast in the media. Cable survived thanks to the strong banks of political capital he had built up both within his party and the public, but the episode threatened the new government's reputation for competence and dominated the top of the news agenda for several days.

Cable, however, got off lightly compared to the man left to pick up the pieces from his gaffe, Jeremy Hunt. As Chapter 5 details, having risen quietly but spectacularly through the ranks following his election to Parliament just five years earlier, by 2012 Hunt found himself laid low by the most toxic issue in British politics, and written off as a 'dead man walking' by virtually the entire media. When evidence linking Hunt's staff to apparent collusion with the business empire of Rupert Murdoch forced his closest aide to resign, most commentators assumed it was only a matter of time – and a short amount of time at that – before Hunt himself was forced to follow. Hunt's survival, which appeared almost miraculous at the time, owed something to luck, as the Leveson Inquiry bought him time to make his case and to have the charges against him ruled on by an independent judge, rather than a show trial in the court of public opinion. But it also owed much to Hunt's own determination to prove his innocence, and even more crucially, to the support he had in times of trouble from the Prime Minister and his party colleagues.

Chapters 6 and 7 look back at some of the crises and scandals in the latter years of the New Labour government. If Jeremy Hunt seemed to have virtually the entire media and the whole of the political Left seeking his demise over BSkyB, the fall of Charles Clarke as described in Chapter 6 shows how politicians can be weakened at times of crisis by enemies from their own side. Clarke, who as Home Secretary had played a leading role in Britain's response to the worst-ever terror attack on the mainland, found himself caught up in the vicious civil war for control of the Labour Party between supporters of Tony Blair and Gordon Brown.

Clarke, a political veteran of the Kinnock era, ultimately ran out of time trying to fix the failings of the civil service machinery which had caused huge embarrassment for the New Labour government over the issue of foreign national prisoners. A target in the eyes of the Brownites, Clarke was forced to pay the price when the issue became a focal point of a dire local elections campaign that led Blair to fear that his hitherto impregnable grip on the premiership was starting to slip away. Clarke's case illustrates not just the perils of holding a portfolio as vast as that of Home Secretary, but also the need for politicians not to take for granted the support of their own side should they find themselves in trouble.

Chapters 7 and 8 look back at one of the greatest scandals of any era in British politics – the scandal over MPs' expense claims. One of the most apparently notorious cases of the scandal, and one of its biggest 'losers' was Jacqui Smith, Britain's first ever female Home Secretary. Smith, a tough former Government Chief Whip, went from dealing with terrorist attacks and fierce political battles to the excruciatingly embarrassing task of trying to explain why she had claimed for reimbursement from the taxpayer for a pornographic movie watched by her husband. Smith then suffered the double indignity of being subject to a lengthy investigation, and ultimately being found guilty, for improper use of the second home allowance – a charge she strenuously denies to this day. In the space of a few months, Smith found her reputation and high-flying career in ruins and the health of her family life at risk under the glare of publicity and deep public anger.

It is not only senior politicians and Cabinet ministers who find themselves embroiled in scandals. Many of the politicians who hit the headlines during the expenses scandal were ordinary backbenchers without big staffs to support them or their party leaderships riding to the rescue. Whether such people sink or swim as they find their homes surrounded by photographers, face journalists raking over every aspect of their lives, with local and national opponents on the hunt, owes much to their own actions and character – and how their families are able to cope. The case of Stewart Jackson vividly illustrates what life can be like for backbenchers when trouble hits.

The expenses issue is not over, as former Culture Secretary Maria Miller found out to her cost. MPs live in the knowledge that they are treading on thin ice when it comes to their expense claims. Even claims that are within the rules and are approved by the new Independent Parliamentary Standards Authority can end up being hugely damaging to the reputation and career of the MP in question if they are spun a certain way. Nadhim Zahawi, rising star of the 2010 intake of Conservative MPs, found this out to his cost when a blunder that had escaped his attention shot him into prominence and onto the pages of the tabloids for all the wrong reasons.

If Chapters 1 to 8 have investigated high intensity periods of crisis of a relatively short duration, Chapter 9 takes a slightly differ-ent approach. Rather than focusing on a specific point of crisis, the chapter explores how low-level but long-term exposure to seemingly relentless negative criticism, pressure and hostility from the media and political opponents (and sometimes so-called colleagues) can affect the outlook, and even the psyche of the person at the centre of it. It does so by looking at one of the most unforgiving jobs in British politics: Leader of the Opposition.

Being Leader of the Opposition is a brutal slog at the best of times. But for William Hague, then a relatively unknown

36-year-old, taking on the job as leader of a party that had been in Government for eighteen years, had no recent experience of opposition, was divided, exhausted and dejected by its shattering defeat at the 1997 general election and facing the ruthless New Labour political machine headed by a hugely popular and charismatic Prime Minister in Tony Blair, was to prove particularly gruelling. Hague describes his four-year ordeal in the job as the 'night shift'. Although Hague prides himself on his rationality and lack of emotion, the chapter explores how far the constant stream of criticism, mockery, challenges to his authority and ultimately the crushing personal rejection, got under Hague's skin and changed him as a person.

The concluding chapter will seek to identify the lessons that can be learned from the tales of scandals and crises in the book. The emphasis will be less on avoiding crises and scandals from happening in the first place – in an age of ever-declining deference and new spaces on the internet and social media for allegations and rumours to take root, they are likely to remain a permanent feature of our politics. Instead, I look at questions such as: what is the best way to handle a crisis? What are the key decisions to be taken and when?

The concluding chapter will also reflect on what the factors were that allowed Jeremy Hunt to survive despite finding himself in the crosshairs of almost the entire media, with an opposition baying for political blood and an angry public enraged at yet another abuse of power and looking for someone to blame. It will also analyse what allowed Chris Huhne to survive for as long as he did, comparing it to the responses that saw Andrew Mitchell driven out of office and nearly into a personal meltdown over what he might or might not have said to a policeman in a brief disagreement of which there is no reliable record.

CHAPTER 1

<u>ANDREW MITCHELL'S HEARTBREAK</u>

*"My first aim was to get back my life, then to get back my reputation
and third to get back my job. But the job was very much third – by a
long way. There was a point where I wasn't sure if I did [want it back].
Indeed, there was a point where I was going to emigrate. We were going
to go. Not only was I going to leave Parliament and cause a by-election,
we were going to leave the country."*

– Andrew Mitchell MP

On 19 October 2012, after twenty-eight days of being at
the centre of public attention and an incessant bombard-
ment by the media over the 'plebgate' (or 'gategate') affair,
Andrew Mitchell resigned from his position as Government Chief
Whip. Mitchell was mentally and physically drained after being, as
he describes it, 'hunted like a wild animal'. He was by now being
told by some political friends at No. 10, to 'lie low, ride things out
and let it blow away – then you can come back'. The same had been
said at the start of his crisis.

His personal friends had wanted him to fight back against the
allegations and torrent of hostile press stories, telling him that to lie
low was a mistake and that he would be 'stitched up like a kipper'.
Mitchell basically accepted the advice of his political friends, but in

truth his ability to make any rational decision was limited. His judgement had deserted him due to the emotional and physical impact of events. Mitchell felt sapped of energy, so that even the smallest movement took too much effort. He needed somebody to take charge, to tell him, 'No, this is the strategy and this is what you need to do.'

Had Mitchell accepted the advice from No. 10 to lie low, he believes it would have killed him. For the twenty-eight days at the centre of the storm he had not been able to eat and had barely slept; he had taken to chain-smoking small cigars. He couldn't get out of bed and would sit with his mobile phone and BlackBerry lined up on the duvet, just sitting there for hours. When he did manage to sleep he woke up with the most terrible foreboding and feeling of injustice – that he had been not only wronged, but conspired against. Having found himself at the centre of a political scandal, Mitchell plunged into a sort of depression. 'Plebgate' had changed his life: it had altered fundamentally the way people perceived him, ruined his reputation and seemingly destroyed his career.

At its peak, Mitchell's family believed he was withering away – suffering from the symptoms of what some might describe as a broken heart. 'I wouldn't have tried to kill myself or anything like that, but if nothing had changed it would have killed me.' Without a fight-back, an attempt to clear his name and regain his reputation, he might simply have faded away.

◇◇◇◇

On 4 September 2012, Andrew Mitchell was moved from Secretary of State for International Development to Government

Chief Whip as part of David Cameron's first major Cabinet reshuffle. There had been widespread unrest on the Conservative Party back benches, with a number of significant rebellions, and the Whips' Office was largely blamed.

George Osborne was among those who felt a change was required. Someone was needed to get a grip of the parliamentary party, someone with experience, charm and a hint, or perhaps more than a hint, of menace. Mitchell was felt to have these attributes in the right combination, so Osborne, William Hague, the Prime Minister and Ed Llewellyn set about convincing Mitchell that he was the right man for the job.

At one level, Mitchell didn't need much convincing. He'd already played a key part in the Whips' Office under the premiership of John Major. The MPs in the Whips' Office of that era formed a very close bond in the most difficult of circumstances. Mitchell, working late into the night with colleagues to keep the beleaguered government afloat, spent more time with them than with his wife and family. Friendships were made during that extraordinary time (when the government was winning by one or two votes late into the night) that became unbreakable. In particular, Mitchell formed a very close friendship with David Davis, later a leadership rival to, and no friend of, David Cameron.

But the Whips' Office had changed enormously over the intervening decades and Mitchell had his doubts as to whether he was the right man. In particular, he was concerned that over half the parliamentary party had been newly elected in 2010 and its ethos perhaps didn't quite have the same reserves of loyalty as in bygone eras. Worse still, he felt he had spent much of his time as Secretary of State for International Development travelling to far-flung parts of the world and felt he didn't know a large chunk of the new MPs, even though numerous Conservative MPs and candidates had attended the 'social action' projects Mitchell and his team had organised in Rwanda and Sierra Leone.

However, he ultimately agreed to the appointment on one condition: it was to be his Whips' Office, with the people he wanted. The appointment of his old colleague from the Major government Whips' Office, Greg Knight, and his Parliamentary Private Secretary, Mark Lancaster, demonstrated that he had got his way: these were his own people. There was a substantial clear-out of those who were deemed to have performed poorly or whom Mitchell thought were better suited elsewhere.

However, this changing of the guard left huge bitterness and resentment among those who were sacked – which would return in due course to haunt Mitchell. Whips are well known for their ability to move quietly in the shadows and to strike when an opponent is at their weakest. Even before 'plebgate', Mitchell had made enemies who wished him ill and were keenly waiting for when the time was right. In these circumstances, his position as Chief Whip was slightly precarious from the start.

The origins of the 'plebgate' story in fact go back over two years before the fateful, and still fiercely disputed, incident by the front gates of Downing Street on 19 September 2012. Shortly after Mitchell became a Cabinet minister in May 2010 he had an encounter with the police, although this time at the back entrance to Downing Street. Mitchell asked the police on the back gate to open it and let him through on his bicycle but they refused. He explained he was a Cabinet minister, showed his pass and told them that he was keeping the Prime Minister waiting for a meeting. It made no difference: he was sent around to the front gate, much to his annoyance, and was late for a meeting in the Cabinet Room.

Mitchell reported the incident to the Head of Security at Downing Street. There appeared to be no hard feelings from the police officers at the time, but the incidents between the police and Mitchell, and indeed other Cabinet ministers trying to access Downing Street, did not end there. Around a year later, on 7 June 2011, the Head of Downing Street Security, John Groves, felt compelled to write a letter of formal complaint to Inspector Ken Russell, the Metropolitan Police inspector in charge of safeguarding Downing Street, 'about the conduct of your Officers who manage access into the rear of Downing Street at D11'.

In his letter, Groves stated that:

Over the last few months there have been a handful of incidents where Cabinet Ministers (including Andrew Mitchell, Secretary of State for International Development) have either not been allowed access through the L Shape Road or have not been recognised/ identified within a reasonable time period … This morning, there were two further incidences where DPG officers refused access to a Cabinet Minister who was here to attend Cabinet. In one incident, Andrew Mitchell was, again, stopped from entering the L Shape road on his bicycle. According to this Cabinet Minister, the Police Officer XXXXXXX said that he did recognise who he [Andrew Mitchell] was but would not let him. No clear reason was given.

Groves went on to say that he could 'not see any just reason why access was refused' and that, as far as he was concerned, members of the Cabinet were entitled to unfettered access to Downing Street at any time of day or night and at any entry point. Police officers had an obligation, he said, to ensure that ministers' access was facilitated as quickly and smoothly as possible, 'not least because they are here to see the Prime Minister'.

Around 7.30 p.m. on 19 September 2012, Mitchell left his office at 9 Downing Street to head to a meeting at the Carlton Club where he was due to speak. He cycled down Downing Street towards the front gates. Mitchell had endured a difficult day dealing with colleagues who had been sacked or not promoted and was feeling tired and emotionally drained. He was running late and probably a bit short-tempered.

Mitchell had been through the front gates of Downing Street several times before that week, but not always without difficulty. He was after all Chief Whip, with an office at No. 9 and one of the three senior ministers who worked in Downing Street, and had gone in and out of the gates either in his car or on his bicycle reasonably frequently. If a car was coming along the street the police would open the gates and, seeing Mitchell riding down Downing Street, would let him pass through at the same time. Sometimes they would simply open the gates for him. On other occasions, the officers would make Mitchell ask for the gates to be opened. Admittedly, the gates are heavy and difficult to open, particularly for any officers who are neither as young nor as fit as they might once have been. Some of the officers resented Mitchell's requests when he could easily have gone through the side gate, whilst others suggested it was an unnecessary security risk. Mitchell was felt by some of the police to be unnecessarily demanding, which perhaps explains how he became embroiled in the saga in the first place.

Indeed a leaked police memo to *The Times* (the sister newspaper of *The Sun*, which Mitchell subsequently sued for libel) shows that Downing Street police asked for advice over Mitchell's repeated demands to open the main gates after an incident on 18 September. Apparently timed and dated 00.48 September 19, 2012, according to *The Times*, the memo's author asked for guidance from a more senior officer, stating;

> [Mitchell] keeps requesting to leave Downing Street via the main vehicle gates. [He was] adamant he WAS GOING THROUGH THOSE GATES. As it was quite late and quiet at this point and in order not to create embarrassment to himself or the DPG [Diplomatic Protection Group] he was allowed on this occasion to leave via one of the main gates.

The email appeared to request backing for officers rather than a discussion about how to handle any further incidents – as if a confrontation was required to end the Chief Whip's ongoing requests once and for all. The opening of the gates was, with little doubt, a source of underlying friction between Mitchell and the police officers that had now been running for well over two years. In most circumstances it would have remained merely a source of mutual irritation – although the email of the night before had probably raised the stakes and sown the seeds for a showdown. So what really made this molehill into a mountain?

On the evening of 19 September, the police made Mitchell ask for the second day running that the front gates be opened. What happened next is hotly contested. Where there is agreement is that Mitchell asked a number of times for the gates to be opened and the police, quite probably with the previous day in mind and wishing to make a point, refused on each occasion. Mitchell was forced to dismount and walk his bicycle round the short distance to the pedestrian side gate. The officer who escorted him, PC Toby Rowland, alleged in a written note of the incident, a version of which was apparently leaked and later described in the media as a 'police log', that, as they walked to the side gate, with 'several members of the public present as is the norm opposite the pedestrian gate', Mitchell raged at him, 'Best you learn your fucking place … you don't run this fucking government … You're fucking plebs.'

PC Rowland wrote in his note that he could not say if Mitchell's alleged outburst was aimed at him individually, '… or the police present or the police service as a whole', a rather odd speculation for what was supposed to be a note of the bare facts. The 'log' records that 'the members of the public looked visibly shocked and I was somewhat taken aback by the language used and the view expressed by a senior government official'.

CCTV footage of the pavement outside Downing Street as Mitchell exited the side gate, which was broadcast by Channel 4's *Dispatches* programme in December 2012, appeared to show that there were in fact no members of the public in front of the gates and only one person walking past. However, the Director of Public Prosecutions would later adjudicate that 'previously unseen and unedited footage of the incident from five different cameras' showed that there were a small number of members of the public present immediately in front of the gate at the relevant time and others immediately off camera but in the vicinity, consistent with the officer's account that several members of the public were present. This evidence, to which the DPP referred in her decision not to charge Rowland and other officers with misconduct in public office or criminal conspiracy, remains hidden from public view at the time of this book's publication.

Mitchell has always denied calling the police officer a 'pleb' or a 'moron' or using any of the other pejorative descriptions attributed to him in the 'log' or in later press articles. He admits that he said, 'I thought you guys were supposed to fucking help us.' Mitchell says he muttered this not directly at the policeman, although it was loud enough for the policeman to respond, 'If you swear at me I will arrest you.' According to PC Rowland's account, he warned Mitchell not to swear at him, and warned him that if he *continued* swearing, Rowland would have no option but to arrest him under the Public Order Act. Mitchell then fell silent and left, saying, 'you haven't heard the last of this' as he cycled off. Mitchell himself claims to have used slightly less threatening language, saying he would take the matter up the following day, although he cannot remember the precise words he used.

That should have been the end of an unfortunate, impulsive but fairly trivial incident, the sort of thing that happens from time to time in daily life. People get annoyed and irritated with each other for many reasons and let off a bit of steam. Swearing in the presence of a police officer, as Mitchell would acknowledge, is wrong and, particularly in the case of a senior government minister, sets a poor example. Mitchell could have behaved differently and probably better (and to be fair to him he did quickly apologise), but nothing he did or said was in proportion to what followed.

Whilst Mitchell was speaking about international development at the Carlton Club he was oblivious to what was coming
next, thinking nothing further of the evening's events. Little did
he know that, once the events were discovered, it would provide
many people with the chance to take advantage, to both his and the
government's great discomfort.

The following afternoon, Mitchell was collecting pictures from
the government art archives for his new office. Ed Llewellyn,
the Prime Minister's long-serving chief of staff, called at around
2 p.m., opening with the line, 'Houston, we have a problem.' *The
Sun* had been given the story about the altercation with the police,
and Mitchell was needed to agree a response with the press team.
Mitchell still didn't believe it was a big story, but Llewellyn was
quick to put him right and ask him if he'd lost his temper, or called
the police 'plebs' and 'morons'. A horrified Mitchell immediately
denied it, only to be told that *The Sun* believed he had said that,
and more, and was planning to run it on the front page.

Together with Cameron's core advisers at No. 10, Mitchell quickly
realised the problem. Who was going to believe the word of a Cabinet
minister before the word of police officers? Whether or not the Prime
Minister and his colleagues believed Mitchell was hardly the point.
The public, pushed on by a popular tabloid, would not. Despite
its support for the Conservatives at the general election, *The Sun*
was feeling distinctly chilly towards the PM and Downing Street. A
host of things had gone wrong for the government, and the Leveson
Inquiry was sapping any remaining News International goodwill.

At the time the allegations against Mitchell surfaced, David
Cameron's government was already facing criticism over the

wealthy and elite backgrounds, and possibly the outlooks, of many of its members. Labour's attacks on a government perceived to be a 'chumocracy' dominated by posh boys and alumni of the Bullingdon Club who didn't know how the other half lived were all hitting home. Even fellow Tories, such as Nadine Dorries, joined in with barbs about Cameron and Osborne 'not knowing the price of milk'. It was a devastating cocktail that *The Sun* believed fed into a distinctly believable narrative of a posh Cabinet minister calling one of 'our boys in blue' a pleb. It was one of the worst possible public relations nightmares No. 10 could have imagined.

Worse still, two young female police officers, Nicola Hughes and Fiona Bone, had been shot and murdered in Manchester by a notorious gangster only the day before. It was the first time in Britain that two female officers had been killed on duty. The tragedy provided a reminder to the public of the dangerous and difficult work that police officers do. It also meant that, politically, any criticism of the police or suggestion that officers in Downing Street were lying would be dangerous, if not unthinkable in that context. To make any such accusation would have been political suicide.

Mitchell attended meetings that afternoon with Llewellyn, Craig Oliver, the Downing Street Communications Director, and others to work out the line to take. He then met Cameron and Osborne at 4 p.m. He told all of his innocence, asserting that he did not use words like 'pleb' or 'moron'. By now he was feeling quite shell-shocked. He could not understand why someone would invent such smears. With the pressure on, his good character under question, and a high-flying thirty-year political career suddenly in doubt, his ability over the next few days and weeks to make rational judgements quickly became shaky.

No. 10, however, was making rational judgements – but they were ones that suited the government and not necessarily Andrew Mitchell. It was at this point that Mitchell needed the strong support and strategic help of his close political and personal friend David Davis. Unfortunately, Davis was away in the USA having one of his many daredevil adventures, this time involving flying light aircraft, and could not be reached.

Mitchell was packed off to the duty sergeant to say he was sorry if he had caused a fuss and that he was willing to apologise to the officer. Mitchell cancelled all his Friday engagements, which included speaking engagements in support of fellow Conservative MPs, and rang PC Rowland to apologise personally for using bad language. Rowland was polite and joked that Mitchell 'was the first member of the public in twenty years to apologise'. So far, Mitchell and Downing Street's attempt to lower the temperature appeared to be succeeding.

The strategy from then on, set out by Craig Oliver and agreed to with some reservations by Mitchell, was to lie low and ride out the storm. Mitchell claims to have had his doubts about it from the start, but, shaken by events and with key allies unavailable, wasn't sure what to do – whether to be a team player or to protect ferociously his own reputation. Everybody in Downing Street was suggesting that the storm would all blow over within a few days. Mitchell therefore packed himself off to his home in Nottinghamshire, where his daughter was about to have her twenty-first birthday party.

Whilst he was there, an email was sent to John Randall MP, his Deputy Chief Whip, from one of Randall's Ruislip constituents, a Mr Keith Wallis, which provided what appeared to be a detailed eyewitness account of the confrontation in Downing Street. Wallis claimed to be a member of the public who had watched events unfold and was disgusted at what he had seen. His account supported *The Sun*'s planned story in pretty much every detail. Complaining about Mitchell's 'yobbish' and 'totally unacceptable' behaviour, Wallis claimed in his email that Mitchell had shouted 'very loudly' at the police officers guarding Downing Street, calling them 'you fucking plebes' [sic] and telling them 'you think you run the fucking country', before continuing to shout obscenities at them.

We now know that Wallis, then aged fifty-two, was a serving police officer and member of the Diplomatic Protection Group that guards Downing Street, but at the time it was devastating to Mitchell's case and the account he'd given to No. 10 and the Prime Minister. His story appeared compelling and believable, and provided what appeared to be independent corroboration of the core allegations against Mitchell. The email seemingly banged Mitchell to rights – an open-and-shut case.

As the headlines began to swirl around Mitchell from around midnight on the Thursday and continuing into Friday morning, he and his family tried to close themselves off in their Nottinghamshire home. By then there were twenty journalists and photographers outside the house in London, ten outside his constituency home in Sutton Coldfield and eight camped outside in Nottinghamshire. At least thirty-eight people were simultaneously hunting the Mitchells. Over the coming days, their children were followed by the press. More hacks were dispatched to Mitchell's aged mother-in-law in Swansea, whilst his 84-year-old father was also pursued for comment. Neighbours were sought out and, whilst most refused to comment or spoke up for the family, one in London laid in to the entire Mitchell family. Meanwhile, his office had received about 1,000 hostile emails. He felt under siege. He would later even be spat at in the street.

With all this going on, Mitchell and his wife had to put their personal feelings to one side and get ready for their younger daughter Rosie's twenty-first birthday party. They were in a house they loved; they had found it as a wreck years earlier and had rebuilt it, pouring their heart and soul into it. That weekend, they moved to the back of the house, put up blackout curtains and kept away from the front of the house. No one could get a picture from across the fields.

But despite the secure and familiar location, Mitchell says he learned an important lesson about the ability to take refuge when at the centre of a political or media storm. 'Sanctuary is not about location,' he recalls, 'it's about a state of mind. When the shit hit the fan there was no sanctuary there. Although it was a physical barrier and they couldn't see us or photograph us, I found no peace at all.'

Mitchell believed that not only were the charges being laid against him false, but he couldn't be at all sure where they were coming from, who was behind it or, most importantly, what was coming next. It was bewildering, yet he was told to keep a low profile in the advice from No. 10. It is interesting to contrast his response to the potentially career-threatening allegations hanging over him with that taken by others who have found themselves in the eye of the storm.

To take one example from the cases covered in this book, Chris Huhne took almost the opposite approach to Mitchell in dealing with his own trials and tribulations. He never once backed away from the media or the limelight – on occasions, quite the opposite. At the time, he made people in the Westminster Village believe that he could not possibly be guilty of the offence he was charged with and later found guilty of. Indeed he was insistent about his innocence and that he would not be going to prison right up to the point where he was forced to admit his guilt on the court steps on the day of his trial. Would a more brazen response from Mitchell have helped him turn the tide or ride it out? Perhaps Huhne's full knowledge of his own guilt made it easier for him to make a clear-sighted and rational calculation of the likely outcomes and options available to him, enabling him to take a more certain and combative approach.

Mitchell tried to focus on his daughter's birthday celebrations, but found it difficult to do anything because of the limitations of making absolutely sure he could not be seen or photographed celebrating. Even within the walls of his own home, it made him pretty useless. Fortunately, the Mitchells had created a big bonfire at the back of the house where they couldn't be seen and he was able to have dinner inside and make a speech about his daughter before celebrating outside. But in reality his mind was elsewhere for much of the time as he was waiting for the next blow to land. 'You absorb what happened that day, but you know more stuff is about to be published the next day because it starts to filter out the evening before,' he remembers.

The full horror of everything that was going on around Mitchell finally hit him with full force on the evening of the Sunday that followed. Over the weekend he had been persuaded by Craig Oliver to do an apologetic doorstep interview for Joey Jones of Sky News early on Monday morning. Henry Macrory, the experienced head of press at CCHQ until a few months earlier, advised him it was a bad idea. Mitchell had brought Macrory on board straight away to help him manage the media storm. It was a good early decision, but Mitchell didn't always take his advice.

Instead, Mitchell decided to be a team player, letting No. 10 make the important moves – something his daughter Hannah certainly regrets, as she blames press officers at No. 10 for persuading her father to avoid conflict with the police and to refrain from telling his side of the story. Only once he had resigned and was no longer a member of the team did he feel able to go against Downing Street's advice. Following instructions, he left Nottinghamshire at 3.30 a.m. on the Monday morning, driven to London by Hannah, who had only recently qualified as a doctor. They got to London earlier than expected and so laid up in the car in Notting Hill, refuelling on hot chocolate whilst waiting for the appointed hour.

Mitchell believed that as it was the first day of the Liberal Democrats' party conference he would be knocked off the news headlines. To his horror, he found his forthcoming live statement was topping the 8 a.m. news. The statement was already giving legs to the story, even before he had actually given it. Oliver's instructions were to apologise and to grovel in the hope that contrition would kill the story off.

It backfired spectacularly. The apology was neither fish nor fowl. Having received contrary advice from George Osborne, No. 10 press aide Alan Sendorek and others, Mitchell, with impaired judgement, was left not completely convinced about the line to take. And as Mitchell himself admits: 'I just can't grovel, I just don't do it well. It's a fault in my personality.' Nor, in his heart of hearts, did he want to apologise at all. What he really wanted to do was go on the attack and accuse 'these people' of lying and using terrible slurs to end his career of thirty years and toxify the Conservative Party.

The mass of advice, his lack of judgement and a feeling that his heart wasn't in it all conspired against his and Downing Street's attempt to put the issue to bed. Instead of drawing a line under the issue, the statement gave it new life. Mitchell knew almost immediately it hadn't gone well. Having done the live statement, he went to the Cabinet Office. As he entered, his phone rang. At the other end of the line, the political blogger Iain Dale, an old friend of Mitchell's, opened with the words, 'Who the fuck told you to do that?' According to his daughter Hannah, Mitchell was given the 'watered-down' statement by No. 10 and their words led to Mitchell being pilloried by the press.

Dale had spotted immediately that it was a disaster, and told him so. By now, two statements by Mitchell, one written and one in person, had failed to cap the problem. Joey Jones, to whom Mitchell had given the interview, spent the rest of Monday outside Whitehall, doing live reports at the head of Sky News' rolling news bulletins. Mitchell went to the Whips' Office to try to work, but found it very difficult to concentrate as the threat to his career mounted.

Meanwhile, his deputy as Chief Whip, John Randall MP, had taken his constituent Keith Wallis's email to No. 10. The email was deadly for a number of reasons. First, it appeared to provide corroboration of the police's version of events from a member of the public who had witnessed the incident first-hand. Second, it was sent to the Deputy Chief Whip by his constituent, whom he was duty-bound to represent. Third, it destabilised a key relationship between the Chief Whip and his deputy. But, crucially, it also undermined the belief that No. 10 had in Mitchell. Key people, including Jeremy Heywood, the Cabinet Secretary, and Craig Oliver, were not convinced by Mitchell's denials.

To make things worse, Mitchell's wife called during the day saying he couldn't go home because the media had surrounded their house in Gibson Square, in the affluent district of Islington in north London. The Mitchell family decided that home for the next few days would be with Mitchell's friend Duncan Budge and his wife and children in Kentish Town. This would mean returning home to Islington in the early hours (as the media left each night between 1 a.m. before returning at around 6 a.m.) to fetch and carry clothes and other necessary personal items. It was far from ideal with everything else going on.

In a phone call late on Monday, John Randall told Mitchell, albeit guardedly, about the Wallis email. Randall read the email to Mitchell, telling him Wallis was a plausible witness; Randall had met with Wallis and had reported this directly to No. 10. The information hit Mitchell particularly hard, after what had already been an awful day of intense scrutiny and pressure. He was beside himself by the end of the phone call with Randall. 'I've been stitched up' he said as he hung up the phone, with his family looking on. He was unable to comprehend what was happening to him. His reputation was somehow being stripped away piece by piece.

His daughter, Hannah, remembers sitting in a chair shaking as the full implications of the Wallis letter sank into the Mitchells. She was certain nobody now would believe them, whatever they said. To her, what was happening was the product of a conspiracy against her father. In Mitchell's own eyes, he had spent the past eight years speaking up for the poorest and most destitute people in the world. People who had known him, admired his work and believed in him would now see him as someone who used vile language and behaved in an arrogant and reprehensible manner. He found it hard to bear.

That Monday night seemed particularly bleak. He felt something terrible was happening to him, a stitch-up that there seemed no way out of – his credibility was being eroded as the evidence against him stacked up. By the Tuesday, Mitchell was in such internal distress that he no longer trusted his own judgement. As he says himself, 'I was caught between the pincers of the press and the police as if Leveson had never taken place. There was nothing I could do. Nobody believed me when I said it wasn't true.'

In his desperation he rang his close friends. Duncan Budge told him to be positive, that the email from Wallis would be his liberation. The Wallis email would quickly be exposed as a fake, Budge reasoned, and the truth would then come out. Mitchell didn't believe him. The forces at work against him, whoever they were, appeared both controlled and powerful. He finally managed to get hold of David Davis, still in Florida, who knew nothing of what was going on and decided to stay up all night familiarising himself with what had happened.

Mitchell also called his close friend Charlie Falconer, the former Labour Lord Chancellor, who was in Australia. His message to

both friends on the phone was the same: an email had arrived
claiming to have witnessed something that had never happened;
he was being stitched up. He did not know how it was being done,
or where it was coming from but the nightmare was happening.
What was he to do? Mitchell says in retrospect, 'I think they both
thought I was going mad.'

As he made the frantic, highly charged calls to his friends, his
family were with him and becoming very worried. Mitchell says:

> It is very difficult for me to find the words to describe how awful
> that night was. It was truly Kafkaesque. I was being systematically
> destroyed and I know it was not true but it had the apparent acqui-
> escence of a senior whip, people in Downing Street and the media.
> I was on my knees with everything exploding around me. I can't
> really find a way to describe the awfulness of it.

Matters did not improve the following morning as the headlines kept
coming. As Mitchell was cleaning his teeth, the Prime Minister called
suggesting the evidence from Randall's constituent was compelling
and it looked a fairly open-and-shut case. Mitchell always called
Cameron 'Prime Minister', but now he dropped the formality:
'David, how will you feel in a few weeks' or months' time when it is
shown that this is a lie?' It was a turning point in the conversation.
Cameron agreed that Jeremy Heywood, the Cabinet Secretary, should
look into it and conduct a short investigation. Heywood was to look
at whether the email was sufficient evidence for Mitchell to be sacked.

Within days the Cabinet Secretary had reported back, briefing
the Prime Minister that the email (from Wallis) 'did not provide

conclusive or reliable evidence' and there was no reason for the Prime Minister to change his view that the Chief Whip should not be sacked. Mitchell's supporters still regard Heywood's response as woefully inadequate: what he found, they say, should have been cause for him having sleepless nights. Heywood had access to the CCTV footage held by Downing Street and the Foreign Office against which to review the claims and factual details in Wallis' email. He also interviewed Andrew Mitchell as part of the investigation, but Wallis refused to speak to either Heywood or his staff, allegedly on the grounds that his emails were 'private communications to his local MP and had not been intended for wider dissemination.' This itself might have led Heywood to suspect that something wasn't right, as might the CCTV which appeared to contradict parts of the police account and that of John Randall's 'constituent', in particular the observation both in the police account and the email from the supposed member of the public that the incident was witnessed by 'several' members of the public and tourists standing by the gates of Downing Street, and whether Mitchell's body language as recorded on CCTV reflected Wallis' (although not the police's) allegation that Mitchell had been shouting 'very loudly' and continued to shout obscenities at the officers. Others who saw the same footage as Heywood told him of their concerns.

Mitchell's supporters have since concluded that Heywood didn't want to make waves in spite of his discoveries. In their view, he could have acted early on to defuse the situation for Mitchell but seemingly chose for reasons unknown not to do so – perhaps sticking to the agreed Downing Street plan to let it all blow over. Heywood has defended his position, arguing that the remit of the review was very limited and that he could only do what he had been asked. Yet having noted that, as he himself said later when addressing the Public Administration Select Committee, there were 'unanswered questions, including the possibility of a gigantic conspiracy or a small conspiracy'. There is a strong sense among Mitchell's friends that he didn't begin to fulfil his moral obligation to try to get to the bottom of it. As one later said, 'Heywood had a duty to trust and to justice as Cabinet Secretary and he didn't fulfil that duty.' But the prevailing view from Downing Street was that No. 10 wanted this all to go away and the best way to achieve that was to say and do as little as possible. Mitchell's wife now felt it was time to view the CCTV footage of the episode, but Mitchell himself still didn't want to push No. 10 too hard at a sensitive time – after all, he needed the Prime Minister's ongoing support if he was to save his job.

Mitchell's attempts to lie low and let the story die away were in vain. In the following weeks, stories about him appeared on a daily basis, in what could only be described as open season. Ingenious links going back years were made; some were pure fantasy. One newspaper wrote a story about how Mitchell had 'luxuriated in the splendour of the Serena Hotel [in Kigali, the capital city of Rwanda, which Mitchell had visited regularly in opposition] surrounded by prostitutes'. Mitchell had never stayed at the Serena Hotel and the only time he'd ever been there was to meet British journalists staying there when David Cameron visited Rwanda.

Alastair Campbell's supposed nine-day deadline about how long someone could remain in the headlines before being finished came and went. However, after many days' constant media pounding,

Mitchell, having taken all the bile and invective to heart, was struggling to function, as lack of sleep, stress and little or no food took their effect on his mental and physical state.

Mitchell is now fairly forgiving of the wider press, with one exception – *The Sun*. He believes the paper went too far and it became a personal campaign of hatred and vilification rather than journalism. *The Sun* argues simply that it had a great story that landed in its lap. What was it supposed to do? Some senior journalists on the newspaper, whilst standing by the original story, admit privately that it probably went a bit too far in targeting Mitchell, based on information fed by the Police Federation. Whatever the rights and wrongs, *The Sun* was unrelenting, piling up the pressure on Mitchell day after day and week after week.

From early on the Police Federation publicly joined in the sport with glee. In March 2012 it had failed to secure enough votes from its membership to go on strike for the first time ever in opposition to government policy. The organisation had and still has a militant element that was determined to cause trouble for the government and 'plebgate' was an opportunity not to be missed. Supported by a Midlands PR agency, there were some members who were apparently prepared to push things well beyond what was truthful to make things worse for the government – whether it was in the email to Deputy Chief Whip John Randall or directly to the television cameras.

Things were so bad for Mitchell that attending the Conservative Party conference became impossible. Had he gone, there would have been a huge scrum wherever he went. His presence would no doubt have distracted from important speeches and policy announcements.

However, the Police Federation tried all manner of stunts to keep the story going, including wearing cufflinks emblazoned with the words 'Toffs' and 'Plebs'. Class was back at the centre of British politics and the Police Federation had placed itself right at its heart, cheered on and supported by a newly dubbed 'One Nation' Labour Party.

Mitchell had been asked quite early on in the crisis for a meeting by Ian Edwards, Chairman of the West Midlands Police Federation. As Edwards was responsible for the area covering Sutton Coldfield, Mitchell's parliamentary constituency, Mitchell could hardly decline, and Edwards had seemed genuine in a phone conversation, apparently commiserating with Mitchell and wanting to clear the air and look to the future. Mitchell agreed on the basis that it would be constructive and was part of his work as a Midlands MP. He also specifically agreed with Edwards that the location of the meeting would not be disclosed.

The date, time and location were all immediately leaked and the Police Federation set about attracting the maximum amount of media interest. Mitchell considered postponing, but decided that it would look like cowardice. The meeting was scheduled for 5 p.m. on Friday 12 October in Mitchell's Sutton Coldfield office. It provided the occasion for another media scrum, with nine camera crews and a host of national media, and the story was elevated to the top of the news above the Jimmy Savile scandal.

Police Federation representatives turned up early to brief the press. The representatives told the waiting media they would be demanding answers and if they didn't get them Mitchell must be sacked. Mitchell gave them exactly what they wanted in a 45-minute meeting, explaining what had happened at the gates of

Downing Street and precisely what had been said. The meeting ended abruptly at 5.45 p.m., the Mitchell camp contest, because the Police Federation officers wanted to ensure the story hit the evening news programmes on national television. Two members of that team told the world that Mitchell had refused to tell them what had been said and that he should now resign or be sacked. On the insistence of Mitchell's wife Sharon, a Conservative press officer had recorded the conversation in Mitchell's office and provided proof that the Police Federation version was untrue. Despite the alarming inaccuracies and untruths in their account, the meeting had given the story further longevity.

On 15 October, after a media siege that had lasted almost a full month, Parliament returned, much to Mitchell's relief. Westminster gives a degree of protection and camaraderie to MPs under fire that is often able to raise spirits. Many MPs at Westminster have been under attack at some point in their careers and know what it's like to feel the wrath of the press. A little sympathy and a few words of support can often go a long way.

But Mitchell knew that getting back to the House was also crunch time. The reaction of the parliamentary party, dominated by new MPs from the 2010 intake, would now be key to his survival. Mitchell attended the Chamber as Chief Whip on the Monday and Tuesday, and was heartened that things had gone as well as could have been expected. Yet he felt the position was hardening against him on the Conservative benches.

Mitchell felt, rightly or wrongly, that for the most part those Conservative MPs who had known him for years wouldn't believe all the awful anecdotes of arrogance and meanness they had seen in the press week after week. However, several others had less faith in him. Many believed Westminster tales that had circulated for years about his abrasiveness and his quick temper and weren't prepared to give the man nicknamed 'Thrasher' Mitchell (a moniker dating back to his school days) the benefit of the doubt. Now few had a decent word to say about him and many were more worried about how it would play for them in their marginal seat. Although many of the 2010 intake had won Labour seats on a rising tide, they hadn't yet had to hold firm under heavy gunfire.

In difficult economic circumstances for the government, many just wanted Mitchell gone. It almost didn't matter whether he had said the offending words or not. It was also time for some revenge, according to one MP close to Mitchell. Sacked whips now moved at Mitchell's weakest point, as did several who were still *in situ*.

No. 10 and Mitchell had agreed that if they could see out Prime Minister's Questions on the Wednesday, it would probably mean that the worst of it was over and some semblance of normality could return to everyday life. Mitchell was only just managing to do his job as Chief Whip with so much going on around him. The situation could not go on, not least because his health was suffering. A line had to be drawn under matters one way or the other.

Prime Minister's Questions was brutal. The Labour leader, Ed Miliband, launched a full assault. Mitchell felt it was a very personal attack and 'absolutely monstered' him, although it was also felt that Cameron dealt with it effectively. Even senior members of the Labour Party later said the onslaught was over the top. However, Mitchell was also facing public criticism from his own side. Whispers started to circulate to undermine him. Michael Fabricant, who had left his job as a government whip in the clear-out that preceded Mitchell's arrival, tweeted that 'several MPs' confirmed having heard Mitchell say in response to Miliband's taunts that he didn't swear at the police. Fabricant, who nonetheless remained Vice-Chairman of the Conservative Party, tweeted that Mitchell's alleged claim had 're-ignited' the story and put 'a whole new light' on the issue. It set a difficult scene for that evening's 1922 Committee of Conservative backbench MPs.

Many ministers and MPs underestimate the power that 'the 1922' still has at big moments for the party. Few members are or ever have been whips. The moment to strike was at hand for those who wanted rid of Mitchell. It was obvious from the beginning that there was a level of orchestration, as the matter was raised early in proceedings. The language used now was less nuanced than usual, with less respect and less ambiguity.

As one of those who spoke against Mitchell later confirmed to me, 'I wouldn't have done it without permission.' In the end, of the twelve Conservative backbenchers who spoke, eight spoke up for Mitchell, but the damage had already been done, because the first four spoke against him in a very forthright way. It looked as if Mitchell had lost the support of the parliamentary party. Mitchell himself had already decided he needed the clear backing of the committee, and the genuine extent of support for him wasn't as clear as it could have been.

His position was destabilised even further when rumours began circulating that his deputy, John Randall, had been to see the Prime Minister the same afternoon to say he would resign if Mitchell didn't go. As the Deputy Chief Whip, Randall was popular among backbench MPs and his departure would have been a shock to the parliamentary party. It would have been very unwelcome and set a dangerous precedent had Conservative MPs been forced to choose between the Chief Whip and his deputy.

Mitchell admits that the meeting of the full 1922 Committee was crucial in his decision to resign. He had met with the committee's officers and had asked for a supportive statement. Although the officers gave their personal support, they refused his request without consulting the full committee. The Whips' Office had also been collecting information from their flocks, as requested by Mitchell, to be fed in by Randall to the Prime Minister as an impartial source of information. The feedback was mixed and loyalties were becoming strained even in the Whips' Office.

The cherry on the top of everything else was that the opposition were threatening to use an arcane parliamentary device to censure Mitchell by docking part of his salary, and to put the matter to full debate in the House of Commons. The notion that Mitchell would have to whip reluctant colleagues to vote for him to keep his salary was too much to take. At a dinner for government whips with Sir John Major that night at the Heraldry Museum, Randall didn't show and Mitchell's last trace of optimism vanished. The game was up.

The following morning, Mitchell decided it was time to go.

He had weathered Wednesday's storm, and opinion was that he could probably survive with the Prime Minister's ongoing support. The worst of the newspaper and TV coverage had also subsided. So why did Mitchell decide to go when he was probably through the worst?

'The Labour motion convinced me it was going to go on and on,' he says: it was the final straw. Having withstood twenty-eight days of incessant character assassination, and what he regarded as lies and distortions, Mitchell decided to go because of a parliamentary motion tabled by the Labour Party to cut his salary. The thought of whipping a parliamentary party dominated by a reluctant and rebellious 2010 intake for his own personal benefit was a hugely embarrassing prospect and he just couldn't do it. He also felt that if he went on until the general election as Chief Whip, the word 'pleb' would be replayed constantly, leaving the party critically damaged. Enough was enough.

'I'd had enough, my family had had enough, and the party had had enough,' is how he explains his final decision to go. 'There is only so much anyone can take, and I'd had to endure more than most human beings in similar situations. My children had exams coming up and I was in despair – it had to stop.'

Whilst David Davis MP performed heroics for Mitchell throughout his difficulty, devising strategies, thinking through tactics, speaking out publicly and supporting him personally, there were others who were not so steadfast. Mitchell remembers meeting one colleague in the cloisters between Portcullis House and the Chamber:

> He said to me, 'You've got to carry on, don't let the bastards get you, you've got to stay as our Chief Whip, I'm right behind you.' He then walked down to the post office, up the stairs to the Members'

Lobby and told his whip I had to go. And then when I was vindicated he put an arm around my shoulder and said, 'I was always
supporting you, I'm so pleased that my faith has been justified.'
And I thought, 'Shall I punch him in the face or shall I thank him?'
I just thanked him.

Mitchell cannot praise his friend Davis enough:

Long before all this, I once said that David was that very, very rare
thing in politics: a man who, if I were caught between enemy lines
lying in a fox hole with a bullet in my leg with the tracer rounds
flying over the top, would come and get me. And I was in that situation and he did. There is no higher definition of friendship than that.

There are some in Mitchell's camp who are deeply unforgiving of
those who let him down. One MP told me:

Anna Soubry was his friend, whom he had helped to get selected
in Gedling in 2005 [she lost that time to the Labour MP Vernon
Coaker]. He gave her a lot of time and effort and support. Yet she
went on *Any Questions* the night he resigned and she begins by
saying 'Andrew Mitchell was a great friend of mine', and proceeds
to rubbish him, saying he was right to ''fess up' and resign.

Soubry had said on the BBC radio programme, 'When we do something wrong we shouldn't mess about, we should put our hands up.
As my children would say, we should "'fess up," apologise and do the
decent thing which is to resign and I am pleased he has finally done

that.' One Mitchell supporter found it hard to contain his anger when he heard of Soubry's remarks: "Fess up? Andrew nearly had a heart attack!' Another of Mitchell's allies notes that Soubry 'will pay a terrible price. I can't tell you when or where, but she will pay a terrible price for that.' When Soubry later described female doctors as 'a burden' on the NHS in a Commons debate, it was probably no accident that Mitchell's wife and daughter – both doctors – weighed in and wrote to the national press accusing her of sexist language.

Soubry isn't the only colleague who comes in for criticism from the Mitchell camp. Theresa May was believed to have been unsympathetic at the party conference and Iain Duncan Smith was making jokes about Mitchell being sent to Rwanda, where there were no gates. Mitchell believes it was some form of payback for when he was whip to the then arch-Eurosceptic rebel Duncan Smith during the fraught Maastricht votes in the early 1990s.

No. 10 does not escape criticism from the Mitchell camp either, with Jeremy Heywood and Craig Oliver criticised extensively for their failures. Oliver, in particular, is believed by Mitchell to have acted directly against his best interests on at least two occasions: once when he stopped ministers going out to defend Mitchell on television, and once when he tried to block the Channel 4 *Dispatches* programme by Michael Crick, which gravely undermined the allegations against Mitchell. Perhaps it is an important reminder for all politicians that when they find themselves at the centre of a storm, they may find that what is in their best interests and what is in the best interests of their party or its leadership start to diverge.

The situation Mitchell found himself in was analogous to Jeremy Hunt's BSkyB ordeal. Both men felt wronged by the accusations being made against them, both felt that the allegations had come out of the blue and both felt that there were larger forces at work in stirring the story up. In Hunt's case it was an anti-Murdoch coalition, in Mitchell's it was the Police Federation.

Hunt had two advantages over Mitchell. First, he had the clear fire break that Leveson provided him with. He could and did make the case that Leveson should hear all the evidence before people decided his fate. It meant he could play for time and people had to accept that a judge-led inquiry was the best place to hear all the evidence. One side had made accusations through Leveson; surely the other side should be heard in the same way? It was a difficult logic to argue against.

Mitchell and No. 10 had no such option, particularly once Heywood had wrapped up his investigation quickly and seen no reason to suggest a larger investigation, during which some of the police's statements could have been put to scrutiny. Mitchell and No. 10 agreed that lying low was the best option to take the sting out of events. No. 10 pointed out that, as Chief Whip, a low-public-profile position, Mitchell could stay out of sight and ride things out. It was a massive strategic error: the Chief Whip is the one position in Cabinet which requires the passive acquiescence of the parliamentary party. At the very least, Mitchell, No. 10, the Whips' Office and others needed to make a pitch to the party that he should be supported. Radio silence was always likely to end in disaster. Hunt, to a greater extent, could last for as long as the Prime Minister continued to support him, though he too would have lost his job had he lost the confidence of the parliamentary party on the day he made his first statement to the Commons when the storm first broke. Of course, the Chief Whip didn't have the advantage of being able to make a statement in the House.

For the Culture Secretary, authority resides in the support of the Prime Minister, but the Chief Whip is the one person in the room who might one day be required to tell the Prime Minister he's got to go. That authority comes from the parliamentary party. Thus, as Chief Whip, the trust of the parliamentary party is absolutely paramount to doing the job and it must be maintained at all times.

The big dilemma for Mitchell once he had resigned was whether he should fight on. All the advice from Downing Street was to continue to lie low, not to overreact, not to fight; in due course (certainly by the end of the current parliament) his career would be back on course. Steeled and spurred on predominantly by David Davis and by his wife, Mitchell chose to fight back. As he rather bluntly puts it, 'My political body was dumped by the side of the road by *The Sun* and the police. David Davis and my wife came and picked it up.' But friends from across the political divide including Peter Mandelson, Charlie Falconer, Robert Harris and Chris Mullin also urged him on.

Having met with Mitchell, Channel 4's *Dispatches* team decided that there was a strong case for his defence that had not been heard. They set about making that defence with the help of Davis and Mitchell. Although the CCTV ultimately obtained from Downing Street was crucial, so was the fact that *Dispatches* proved that Keith Wallis, the constituent of Deputy Chief Whip John Randall whose email had done so much damage, was in fact a police officer. A Met Police Assistant Commissioner visited Mitchell and Davis in the

House of Commons in early December 2012 to tell them directly of this new evidence and inform them that Randall's constituent, PC Wallis, had been arrested over the previous weekend. It left Mitchell speechless, literally unable to speak for several minutes. Once he had gathered his thoughts he called Ed Llewellyn and demanded to see the Prime Minister. Mitchell's fight-back was in full flight by mid-December.

When the *Dispatches* programme aired, it painstakingly re-examined the allegations against Mitchell. Remarkably, Wallis admitted to the programme that he wasn't even present at the scene of which he had claimed to provide an eyewitness account. He later pleaded guilty to misconduct in public office for falsely claiming to have witnessed the incident and was sentenced to twelve months in jail. The impact was extraordinary. The Prime Minister watched the programme in his Downing Street study; his jaw allegedly 'hit the floor'. Suddenly, the attitude of the press changed and Mitchell's side of the story could finally be heard. Chris Mullin and Robert Harris published prominent articles, as did Mitchell himself in the *Sunday Times*. Letters and emails started to pour in to support Mitchell, rather than castigating him as they had in September.

The night *Dispatches* went out, Mitchell, by coincidence, had arranged for all his old private office people from the Department for International Development and all his parliamentary office staff to have dinner at his house. They arrived as the programme aired, and as it ended, the entire party stood up and cheered, with some hugging Mitchell. 'I knew that was a really important moment,' he says now. 'I owe my reputation, my life even, to those investigative journalists. *Dispatches* were the right people because we knew they didn't like politicians, and especially Tories, but we also knew that Michael Crick would pursue justice. If he had thought we were not telling the truth he would have pursued us without fear or favour.' Mitchell now regards the meeting with Karen Edwards, the producer, as probably the most important of his life. 'She listened to me and believed what I said. Once again, though, it was David Davis who worked out how to get my side across.'

THE AFTERMATH

So why did 'plebgate' get legs as a story in the first place? It has to be considered in the context of the longstanding and sometimes bitter struggle between the Government, with its austerity policies, and the police represented by the Police Federation, the powerful and wealthy union into which every policeman and policewoman is automatically enrolled.

In all probability, PC Rowland would not have expected his recollection of the event to be splashed in *The Sun* by colleagues following a more political agenda. But when it was, it seems that the 'plebgate' storm in a teacup presented the Police Federation and elements of the police that opposed the government's handling of police matters with a golden opportunity and a handy stick with which to beat the government. As one of the police officers on duty at Downing Street on the night of 19 September 2012 said in a text exchange, 'The Fed need our help'.

The Police Federation has since been the subject of damning criticism for its role in escalating the 'plebgate' scandal. The three Federation representatives who had met with Mitchell on 12 October 2012 were subsequently referred by their respective forces to the Independent Police Complaints Commission (IPCC) after a recording of the meeting was broadcast as part of the *Dispatches* programme. The recording appeared to show that the comments they had made to the waiting media ahead of that evening's six o'clock news bulletins did not accurately or fairly reflect what Mitchell had said in the meeting. When the House of Commons Home Affairs Select Committee launched its own investigation, it found the evidence it received from the three men, Inspector Ken MacKaill of West Mercia Police, Detective Sergeant Stuart Hinton of Warwickshire Police, and Sergeant Chris Jones of West Midlands Police to be 'misleading, possibly deliberately so, and lacking in credibility'. Among a litany of serious criticisms it made and irregularities it identified, the Select Committee found DS Hinton to have been 'mendacious' and Sergeant Jones to have misled it. Both were threatened with contempt of Parliament unless they returned before the Committee to apologise.

The Select Committee also concluded that the 12 October meeting with Mitchell was convened on the basis of an anti-cuts campaign run by the Midlands regional branches of the Federation and their media relations advisers, the Gaunt Brothers. It would not be surprising, the Committee noted, that when the full set of circumstances were taken into account, some people would conclude that the regional branches of the Federation had set up the 12 October meeting with the aim of securing the resignation of a Cabinet minister.

The total number of police officers involved remains to be discovered but the Police have a reputation for protecting their own. After a lengthy investigation, the Director of Public Prosecutions found that it was 'clear' that information was leaked to the media by an officer unconnected to the incident, although the DPP did not reveal the identity of that officer or any links he or she may have had to the Police Federation, or indeed how the officer obtained Rowland's email in the first place. The DPP also found that there was information, albeit not evidence that would be admissible in court, which suggested that an officer's partner had contacted the media, introducing the word 'morons' into the press coverage of the incident, despite the fact that no officer had ever claimed that Mitchell used the word 'moron'.

The DPP opted against prosecuting the officer who had leaked to the media, but on 26 February 2014, the Metropolitan Police announced that PC James Glanville, who had not been on duty during the original incident but was present at the Diplomatic Protection Group office later that night, had been sacked for gross misconduct, having been found to have passed information about the incident to *The Sun* newspaper. Glanville had provided the newspaper with a copy of PC Rowland's email describing the confrontation to his supervisors.

At the end of April 2014, PC Gillian Weatherley, a police officer who had been on duty at the Downing Street gates on the night of the Mitchell incident, and who went on to exchange several messages with PC Glanville over the following three days, became the third Met PC to be sacked for gross misconduct over the affair. Weatherley was found to have leaked information about the 2012 incident and subsequently given 'inaccurate and misleading state-ments' to the Met's own investigation into alleged misconduct by officers. Weatherley is also alleged to have boasted about her involvement in the affair in text messages as it became public, including making the claim, 'I can topple the Tory government.'

A fourth officer, Susan Johnson, was later dismissed for breaching professional standards of honesty and integrity, having failed to inform her superiors that Wallis had copied her into the email he sent to his MP, and after evidence was found of contact between someone closely connected to her and *The Sun*. After Johnson received the copy of Wallis' email, she sent him a text message congratulating him on his efforts, saying: 'Brilliant Keith. I love it. Big hugs x'.

Days later, when Wallis reported to her that he had met his local MP, John Randall, to discuss his email, and that Randall had believed Wallis' false claims to be an ordinary member of the public, Johnson replied via text: 'Brilliant. Good to hear. Well worth the email.'

From the media's perspective, the fallout from the Leveson Inquiry into the culture, practices and ethics of the press was still in the background. The print media in particular felt that the government had been weak in conceding the Leveson Inquiry in the first place and they didn't much like where it was heading, with legislation and potentially huge fines on the horizon. The media wanted to give the government a good kicking to send out a warning of what might be to come, and a story such as this, with a whiff of scandal and class-based popular outrage, was the perfect vehicle to do it.

Whatever the full truth about the matter and the extent of the forces against him turns out to have been, Andrew Mitchell wilted in the eye of the storm. The sense of injustice at the destruction of his reputation and Cabinet career, the relentless tide of allegations,

and the hostility he had to endure almost broke him. Some of the
subjects I have interviewed for this book have been remarkably
philosophical about their ordeals and the impact on their careers
and personal lives; others have gained perspective with the passing of time. For Mitchell, the scandal that engulfed him left him
almost unable to contemplate a future life in his own country. He
says now:

> My first aim was to get back my life, then to get back my reputation
> and third to get back my job. But the job was very much third – by
> a long way. There was a point where I wasn't sure if I did [want it
> back]. Indeed, there was a point where I was going to emigrate.
> We were going to go. Not only was I going to leave Parliament and
> cause a by-election, we were going to leave the country.

The restoration of Mitchell's health and self-esteem owes much to
others. His supporters, led by his wife and David Davis, helped
launch the still ongoing fight to clear his name after his fall from
office. Crucial assistance came from the Channel 4 *Dispatches* investigation, which helped to turn the tide of opinion about 'plebgate'
to the extent that the affair is now known as much for suspicions
of an appalling conspiracy by an as-yet-unknown number of police
officers as for anything Mitchell is claimed to have said to PC Toby
Rowland. Mitchell eventually got the chance to have his side of
the story heard. But he remains ensnared in the cross-fire between the
Government and the Police Federation, as PC Rowland (to whom
the Police Federation gave its full support) is now suing Mitchell for
libel and slander for claiming that PC Rowland's note inaccurately

recorded what Mitchell said. Mitchell's own libel action against *The Sun* still continues, with the publication lining up with the police.

Meanwhile the Home Secretary, in an unprecedented assault on the Police Federation, pointed to the conduct of senior echelons of the Police Federation and the actions of some of its members over and in the wake of 'plebgate' as one of a number of crucial factors in its membership's contribution to the public's loss of trust in the Police.

Mitchell's political body may have been 'dumped by the side of the road', to use his own colourful phrase and he remains a 'political football'. But although he lost his Cabinet job, he was later thrown a lifeline. And although the battering he took left him drained, the chance to claim back what he believes was stolen from him has given him renewed energy. His determination to see himself fully vindicated and to bring his detractors to justice is fearsome.

CHAPTER 2

LIAM FOX HUNTED DOWN

"I'd been on the front line of politics for a long time and had my skir-
mishes but I've always thought that medicine's quite a good preparation
for a crisis, as you see things in perspective. A baby with a cord wrapped
around its neck feels like a crisis, it really does. Politics is stressful and
it's an irritation, but it doesn't feel quite the same, and it's only if you
have been in life-and-death situations that you can understand what a
true crisis really feels like."

– Liam Fox

In essence, the case against Liam Fox in the growing storm that led to his resignation on 14 October 2011 was one of foolishness: foolishness in involving his best friend in his political career and foolishness in allowing the suggestion that Adam Werritty could pass himself off as his 'adviser'. Fox described it as allowing a 'blurring of the boundaries' between his personal and professional life. Benedict Brogan of the *Daily Telegraph* said at the time: 'Let's say it, there's something a bit weird about allowing your mate to hang around the office. But I can well imagine Dr Fox being oblivious to the problem.'

And therein lay the problem. For Fox, his relationship with Werritty was completely normal and above board; he simply did not see any conflicts of interest or any perception of wrongdoing that might result from their actions. Fox simply didn't see the train hurtling towards him. He had an important job to do and didn't particularly care what other people thought of how things looked.

As one commentator at the time put it, 'A theory in Westminster [is] that he doesn't really give a toss what people think of him.' When *The Spectator*'s James Forsyth asked a political ally of Fox's to explain how the Defence Secretary had got himself into his difficulty, he received the response, 'Because he's a reckless bastard with no judgement.'

That may be too strong a description, but as Forsyth wrote in the *Mail on Sunday*, Fox 'prides himself on not playing by the safety-first rules of the 21st-century political game … This conceit may well be his undoing.' The biggest crisis of Liam Fox's political career highlighted not only his huge talent and ability, but also his tendency towards hubris.

Bill Shankly, the manager of Liverpool FC in the 1960s, once said, 'Some people believe football is a matter of life and death. I am very disappointed with that attitude. I can assure you it is much, much more important than that.' There are some who believe that politics should be seen in the same vein – but not Liam Fox. Fox has seen too many real life-and-death dramas to pay any such lip service to personal political crises.

Fox was brought up as a Scottish Catholic in a council house in East Kilbride, a no-nonsense, straight-talking part of the world.

He went to a state school and on to Glasgow University, where he read medicine, eventually becoming a general practitioner in Beaconsfield. The world of medicine is unforgiving, shocking and often fatal. Doctors often have to desensitise their emotions due to the frequently challenging circumstances they can find themselves in – and still they must function at peak performance.

As a doctor, Fox dealt with exceptionally serious situations. As a GP in Beaconsfield he attended a major road traffic accident where a fire engine had been involved in a head-on collision with a lorry. As the attending doctor, he worked for hours alongside the emergency services cutting men from the fire engine:

> That was real stress – that was probably the most stressful thing that I ever did. It was a really horrible, mangled crash with several fatalities as it turned out. And we had to do some pretty unpleasant things to get them free. I was feeling OK at the time, but I remember about four hours later going home and being unable to hold a cup of tea steadily.

Although Fox had been in the front line of politics for a long time, he had had only skirmishes with potential political storms. His profile and senior positions in the Conservative Party and then the coalition government ensured he was under constant surveillance from the media, but there was no big political preparation or experience for what was heading Fox's way in 2011.

Possibly the nearest to real pressure he felt was during the 2005 Conservative leadership campaign, when the press were camped outside his house, or prior to that when he was Party Chairman during the general election campaign. It certainly provided a taste of what it might be like to be exposed to extensive scrutiny. But there was a difference between these earlier exposures and what came in 2011. In opposition, Fox didn't have the physical protection of armed guards that he had when Secretary of State for Defence. The isolation this security created was, as we will see, to make a difference to how events played out.

There had been talk around Westminster about Fox's private life for years. Most of it was smears and innuendo, and Fox had heard it but simply ignored it. 'I tend to treat gossip as gossip,' he says. When pressed in 2005 he said, 'I know that some people use smears and I have heard them for years. They'd say, "Why are you not married? You must be a playboy, or a wild man, or gay, or whatever." To which I'd reply, "Well, I'm getting married in December and I'm perfectly happy with my private life."'

In December 2005 Fox married Jesme Baird, also a doctor, who worked at the Roy Castle Lung Foundation. It was 'a wedding that took place against a background of gossip, innuendo – or "up yer endo" as they like to say in Fleet Street on these occasions – and political intrigue', according to *The Week* magazine.

In the run-up to the big day, the internet was ruthless and the media speculated privately and sometimes publicly about Fox's forthcoming wedding, particularly as he had moved into his forties as a confirmed bachelor. The press could not resist, because only a week or two earlier Fox had appeared in the headlines after entertaining UK students in a hotel bedroom in Paris, where they had emptied the contents of the minibar and one student ended up staying the night on the sofa in Fox's room. He was tackled shortly afterwards by Patrick Hennessy, then political editor of the *Sunday Telegraph* (and now Ed Miliband's spin doctor), asking why he would want to get smashed with a bunch of students.

Fox's reply was matter-of-fact and indifferent to the underlying suggestion of homosexuality running through the press:

> I did *Question Time* from Paris and I was there for three days. They were a nice bunch of students. They came to the programme, they were in the audience and they were desperately keen to get to talk to a British politician. And they invited me to a barbecue, so I went, 'Why not?'

Why not indeed? Why should Fox play to the safety and conformity standards of the 21st-century politician? Fox was, as he remains, a man who really knew how to party, whether dancing, drinking or singing.

It didn't stop a sneering press implicitly suggesting that his engagement was something to do with a run at the Conservative Party leadership that December. Hennessy wrote with a suggestive hint of irony: 'As is the case with many politicians who reach their early forties as a bachelor, Dr Fox has been dogged by persistent rumours about his sexuality ... However, he has put all that to rest by announcing his engagement last week to Jesme Baird.'

It is very difficult to delve into Fox's biggest political crisis without seeing the unpleasant undercurrent, almost throughout, of homophobia. His relationship with Werritty was seen through a prism of strangeness, an attitude that there is something not quite right about the relationship between two men. The closeness of the friendship was described as 'surprising' by James Kirkup in the *Telegraph*. Perhaps this is part of what Fox was referring to in his Commons resignation statement when he said, 'I believe there was, from some quarters, a personal vindictiveness – even hatred – that should worry all of us.'

The press loves a good 'nudge nudge, wink wink' story, as William Hague found with his relationship with his special adviser Christopher Myers. Sections of the media, as well as political bloggers and Twitter users, strongly insinuated that the Foreign Secretary might be gay. The same was intimated of Fox and Werritty.

It was written that Adam Werritty had been 'close friends' with the Defence Secretary for about fifteen years. They met when Werritty was a twenty-year-old student at Edinburgh University. Fox then appointed Werritty executive director of Atlantic Bridge, a charity established to build strong relationships between the US and UK. Werritty was alleged to have lived rent-free in Fox's London flat for several years after 2002.

The two men were then said to be fond of dressing alike, according to one Sunday newspaper. The paper even found a behavioural expert to say, 'When people are very close and friendly there is often a tendency to start looking alike, even down to the posture they adopt and the way they dress.' This was surely an insinuation that the pair were probably gay.

That Adam Werritty and Liam Fox were close friends no one can doubt. But was this friendship really as odd as many in the media made out at the time? The two are believed to have met at a Burns Night supper event organised by Edinburgh University Young Conservatives in 1998, when Fox was Tory frontbench spokesman for

Scotland and Constitutional Affairs. Despite the age gap of seventeen years, the two men had a lot in common besides the obvious shared interest in politics. They had similar backgrounds: Fox's father was a school teacher, Werritty's a university professor. Both were educated at state schools; both loved the United States; they had a shared passion for rugby and partying; both had similar right-wing ideology and a love of Margaret Thatcher. It would have been more surprising if they hadn't got on and enjoyed each other's company.

The partying was, at times, fairly spectacular. Fox's thirty-seventh birthday party was fuelled by huge amounts of alcohol that included (according to reports at the time) a multi-bottle lunch, a couple of Scotches in the afternoon and a bottle of champagne each before dinner. By midnight the party was on Sambuca and ended with Dr Fox 'crawling back' to his Edinburgh hotel room at five in the morning. Who knows how close this account actually was to reality, but other reports followed, including stories about Fox and Werritty going out on karaoke nights, where Fox would sing under the name 'Barry from Bournemouth'. Fox certainly enjoyed a good party in his younger days, perhaps a spill-over from his time as a junior doctor.

Having held the shadow defence brief since the start of David Cameron's leadership, Fox became Defence Secretary in 2010 after the formation of the coalition government. In office, Fox had embarked on major reforms of the Ministry of Defence and the Armed Forces to bring them into line with Britain's defence needs in the modern age, whilst tackling the multi-billion-pound black hole in the ministry's finances. As of the beginning of October 2011, he appeared to be riding high, having played a prominent role in the courageous British and French military campaign to protect the Libyan rebels from being slaughtered by Colonel Gaddafi, and with none other than his political hero Baroness Thatcher attending his fiftieth birthday party celebrations as his guest of honour on 24 September. Two weeks later, Fox was forced out.

There had been background chatter about Fox intermittently through the summer of 2011, but nothing that would have caused him alarm. There had been a difficult story in *The Sun* about taking his staff on holiday to Spain, but nothing career-threatening. The original story that led to Fox's difficulties was broken by *The Guardian*, taking its main source of information from an American businessman called Harvey Boulter. The previous June, Fox had stopped over in Dubai en route back from visiting troops in Afghanistan and agreed to meet Boulter at the suggestion of his friend Werritty. He and Werritty held a meeting with Boulter at the five-star Shangri-La Hotel. It was a meeting that Fox should never have agreed to, as he later admitted. Had they known about it, his civil servants would probably have strongly advised against it or stopped it altogether.

Boulter was the chief executive officer of Porton Capital Inc., and the purpose of the meeting that Werritty had set up was to discuss mobile phone encryption technology for use by British troops in Afghanistan for 'welfare' calls home. Towards the end of the meeting, Boulter raised the subject of legal proceedings which had just begun in London between Porton Capital and the American company 3M over BacLite, a screening test for the detection of MRSA in hospital patients. Porton Capital was demanding up to $41 million in disputed proceeds from 3M, who had bought the test in 2007. A Ministry of

Defence agency, Ploughshare, which had helped to develop BacLite, was also one of the claimants in the proceedings. Fox, however, knew nothing about the details of the lawsuit and didn't enter discussions with Boulter on the dispute or the court proceedings.

Boulter was later sued for blackmail by 3M in New York after sending 3M's lawyer two emails referring to his meeting with Fox, and claiming that unless the case was quietly settled, David Cameron's Cabinet might 'very shortly' be discussing the knighthood recently bestowed on the chairman of 3M, Sir George Buckley. The implication was that Fox was a contact of Boulter's who might use his political influence to rescind Buckley's knighthood. The suggestion by Boulter was utterly implausible as neither Fox nor the Cabinet could rescind a knighthood through discussion or anything else. *The Guardian* should have known that this was the case, although it may have concerned the Americans.

Boulter would later agree to apologise to Fox and pay damages and costs, admitting in a joint statement read out in court that there had been no discussion between them of Sir George Buckley's knighthood at the June 2011 meeting in Dubai.

Whatever the authenticity of the information, *The Guardian* began to run the stories from Harvey Boulter. Boulter stoked the stories and gave interviews suggesting that Fox was lying about what was said and what had happened at their meeting. It was bad timing for Fox as, with the exception of Britain's military campaign in Libya, the news agenda was pretty thin and this story had the alluring whiff of conspiracy, exotic locations and shady deals.

By setting up the meeting, Werritty had embroiled Fox in a fight – and it was one in which the Queensbury Rules would not be adhered to. More problematically, however, the story drew attention to the role of Werritty himself in Fox's arrangements. On 19 August, *The Guardian* reported that Werritty had brokered the meeting with Boulter, noting that he described himself as an 'adviser' to Dr Fox despite the fact that he was not an employee of the MoD. Fox had already found out in June that Werritty was using business cards bearing the parliamentary portcullis and describing himself as his adviser, and had told him to stop.

The revelations about Werritty's activities in brokering meetings between Fox and private businessmen, and his branding himself the Secretary of State's 'adviser' despite his lack of an official government position had led to growing questions about Werritty's access and influence. Whilst Fox had been able to stonewall a question from the witch-hunting Labour MP John Mann in September about the number of official overseas visits Werritty had accompanied him on, by 5 October it was revealed that Werritty had visited Fox at the Ministry of Defence fourteen times since Fox had taken office. Fox's assertion that his meetings with Werritty at the ministry were 'not in an official capacity' did nothing to dispel the confusion, and growing suspicions, surrounding the issue.

Fox himself was preoccupied with the Libyan campaign, which was taking up most of his time. He regarded the *Guardian* stories about Boulter and the growing questions about Werritty's role as an irritation and a distraction. He now admits that he probably didn't focus on dealing with it early enough: 'You could say that I should have tried to head it off earlier and tried to put a stop to it. But I was trying to do something that was really quite important and time-consuming.' The Secretary of State was responsible for operational decisions in the ongoing military efforts in Afghanistan and the Libyan campaign, even down to the level of approving military targets. But the media, and his political opponents, wouldn't let up and Fox's slow reaction to events allowed the story to gather pace.

As would be expected with such excellent base material, the press went to town. Fox regrets that at this point he did not put a stop to the relentless stream of stories with the threat of legal action. But he had failed to grasp how damaging all these allegations could be if they were allowed to accumulate unchallenged; he should have understood that once the pack scented blood, unless he put a stop to the whole thing he was providing a green light for journalists to write almost whatever they liked. Indeed, at one point the *Daily Telegraph* ran a story with pictures of Fox with a topless star from the early 1990s as if it was only the previous week. Fox's own inaction and failure to focus on the personal consequences of these stories had allowed events to run out of control.

The Defence Secretary had clearly not read a manual of how to handle and survive a crisis, and he wasn't getting much advice. There didn't appear to be anybody telling Fox to focus on the growing storm around him, to try to put it to bed by giving a detailed account of his own rebutting the allegations in full, as, for example, George Osborne had done when faced with the allegations of soliciting donations from a Russian oligarch in Corfu. That would have left the story with nowhere further to go.

Indeed, Fox even ignored his own advice that he had given to Osborne when in the jaws of the Deripaska scandal. In the midst of Osborne's difficulties, Fox had told him that in a crisis it is very difficult for the person or people at the centre of it to behave rationally. So for several days Fox didn't let Osborne go far without him, even going as far as to suggest that the young shadow Chancellor should not even get into a taxi unless he was with him. Being Secretary of State for Defence was a hindrance in this sense for Fox. Because he had armed protection with him at all times, it was it impossible for people to just drop in and out of his daily routine. He couldn't get the same kind of collegiate support that he had been able to provide to Osborne. The MoD's security had effectively marooned him from his friends and the people that could give him the best advice. But he also failed to lift his head and look at what was going on around him.

On 6 October, Fox finally issued a statement. Dismissing what he described as 'baseless allegations' about his links with Werritty, he asked Ursula Brennan, the Permanent Secretary of his own department, to carry out an internal inquiry to establish whether there had been any breach of national security or the ministerial code as a result of Werritty's access to him. But he remained largely focused for almost all of this time on what was happening in the MoD and in Libya, and a day later, Fox was in the Libyan town of Misrata, surrounded by death and destruction. A local man showed him heart-rending pictures of his dead children – once again demonstrating to Fox how unimportant his own political squalls and crises were when lives were at stake. It did not help his cause that bombing missions had degraded communications facilities across the country, so there was no phone contact and Fox therefore had little idea what was happening back at home for around three days.

In those circumstances, Fox believes that the ongoing political attacks against him at home by his political foes and those in the press who were pursuing him should have been curtailed whilst he had no means of communicating or fighting back. Whatever the rights and wrongs, Fox's expectation was surely unrealistic. If he believed it, he should surely have tried to reach out to the various editors explaining that he needed to be out of the country on urgent matters of state for which he was personally responsible as Defence Secretary, and that he would deal with all of the issues, in full, as soon as possible on his return. At the very least, he should have made sure that one of his aides or allies in the UK was in charge of the situation whilst he was in Libya and largely out of contact.

Once Boulter had started making his accusations, Fox had agreed to allow the MoD's lawyers to take a detailed statement about the meeting that had taken place in Dubai from which everything else flowed. The lawyers appeared relaxed about what they heard and thought the accusations were going nowhere. Legally, perhaps – but politically it was quite another matter.

Unlike other scandals and crises in this book, in Fox's case there was little incoming advice about how to handle events from either Conservative Party Central Office or No. 10. In fact, Fox personally had very little contact with No. 10 officials at all. One is left pondering why an often assertive No. 10 backed off. Was it slightly wary of Fox? Was it concerned about the reaction there might have been if it stepped into his territory? Or did it, like Fox, fail to see how big the crisis was? Fox is an extremely capable and single-minded politician, not one to take direction easily. Perhaps No. 10 was waiting for Fox to ask for its assistance. He did not. The Downing Street machine only got as far as talking with his outer office by the time of Fox's resignation.

Fox relied on his two officially appointed special advisers, Luke Coffey and Oliver Waghorn, for most of his guidance. Fox's wife, Jesme, was also in the loop and remained calm throughout the whole affair. She only became really irritated when her mother or Fox's family were being doorstepped, because she felt it was nothing to do with them.

When crises get serious, it is almost standard practice for the press to start turning up at the homes of friends and family, even frail elderly relatives, knocking on the door or calling them up asking for their thoughts on the episode and whether the person in the line of fire should resign. It is one of the biggest intrusions during such high-profile crises, with the person at its centre feeling a combination of responsibility for the inconvenience and distress, and, in all likelihood, a degree of embarrassment. Fox, as with others, found it beyond the pale. But his family handled it well, telling the journalists in most cases to simply get lost. The worst intrusion was against Jesme's elderly mother, a widow living on her own, who was quite frightened by the experience. But all remained supportive and no one suggested Fox should resign or throw in the towel. Instead they rallied around and offered strong support.

Fox felt the impact on his family and friends was distinctly unfair:

You accept it yourself on the front line of politics because you know that's what you're up for. I felt very sorry for Adam [Werritty] because he was being torn apart and not able to answer. And that did bother me because it is something you can't do anything about. But you live and learn.

Unfortunately, there was very little that Fox could do to protect himself, let alone his family and friends, including Werritty. It demonstrated the inability of even the most powerful people in politics to protect those close to them once a scandal or crisis has exploded. Fox's constituents weren't telling him there was a problem either. If anything, he was getting feedback from constituents and local Conservatives that they were angry with the media, especially the printed press, for its coverage. Nobody was suggesting outside of the Westminster bubble that much was amiss in an admittedly complicated story. Rather, many were left wondering what it was all about – but that didn't stop a frenzied pursuit of Fox.

The reports did not move the support of Conservative MPs, either. Most felt that Fox had probably stepped a little over the line, but certainly not to the point where he needed to resign from his job. The parliamentary party liked Liam Fox for his Thatcherite, no-nonsense views and his resistance to blindly accepting the prevailing politically correct orthodoxy. It was felt that he spoke up for and represented in Cabinet a view in the party that had been side-lined by the Conservative modernisation programme.

He had many friends and they were very happy to go out to bat for him in public, whether in the House of Commons or the TV and radio studios. His friend Greg Hands and others wanted to save him. Hands, a PPS at the time to George Osborne, said on BBC *Breakfast* that there was 'insinuation, innuendo and smear' in many of the allegations swirling around the Defence Secretary.

Chris Grayling, a close ally and Fox's leadership election campaign manager in 2005, told BBC Radio 4's *World at One*:

I think this will blow over in a while. He has been a very good
Defence Secretary, trying to deal with difficult circumstances in the
MoD, a huge mismanagement of the procurement programme by
the Labour Party, all the challenges in Afghanistan and Libya … I
think this will soon be forgotten.

There were more than enough supportive MPs who were willing to
go into battle for Fox and provide the public voices of defence. A
number of his MP friends and colleagues saw the press stories as a
vicious attack on Fox's character.

Fox's own recollection was that he was fairly calm throughout the crisis, but that the pressure grew to a feverish pitch. By
the time of his return from Libya, the scale of the crisis had
started to creep up on Fox. Because it had appeared in August
and September, he thought it was just going to keep turning
up and blowing itself out. But there had been extensive press
coverage again over the previous weekend and still there was no
lull in the storm. Stories were running about Fox being involved
with Israel and questions were being asked in print as to whether
he was a Mossad agent. The rumours were becoming increasingly
far-fetched but all the same were treated with a surprising level
of seriousness.

There seemed to be no way of getting on top of events. A
quite staggering level of additional material was being turned up
throughout each day. Increasingly, it didn't seem to matter whether
the new allegations had anything to do with the somewhat obscure
nature of the crisis surrounding Fox, nor whether there might have
been a rational explanation.

When Fox was away at the Conservative Party conference in early October, a story about his involvement in secret espionage, personal foreign policy initiatives and arms sales first began to get legs. It sounds absurd to suggest this now, but at the time British commentators were seriously asking whether Fox was running an alternative foreign policy to that of the British government. Fox, it was alleged, was globetrotting around the world meeting all sorts of shadowy people and putting his personal foreign policy forward on behalf of Britain. This was a proposition that was seriously entertained by media commentators at the time. The atmosphere created by such frenzied pursuits creates an artificial environment where almost anything can be suggested and possibly believed, no matter how preposterous.

Questions started to be asked about Fox's dealings in Sri Lanka. He had attempted to assist with the negotiation of part of the peace process in the 1990s and had kept up with his contacts since, wanting to continue to help. But there were other groupings in the Tamil diaspora with a different point of view. Fox had also made enemies with his pro-American and pro-Israeli stances. It made for a multifaceted and wide-ranging attack on Fox from people who had been waiting for just such an opportunity. Fox felt he could have seen any one of the attacks off on its own, but now, he found, 'They all piled in. It was a whole lot of stuff rolled in, and you know, people now look back and ask, "What was it really actually all about?"' Fox believes, with some justification, that although he made mistakes, there was an element of 'we'll teach him a lesson' and a settling of old scores and enmities during the crisis – which is why it became such a feeding frenzy.

The intensity made him wonder whether he could tough it out, and question whether it was practically possible to do so if it continued at the velocity and scale the crisis had reached. Unlike Andrew Mitchell, it did not affect Fox's health to any great degree or cause him to lose sleep. The impact was more subtle than that. Gradually, the need to respond to the growing stream of allegations began to crowd out what Fox was able to concentrate on and think about. As he puts it:

> When you're running non-stop and you have to constantly think what to say to the press ... and I'm supposed to be doing specific targeting for the Libyan campaign, literally choosing which targets we were going to hit on the ground, worrying about the collateral damage and civilian casualties and so on ... And all the time I'm getting a barrage of 'The Sun says this ... The Sun says that ... what do I do about it?' There comes a point when you have to accept that it's not possible, I can't do this.

Fox had tried very hard to ignore all that was going on around him and get on with business as usual. This in itself irritated some in the press, who suggested that he wasn't taking the crisis seriously, or was shirking his responsibility to answer the allegations. They delved into every nuance of the story, looking for changes or amendments to Fox's response.

There were also those in the media who didn't like the fact that he could largely avoid them if he wished to do so. The comic nature of events was recognised when the press did manage to close in on him. At one point he had a BBC journalist, among many others, chasing him around St Pancras station saying, 'Dr Fox, do you think this is a witch hunt?' Every crisis has its comic moments and a little gallows humour, and Fox must have seen the pantomime absurdity in this.

Having returned from Libya, instead of focusing on bringing a military conflict to an end, Fox was summoned to the House of Commons on Monday 10 October to give a statement to the House of Commons, where he was forced to give a full account of his relationship with Adam Werritty, his contact with Harvey Boulter and his contacts in Sri Lanka. He found it awkward and slightly embarrassing having to publicly account for these events in some detail. He denied any wrongdoing, but apologised for his error in judgement, accepting that it was a mistake to 'allow distinctions to be blurred between professional responsibilities and personal loyalties to a friend'. He further apologised to the Prime Minister, to the public and to the House.

Despite this, the papers reported that Fox had emerged relatively unscathed from the ordeal. The *Telegraph* declared that Labour had given up soon after their initial unsuccessful attack: 'The Labour benches thinned out very quickly as their quarry made his escape. The history of these occasions tells us they favour the minister in trouble. But the Defence Secretary put on a confident and combative performance. Dr Fox has escaped to fight again.'

Whether he had escaped or not, that Monday was a torrid day for Fox. The Prime Minister received the interim report from Fox's own Permanent Secretary of her investigation, which found that material from Fox's diary at the MoD had been made available to Mr Werritty in a manner that was 'not appropriate'.

Downing Street's line in response was that it was clear that 'serious mistakes' had been made and the then Cabinet Secretary, Sir Gus O'Donnell, was ordered to take over the inquiry from the Permanent Secretary at the MoD. Later that day, the Ministry of Defence released a list of forty meetings between Fox and Werritty either in the MoD's Whitehall offices or on trips overseas, adding further fuel to the fire.

As much as he had tried to focus on his responsibilities in this most fundamental of offices of state, the scandal had slowly got under Fox's skin. It was a gradual process, but it got to a point where, quite subconsciously, he reached a tipping point. He suddenly felt weighed down by events and thoroughly fed up. It now went through Fox's mind that perhaps he should resign just to put an end to it. He decided to continue and see how the next few days panned out.

In spite of the Cabinet Secretary's inquiry ordered by Downing Street, the Prime Minister continued to be supportive of Fox, and personally called to ask if he was all right. Former rivals for the Tory leadership, the pair had what could be described as a good working relationship. Fox had known Cameron for a long time; they even used to play tennis regularly when the former was at the Home Office. Cameron would probably have stood by Fox had he wanted to continue but the clamour against him had become so intense that it is difficult to see how things could have been handled differently. Fox had a strong feeling that if certain parts of the press couldn't nail him on something of substance they would gradually destroy his reputation anyway.

Fox was putting a brave face on things, staying calm, not least because his role as Defence Secretary demanded that he looked in control. A Defence Secretary who looked damaged, weak or indecisive was sure to be finished. As Fox says, 'You can't look as if you're panicked, and it was not like I was losing sleep over it, that I would get up in the morning and think, "Oh God, here we go again." It wasn't affecting me emotionally, I would say. It was, though, irritating beyond belief.'

Worse was to come on 11 October as the Tory wall in support of Fox cracked and he drew fire from his own side. Patrick Mercer, a senior Tory MP and former soldier who later become embroiled in his own scandal, sniped at Fox, suggesting that 'the last thing ... busy civil servants and busy uniformed staff need inside the MoD is this sort of distraction with their boss'. Jim Murphy, then shadow Defence Secretary, was in full cry, suggesting Fox had broken the ministerial code and should be investigated by the independent adviser on ministers' interests.

On Wednesday 12 October, Fox travelled to Paris in his capacity as Defence Secretary, but a press conference scheduled for that day was cancelled due to the overwhelming interest in the feeding frenzy now surrounding him. The scandal then dominated the weekly session of PMQs. The session was not pretty for the Defence Secretary. It was becoming untenable, even for someone so experienced and robust. The same day, a newspaper report revealed that a younger man had been present in Fox's flat at the time of a burglary the previous year, throwing the gay smears and innuendo back into the mix.

Fox had finally reached his personal tipping point: he decided to resign that Friday, 14 October. Things had become impossible. There was also evidence that Conservative MPs were now predicting openly that he was going to have to go. A Tory whip with a rather big mouth had told a Labour MP that Fox would have to quit when the inquiry by the Cabinet Secretary reported the following week. The Tory told his Labour friend, 'You will get your scalp' – and the Labour friend promptly told the *Daily Mail*. The BBC's political editor, Nick Robinson, had also helpfully compiled a list of Fox's sins.

Having spoken to his wife, Fox met his two special advisers to tell them of his decision. They tried to convince him to carry on. Ed Llewellyn and Craig Oliver were also pushing him to continue, suggesting various media strategies to deal with the ongoing crisis. But he told them all they were behind the curve: the point of no return had been passed. He had made his decision and would not be persuaded to change his mind.

Fox's steely resolve saw him call the Prime Minister whilst he was doing a constituency surgery to say, 'I've decided to go.' It had become impossible, he said, to carry on with so many stories and accusations flying around. The stories, he told the PM, were fundamentally untrue, but he needed time to think about how to deal with them. 'At the moment it's impossible, I can't get a hearing.'

Fox felt that he was unable to talk about anything to do with his job. The opposition and the media had decided it was time to take a scalp, which meant he was unable to concentrate on any of the things that needed to be done. He would have to give up the job he loved, partly for his own sake, but also for the sake of the government.

Fox's resignation was announced that afternoon. In a letter to the Prime Minister, he repeated the apology he had made in his statement to the House of Commons on the Monday, saying he was 'very sorry' for allowing the distinction between his personal interest and his government activities to become blurred. Acknowledging that 'national interest must always come before personal interest', he announced that he had decided, 'with great sadness', to resign as Secretary of State for Defence.

In response, Cameron acknowledged that Fox had been a key member of his team since becoming leader of the Conservative Party, and stated that Fox had done a superb job both in opposition and in government. Cameron added that he and Fox had worked closely during that time and that he valued the friendship of both Fox and his wife Jesme.

Could Fox have possibly seen it through? Would the frenzy have burnt itself out as some were telling him? Fox took the view that to continue and say 'I'm going to survive in this office come what may' could score points for its bloody-mindedness but wasn't in the interest of the government. He chose the course he was going to take and simply didn't want to be seen as one of those ministers who cling on without any sense of self-respect.

Could he have handled it differently at the beginning? He accepts that burying his head in his work and not acting quickly to try and kill the scandal was a mistake:

I think that your instinct is to get on with your work and I think probably we should have stopped and said 'we have to deal with this and then move on, rather than just try to continue'. But it was slightly more difficult when you're in the middle of a war and in the circumstances I might possibly do the same again. Then, of course, as with all these things, you are a little bit at the mercy of events. Would things have been different if we had caught Gaddafi a week earlier?

The sensation surrounding Gaddafi's capture and death, which took place on 20 October 2011, probably would have allowed the story to move on and might have taken the heat off Fox because he had achieved a successful outcome – a tyrant defeated.

At least Fox can feel comfortable with himself that he had dealt with the crisis in his own way and kept the respect of his close friends and family:

> You never know with all these things. I think, as with anything in life, it's not whether it hits you or not, it's how you deal with it when it does. I hope I dealt with it in a relatively matter-of-fact way, I didn't go gushing and complaining, and I kept my counsel. I was very fortunate because I do have very close friends and family and so that becomes a strong insulating element.

THE AFTERMATH

Looking back, there may be a fairly simple explanation for what went wrong with Fox's connection to Adam Werritty. Werritty had been one of his team in opposition, when Fox had a limited number of special advisers. Although Werritty wasn't an adviser, working rather as a paid intern, he became integrated into the team and would therefore meet up with Fox when he and his team went abroad. In opposition, where these things are less prone to civil service rules and regulations, it was a perfectly ordinary dynamic as far as Fox was concerned. But despite this explanation, he should have checked when in government to make sure everything was above board.

However, it is also worth asking questions about how the civil service could have better assisted their busy and preoccupied Secretary of State. What were the civil servants doing and saying to him at the time about Werritty? They may well have had concerns, but did they raise them in the proper way? Shouldn't the civil service have put in writing any concerns they had? They could have raised the matter officially at any time through the Cabinet Office, and the Cabinet Secretary would then have been forced to raise it directly with Fox. Fox himself has refused to attribute any blame. However, one wonders how strongly civil servants felt at the time if no one ever officially raised concerns about Werritty in a note or memo.

Whatever the rights and wrongs, once Fox had decided to 'stop this nonsense', as he puts it, by resigning, unlike many other former Cabinet ministers in a similar position, he wasn't met with a void. He was still resident at Admiralty House for some time after his resignation and also had full personal protection from his security officers. Ex-ministers have often commented on the strange sensation of getting up the day after losing their job to find that nothing remains of the trappings of high office that had surrounded them for months if not several years – leaving them feeling they have been completely abandoned. Fortunately for Fox, his tenure in high office did not end so abruptly. In his case, the symbols of power were withdrawn gradually, so allowing him a steadier transition back to normal life.

Just as he was during the crisis, today Fox is matter-of-fact about the life of a politician:

I can understand why people have difficulty with the adjustment. But let's face it, that can happen to you in democratic politics anytime. You can find yourself a Cabinet minister one day and not even a Member of Parliament the next, if you lose an election. It is something we all subconsciously think can happen. You're always aware of the fact that at any time the rug can be pulled from under you.

In the days after his resignation he returned to his constituency home in Somerset, where he found the usual crowd of journalists gathered outside his home. They were positioned at the end of the drive. When asked by Fox's wife why they were there, they replied that they were waiting in case Fox made a statement. He let it be known that there was not going to be any statement. They stayed for a day and a night after his resignation and then just fizzled away, until they were eventually gone. Fox and his family's lives were finally returning to normal. The news hounds had their scalp; there was nothing else left for them.

Fox sat down with his wife Jesme and discussed the events of the previous weeks. They tried to make sense of the events that had led to his downfall and rationalise them. They also planned what he would do next, and quickly put in place a plan for how to deal with both the past and the future. This was made easier because there were lots of events in the diary – he had a lot of engagements, foreign trips coming up, conferences he had been invited to – and they all stood by the invitations. Fox had plenty to occupy him. All this helped his adjustment to new circumstances.

On the night that Fox resigned, he had a diary commitment to speak at a big dinner hosted by the Tamworth Conservative Association with hundreds of people in attendance. He had to decide whether to go ahead and do the dinner or to pull out. Fox was in a quandary what to do. He used to tell his patients who were in a car crash to 'get behind the wheel again as quickly as you can'. Now he felt he should take his own advice and get back out there, even though he knew it would be a test of his character:

> I really wasn't looking forward to it and there was a bit of me that thought, 'It would be so awful, I'm not going to do it.' But there was a bigger bit of me saying 'Go and do it. Apart from anything else, people paid and it's your duty to go and do it.'

However much he had been dreading it, honouring the commitment was one of the best decisions he ever made. The local activists were fantastically supportive.

> Within a couple of days I had done my first big public event and that was really instrumental in recovering – I think it is a big mistake to hide away, but I suppose it depends on your personality. My approach was to get back out there. I set myself a very clear rule that I wasn't going to talk about politics, I was only going to talk about policy and so I was never going to comment on the day-to-day running of government or personalities. I have stuck to that rule absolutely rigidly.

Out of office, Fox now takes a different view of ministerial status. He doesn't believe it is healthy for government ministers – and Cabinet ministers in particular – to be in office for too long without a break because this leaves them with a skewed view of reality.

> My view is that it would be healthier for ministers to do four or five years on the front line, have a break and come back. I think that would be much more refreshing for them. I now think my own seventeen consecutive years on the front bench without a break was too long. You have too much output and not enough input. The one thing since I've left the government was that I had tonnes of time for input plus I had a fair idea of what I wanted those inputs to be. I have had a relationship to reading novels that someone stumbling across an oasis in the desert would have with water – I couldn't read enough of them, it was like a terrible thirst.

He has also spent more time at home, seeing friends and playing a bit more sport. He leads a normal life again, which is not a bad way to come out of the biggest crisis in your political career. But Fox is a fighter, a strong and determined character with a real sense of what he believes. If anyone had the character and self-belief to cope in a crisis it was him.

CHAPTER 3

CHRIS HUHNE
ON THE ROAD TO NOWHERE

"Prison is not something I would opt for. I don't think anybody would think it is easy or pleasant – I don't think it's likely that Thomas Cook will be putting the British prison system on their favoured fortnight. However, I knew I had to spend two months there and you get through it. The worst part of the penalty in all this was losing the job I loved."

– Chris Huhne

Of all the falls from grace in British politics in the last decade, arguably one of the most spectacular was Chris Huhne. He has the ignominious distinction of becoming the first Cabinet minister in British history to resign as a consequence of criminal proceedings. He was subsequently convicted of perverting the course of justice, contrary to common law.

Some say Huhne was unlucky, whilst others believe he was overly arrogant and calculating as events unfolded. Whichever it was, the chain of events that led to Huhne and his ex-wife, Vicky Pryce, going to prison are remarkable and serve as a warning to all politicians that something that may appear to you as a trivial-seeming misdemeanour can return with a vengeance to strike down even the most high-flying of careers.

The damage was ultimately self-inflicted, but it was nonethe-less extremely painful, blowing Huhne's family apart, destroying his career and severely damaging his personal reputation. It was certainly a significant price to pay for falling in love with Carina Trimingham.

⋄⋄⋄⋄

Whilst technically Chris Huhne's problems began with his wife taking his speeding points and fine back in 2003, the real trigger for his problems was an affair with Carina Trimingham. That affair began in mid-2008, after a period when the two had been working very closely together and found they were attracted to one another.

Huhne had first got a warning that the media might be onto his affair with Trimingham in the run-up to the 2010 general election. He was the subject of a fairly routine tabloid investigation, the sort which usually features celebrities or high-profile politicians, put in place by *News of the World*'s then chief reporter, Neville Thurlbeck. Thurlbeck had previously broken stories about the private lives of David Beckham and Max Mosley, whilst also outing the former Cabinet minister Nick Brown as gay, and breaking the story that Jeffrey Archer had committed perjury in his libel trial against the *Daily Star*. Thurlbeck was later sacked from the paper in the wake of the phone-hacking scandal, before pleading guilty when subse-quently prosecuted on hacking-related charges.

Thurlbeck had received a tip-off from 'a nosy teenager', as he put it, and had followed it up. He hired a private investigator – retired policeman and so-called 'silent shadow', Derek Webb – to tail

Huhne's lover from his Eastleigh constituency to her London home. Surprisingly, the story of Huhne's affair didn't make it into the newspaper, apparently because it was felt by the *News of the World* that Huhne wasn't yet a well-known or significant enough political figure.

Those close to Huhne don't entirely buy this story. They argue that private surveillance is an expensive business and the *News of the World* must have thought Huhne sufficiently high-profile before it began. They suggest it was not coincidental that the surveillance happened at the time when Huhne went public as the only senior frontbencher calling for a renewed police investigation into voice-mail hacking at the *News of the World*. The surveillance of the affair, and the decision to back it financially, may, they believe, have been either revenge or a warning not to pursue phone hacking.

Huhne now believes he was probably foolish to place himself in the firing line of a newspaper that was desperately trying to survive a major scandal, but the line had been agreed carefully with his party leader, Nick Clegg, before he went public. Huhne and Clegg agreed that the evidence was very clear: there was not just one rogue reporter at the *News of the World*. It appeared that many reporters were involved in illegal activity. Huhne, who had worked in a newsroom, was convinced that illegal practices were widespread at the paper.

The only reporter on the *News of the World* who had been convicted in relation to phone hacking at that point was the royal reporter, Clive Goodman. According to the court case, Goodman had been hacking into the voicemails of people such as Gordon Taylor, the chief executive of the Professional Footballers' Association, Max Clifford and Simon Hughes MP – yet none of them had anything to do with the royals. Huhne believed that a royal correspondent would be interested in the royals, not in politics, football, or in any of these other fields where phone hacking had taken place.

Having left the story of Huhne's affair in the pending file, the *News of the World* returned to it after the general election. It renewed its investigation and this time got pictures of Huhne and Trimingham together. By now, Huhne was much more significant, as a Cabinet minister in a rare coalition government rather than a mere Liberal Democrat spokesman.

The *News of the World* was now going to run the story and Huhne had no way of denying it. The question then was: did he want to leave the situation unresolved? This in turn would mean further endless speculation about what he would do next – a 'will he, won't he leave his wife?' situation. It would become a real-life, real-time soap opera, with wall-to-wall coverage in all the newspapers about what might happen next.

In fact, Huhne had already made his decision. But the revelations would jeopardise all his plans for a smoother transition for his family. Huhne had hoped to get his youngest son through his A levels before telling his wife and getting a divorce. He now decided that the sensible course was to bring his existing plans forward and announce that he intended to leave his wife and live with Trimingham. This, thought Huhne, would make everything clear so it was no longer a story. Reflecting on the choice to go public about his decision to leave his wife, Huhne recalls, 'That was a decision which I had already taken, but I obviously hoped the timing and the circumstances would be ones of my own choosing, rather than those of the *News of the World*.'

Huhne had been married to Vicky Pryce for over twenty-five years and they had three children together, in addition to Pryce's two children from a previous marriage. They had shared many good times during their long relationship but were said to have drifted apart – although not by Pryce, who believed her marriage was secure. Huhne was adamant that his attraction to Trimingham was not superficial or a passing phase for a middle-aged man, as is so often the case. After his marriage split, he ventured that he had fallen deeply in love with her.

The equation may have been simple to Huhne, but it did not make the fallout from it any easier. He had to go home and break the news to his wife, then pack his bags and leave. The press were desperate for every detail and reported it in unflinching terms that made it difficult to have any sympathy for him. The *Daily Mail* reported that he had:

> ended his 25-year marriage during a televised football match, his ex-wife revealed yesterday. Vicky Pryce said his admission that he was cheating came in the half-time break of a World Cup match in June 2010. According to Miss Pryce, the Liberal Democrat Cabinet minister immediately went off to draft a statement to the media before heading to the gym.

There were strong elements of truth in the *Mail*'s report, but it didn't tell the whole story. On the day Huhne told his wife of his affair and his decision to leave her (Saturday 19 June 2010), he had travelled back to London from his Eastleigh constituency with Trimingham, where the two had stayed the previous night at his constituency home. Huhne had held a constituency surgery that evening in Eastleigh. Pryce remained at their home in Clapham.

On the Saturday morning and as part of their now normal subterfuge, the lovers left the house separately, minutes apart, and headed for the railway station where they stood apart on the platform. They boarded separate carriages before Huhne joined Trimingham in the first-class carriage for breakfast. On arrival at Waterloo Station they again kept their distance, leaving the station by different exits before meeting again at the taxi rank.

As the couple were queuing for a black cab, they noticed a press photographer taking pictures. After all the deception on their journey, they immediately knew that there was something afoot but weren't sure exactly how serious it was, as they hadn't been challenged about their affair up to that point. With the media seemingly onto the couple, they still had some time before a query about their relationship would eventually arrive through the Deputy Prime Minister's office.

Huhne's instant reaction was that he needed to talk to Jonny Oates – the Liberal Democrats' communications chief in Downing Street and later chief of staff to Nick Clegg – who confirmed that there were newspapers, particularly the *News of the World*, asking about an affair. They agreed the line Huhne would take as a result of the enquiries. After Huhne's conversation with Oates, a telephone call from a newspaper quickly followed asking about the truth of the story in circulation about an affair.

With the story rapidly gathering speed and likely to break at any moment in the world of 24-hour news, Huhne's priority now was to get home to see his wife and explain what had happened, so that she would hear the news from him, rather than a journalist. Huhne was keen to limit both the longevity of any story and the damage that the affair would do to his own reputation. He was also aware that he urgently had to speak to his children. Fortunately, he managed to get hold of each of the children on the phone and talk to them individually before they heard anything from the press.

His circumstances and subsequent choices were widely reported at the time as similar to the situation Robin Cook faced in 1997 when his affair with Gaynor Regan, his then secretary, was suddenly about to become public. Cook also had to make an instant decision to tell his wife and choose between the two women. He ended his 28-year marriage just before he boarded a plane at Heathrow.

With the story about to become public, Huhne arrived at his family's London home and wanted to talk to Pryce as privately and quietly as was possible. He took the first possible opportunity when she came downstairs to the kitchen, having been watching TV upstairs. Huhne told her they needed to talk. They sat down in the kitchen and he told her of the affair. The pair went on talking until neither had anything more to add – which Pryce has contested was not very long.

Pryce had had no idea about any of it and found it hard to take in. It was an enormous shock. She had not had the slightest inkling that Huhne was having an affair. However, Huhne did not then walk out and leave the family home – although he did draft a statement and go to the gym. But he remained at the house until the following evening, when his wife told him to leave.

According to Huhne, despite his admissions of infidelity and his love for Trimingham, and despite the shock, anger and devastation

Pryce must have felt, the couple's parting was, in fact, not decided upon at this point. The matter had been left open during their discussion in the kitchen on the Saturday evening. But with the Sunday papers wanting to know the truth of what was going on, Huhne put out a statement aimed at killing any chance of an ongoing soap opera and designed to try to minimise press interest and intrusion. The short statement made it clear that Huhne was having an affair with Trimingham, that it was a serious relationship and that he intended to leave his wife to be with her.

Huhne achieved his purpose with the statement in that there was no further immediate press intrusion; the sting had been taken out of the matter from the media perspective for the time being. Huhne was no stranger to controversy, either within the Liberal Democrats or in the wider Westminster world. He was a man known not only to speak out bluntly but also to avail himself of the dark arts of politics in the shadows. He was well connected with journalists and knew how to undermine his opponents and competitors whenever necessary – usually without leaving any fingerprints. His political life had not been a quiet one and he had experienced media attention before.

Although the coverage of his affair and separation from his wife was unpleasant, it was fairly short-lived, with very little follow-up after the original story. Most of the press didn't even run pictures of Trimingham and Huhne together – that came later. In media terms, Huhne felt the exposure of his affair was more a squall than a storm – quite low intensity.

One suspects that Huhne was more reluctant to leave the family home and his wife and children than he would ever publicly admit. He is clear that he had already made up his mind to leave before the news broke, but events, as he acknowledges, still conspired to force his hand earlier than he would have liked or expected. In these circumstances Huhne's legendary political logic and his supreme confidence in his own political nous would have kicked in and possibly outweighed immediate family considerations.

Pryce later told of her shock and humiliation and described the episode to a national newspaper:

> I was watching the World Cup and it was half-time. I came down to have something to eat and my husband came in and told me he had been found out by the Press for having an affair, and that he was about to make a statement. I discovered it just like that. It was only over a few minutes of conversation that I learned that my marriage had basically come to an end.
>
> 'He went to the study and wrote [the statement] and sent it off then he went to the gym. That was that.

Chatter in the Westminster press lobby in the days that followed was unkind to Huhne, suggesting he had announced the end of their marriage in order to save himself from some difficult press and to stop his career from being weighed down by ongoing questions about personal life. Certainly the majority of the media believed his decision was based on his desire to keep hold of his job and a Cabinet career, and that he was prepared to sacrifice his marriage to do so. The press saw him as fair game thereafter and there was a steely determination among a number of them to pursue him.

Whatever the truth of Huhne's motives, the outcome was now decided: he was in love with and had chosen Trimingham. From that point onwards the whole Huhne family experienced a terrible ordeal that ended with both parents going to prison.

At the outset, the political ramifications of the affair for Huhne were not nearly as severe as the personal difficulties. He had spoken as early as possible to Nick Clegg and his advisers, and the general view at Westminster was that this was just another politician who had got into a mess in his private life. Francis Maude, his Conservative Cabinet colleague said, 'What goes on in people's private lives is a subject that fascinates the tabloid press but is irrelevant to the job they are trying to do.' For most MPs it was a personal not political matter, one they may have joked about in private but were silent or sympathetic on publicly.

The attitude to affairs had changed in thirteen years of a Labour government. As Prime Minister, John Major had been dogged by these matters, but the reaction within the Establishment had now developed beyond the times when an affair automatically signalled an entire political career going up in smoke. There are now numerous examples of people in public positions having had complications in their private lives – the same sort of complications which also exist for many people in other walks of life – and being able to work through them without it ruining their career.

However difficult the matter was for Huhne and Trimingham, things were very much worse for Pryce. She had not been expecting the curtain to be brought down on her marriage at that point, and certainly not by a public statement. Having left the matter open in his face-to-face talk with her, Huhne had gone ahead unilaterally and made the end of their marriage final through the media. This added humiliation must have been exceptionally painful for his wife, already reeling from a terrible shock.

Pryce had been chief economic adviser to Vince Cable at the Business Department and she continued in the job briefly under the coalition. She had handed in her notice several weeks earlier, more than a month before the general election. There was no truth to reports that she had resigned because Huhne had joined the Cabinet. But after the initial shock of what had happened died away, Pryce was left thinking about her next move.

DEALING WITH THE CRISIS

Huhne had run for the leadership of his party twice. In March 2006 he lost to Menzies Campbell when he had been an MP for just seven months, and then by the narrowest of margins (511 votes in a turnout of more than 40,000) to Nick Clegg in December 2007 following an often rancorous campaign. His campaigns for the leadership had already enabled him to adjust to greater scrutiny from the media, as he recalled to me:

> When you get involved in a leadership campaign, you realise that there is an entirely different level of media attention to the one that you would expect in politics. My first experience of it was shortly after the 2005 election and the difference was massive.

The Liberal Democrats, as a small third party out of government for nearly seventy years, were not taken particularly seriously by the media. Individual MPs had to fight to gain any form of recognition and much of what they said was considered meaningless as it would never be implemented, there being no chance of them forming a single-party government. The leader of a party however, was nonetheless able to get their fair share of coverage, which placed those vying for the position on a different political plane from the ordinary Liberal Democrat MP.

In his tussle with Menzies Campbell, Huhne suddenly became a serious candidate, so the level of media interest rocketed. Instead of no one turning up to hear his views, now there were regularly four or five television cameras and twenty or thirty journalists. These leadership campaigns were a foretaste of his future, because they were quite compressed by time, fiercely fought and generated a lot of heat. For example, there were a number of attacks on Huhne about his personal finances. Huhne got a flavour of the political rough stuff.

Although it did not put him off, he didn't like it at all and one attack during those elections made a mark on him. A leaflet put out at a leadership husting accused him of having investments which were inconsistent with the political positions he had taken. The leaflet claimed Huhne had invested in a company which was involved in surveillance, even though he was in favour of civil liberties and opposed to excessive intrusion into the private lives of individuals. In the great scheme of political shenanigans this might appear pretty mild – but even those politicians with 'balls of steel', as is often said of Huhne, are sensitive to charges of hypocrisy.

Despite the sensitivities, Huhne did learn from this experience in the spotlight – which helped him to remain steady under enormous media pressure.

I think one of the lessons, which is a very early lesson people have to face when they have a lot of media pressure, is whether or not you react and put out a denial. You may feel a particular story is deeply unfair and untrue and you want to rebut it, but sometimes it actually makes sense not to do so because in doing so you give the story more legs than it would have if you merely ignored it. It's always a fine judgement to make in the media storm as to whether you rebut something and risk other newspapers, who haven't run that story, picking it up. Sometimes it is better to ignore it and hope that the story goes away.

It is interesting that Huhne's approach appears to run directly counter to the 'standard procedure' of how to deal with a political crisis – which involves getting as full an explanation of events into the public domain as soon as possible. This is something that many law firms also advise their clients to do in similar situations where a crisis or serious scandal is underway. In such circumstances, it can also be effective to use a law firm to make media organisations aware of potential libel consequences of the story. But, as Huhne would counter, this requires a matter of judgement as to whether the matter is serious enough to warrant such a response – and most political stories are not.

Huhne also set great store by how those at the centre of the storm conduct themselves personally. He felt that even when in the most difficult situation, the appearance of coolness and calmness under fire was essential. However a person in the limelight might feel inside, it gave a perception of authority and might avoid making things worse. Sometimes, he felt, the more you say the worse it gets: much better to quietly and authoritatively go about your daily business and give off a feeling of being in control. 'Sometimes it is better to just try and face it down.'

Huhne's view of how to deal with a crisis is formed from his view of media behaviour, which is the driving force that propels any crisis forward. 'The one thing about a media storm is that it is a very contagious event: it's like a stock market panic or a house price bubble – it's almost by definition a bunch of people behaving like lemmings, and you have to be very, very calm in those circumstances.'

Even so, for all that Huhne had learned about the rough-and-tumble of politics and about being under media pressure, he had not yet had to face the challenge of stories about his family or personal life, or deal with doorstep interviews from photographers and journalists camped outside his house.

After a fairly quiet summer following the announcement of Huhne's affair and the end of his marriage to Pryce, the real crisis for Huhne began to unfold as newspapers began to pick up things that were attributed to Vicky Pryce or those around her. Pryce was contacting newspapers to damage Huhne out of revenge for the affair and its repercussions on her and her children. Pryce may have been getting advice from those around her at this time, such as her neighbour Constance Briscoe, who was a public figure herself by virtue of being one of the first black women to sit as a judge in the UK, and who had also been left by a long-standing partner. Pryce and Briscoe must have had plenty to discuss, and they certainly had a significant level of contact. Huhne's team established that between June 2010, when Huhne left Pryce, and October 2012, Briscoe rang or texted Pryce 848 times, and Pryce rang or texted her 822 times.

The first newspaper contacted to run a story was the *Mail on Sunday*. Briscoe told the paper that Pryce had told her back in 2003 about certain events that had taken place. The *Mail on Sunday* decided not to oblige, in part because it was concerned that this was merely fallout from the messy break-up of a marriage, rather than a story of genuine wrongdoing.

The first allegation actually put to Huhne was that he had passed speeding-fine points to a member of his office in Eastleigh called Jo White. That was the allegation the *Mail on Sunday* put to Huhne and it was easy for him to deny as it was demonstrably untrue, given that White hadn't had a driving licence at the time.

Huhne knew that the interest in the speeding points was no accident. In 2003, a car used by him was caught speeding by a camera in Essex. Huhne had been in Strasbourg that day, carrying out his duties as a Member of the European Parliament, returning to Stansted Airport late that night. A few weeks later, he was seen by police using his mobile phone in stationary traffic on the Old Kent Road in London – he had been phoning ahead to alert a political meeting in Kent that he was caught in traffic and would be horribly late.

This was the point at which, on totting up the points on his record, Huhne would lose his driving licence. With the points from the Essex speeding incident he had nine, and this new offence would mean he had reached twelve and the automatic loss of his driving licence. For many people, losing their right to drive would be highly inconvenient but manageable. But Huhne was seeking to become an MP in the UK Parliament at Westminster and was in the middle of a selection campaign for the Eastleigh constituency. Having a driving ban would have been embarrassing for Huhne, but more to the point, he had to get around the constituency from Liberal Democrat member to Liberal Democrat member, to actually see them in person. He was determined to get the nomination, and so the straightforward, practical issue of needing a car was central to his political progress.

Knowing that Huhne already had nine points on his licence, and after some debate, his wife Vicky Pryce had eventually signed the form saying it was her driving the car and therefore taking the points. There was no further discussion of the matter after that for some years.

When the issue of the speeding points resurfaced in 2010, Huhne felt it would fizzle out quickly as an issue. By this time, the offence was already seven years old, and the CPS had never prosecuted anyone else for an offence of this sort that was so long passed. At any rate Huhne thought, it was also an offence that the public was familiar with, and most of the time people got away with it. The AA had found through polling that this type of offence happens in many households across the UK, possibly running into many thousands. However, Huhne's confidence that the story would quickly run out of steam would turn out to be a serious misjudgement. It did no such thing.

The first skirmish with Pryce had been dealt with fairly easily, but she then talked to a *Sunday Times* journalist, Isabel Oakeshott. Suddenly, the story was on the front page of the *Sunday Times*. The main question of fact in the article, and indeed the subsequent criminal case against Huhne, was whether he had caused Pryce to accept three penalty points which he had allegedly incurred whilst driving from Stansted Airport to London on the evening of 12 March 2003. If he had done so, he had perverted the cause of justice. When asked about the allegations that Huhne had convinced 'someone close to him' to accept penalty points for speeding, Pryce told the paper, 'Yes, he did. But look, there is such huge pressure on politicians to be everywhere at once, especially early in their career, so that they are visible – huge pressure – and he does drive a bit like a maniac.'

The revelations kept running on the front page of the *Sunday Times* for four weeks. After several false alarms, Huhne was now very much in the middle of a storm. With his background in newspapers, he understood the implications of a serious heavyweight Sunday newspaper giving the Pryce story credence. He also knew the fundamentals of the story were true: that he had been driving and that Pryce had filled in the forms and taken the speeding fine and points. But he was determined to brazen it out rather than lose his job. He could still see many reasons why a case against him might not progress.

The *Sunday Times* was persistent in pursuing Huhne, probably because it knew it was onto a real political scandal. Privately, Huhne also believed that it was part of an attempt by the Murdoch empire to dent those pressing on the phone-hacking issue.

Regardless of the *Sunday Times*'s motives, after the stories had been published, a backbench Labour MP, Simon Danczuk, lodged a formal complaint about Huhne to Essex Police on 15 May 2011. Essex Police issued a statement saying that they took such allegations 'extremely seriously' and would review the claims. A few days later, Essex Police announced that they were launching a formal investigation into the allegations.

The police interviewed Huhne and Pryce separately in late May. Soon afterwards, a tape recording emerged in which Huhne was heard urging Pryce not to talk to journalists about the speeding incident, whilst Pryce tried to get Huhne to admit his guilt on tape. On 21 June, the police visited their former marital home in Clapham as part of their investigations, and both Huhne and Pryce were re-interviewed by detectives at police stations in Essex on 20 July. At the end of July, Essex police announced that they had handed over a file of evidence regarding 'a 2003 speeding offence' to the Crown Prosecution Service (CPS) for a decision as to whether to bring charges.

Over the next few months, the CPS would twice send the file back to detectives at Essex Police asking them to carry out further investigations. Any decision as to whether to bring charges against Huhne and Pryce was also put on hold pending the outcome of legal action which the police had brought against the *Sunday Times* to force the paper to hand over emails and other evidence it held in relation to the case.

With the story very much in the open, with Essex Police investigating, the CPS taking it seriously and a national newspaper constantly pulling at the threads, why didn't Huhne realise his number was up, admit the allegations, step down and then look to be rehabilitated? Ever the rational calculator, Huhne believes that 'there was no conceivable short-term option of that sort'. He believes that the police and the DPP would have prosecuted come what may. They would have prosecuted not just him but Pryce as well, whatever the legal advice she had taken or assurances she had received from Isabel Oakeshott. There would be an attempt to prosecute and both would end up facing a prison sentence. This was clear to Huhne from the outset once the *Sunday Times* article had appeared.

Huhne's dilemma was that he didn't think he had done anything seriously wrong in the grand scheme of things. In his own words:

> It was not a murder charge, not carousel fraud with £29 million squirrelled away, not even keeping a secret Swiss bank account – and 1,100 people have just been given immunity from prosecution and anonymity by the Treasury for lying about what they actually owe in taxes and having repeatedly lied on their tax returns. I think most people would regard sending back a form about a speeding offence as being of a lesser order of magnitude than any of those things; and for such disproportionate consequences for your family, for your career, not just for me but for my ex-wife as well, I think frankly that most people would do what I did.

For Huhne, seeking to ride out the allegations was not about standing firm against his ex-wife. He saw what Pryce was doing as 'unbelievably self-destructive'. He was desperate to try to find a situation where they could agree to have the case dismissed against both of them. Indeed, in the summer of 2011, after the initial investigations, his QC did open discussions with the CPS as to whether if he pleaded guilty they would drop the charges against Pryce, but the answer was no. The couple were now into a long and painfully slow and expensive legal process.

The media pressure was very high for about four weeks after the local elections in 2011 as the *Sunday Times* kept the story going with front-page splashes. Huhne largely relied on his own experience of the media to deal with the situation, even at its most intense. Whilst other cases described in this book demonstrate the difficulty that those at the centre of storms face in maintaining the ability to think straight at times of great pressure, with many finding it enormously difficult to make rational decisions as to how best to get out of their predicament, Huhne appeared to have no such doubts about the wisdom of his actions.

He had been in journalism for nineteen years and felt he knew how the media operated. He believed he could second-guess them and knew when they were flying a kite. But he had the problem that this issue touched on intensely personal matters involving his wife, his children and an affair. In addition, if he took people into his confidence to solicit their help he would have to admit to them that he was guilty of the charge. He therefore had to handle the intense media pressure alone. There were journalists and photographers pitched outside his house, although 'fewer than you'd think', he says. Huhne felt very much that it was a campaign being waged mostly by two newspapers – the *Sunday Times* and the *Mail on Sunday*. The other papers were picking it up to some extent but they weren't adding anything new to the story, merely adding to the momentum by echoing what the *Sunday Times* and *Mail on Sunday* were reporting.

The intense phase of the scandal – Huhne's time at the centre of the storm – lasted for about twenty-eight days, much longer than Alastair Campbell's fabled view about how long a minister could survive if constantly in the headlines. In one respect, Huhne was fortunate that the police launched an investigation into his case, as it meant that he had an excuse not to make public comments – and he didn't, except to say that he 'welcomed' the investigation. As soon as the police started investigating, the stories were stopped in their tracks, at least for a while. Huhne was able to put out the stock response: 'Look, it's under investigation, let the police get on with it.'

So Huhne did not feel he was under constant pressure for two years. The allegations and the burden of the investigation ebbed and flowed. Many scandals and crises constitute particular pressure points and inevitably distract those at the centre from their job. However, Huhne seems to have been an exception, displaying an almost robotic ability to focus on the job at hand:

> It is inevitable if you're doing a high-profile, high-pressure job, as any secretary of state is; if you're running a department then you're under massive pressures from all sorts of different places. The key attribute you need to have in running any organisation is the ability to prioritise what needs to be done when and deal with it. Once the police investigation had started, it was relatively easy to put it in a box and to get on with the job. Then the key issue was being dealt with by my legal team, who were dealing with the police and then the CPS.

Huhne believes this kind of compartmentalised thinking is simply a skill that all senior people in politics or high-profile positions need to have in order to be successful. He was fortunate enough, unlike a number of other politicians, to have actually run things before going into politics. He had run a business, and had been responsible for running parts of newspapers including the business section of *The Independent* and the *Independent on Sunday*. Having to take lots of decisions very quickly, against a deadline, means having an ability to prioritise what's important and an ability to focus in on those key tasks. 'If you can't do that, frankly, you can't be very good at the job,' he says.

On 3 February 2012, the Crown Prosecution Service announced that it would be charging Huhne and Pryce over the 2003 speeding-points case. The then Director of Public Prosecutions, Keir Starmer, said in a statement that the CPS had concluded there was 'sufficient evidence to bring criminal charges against both Mr Huhne and Ms Pryce for perverting the course of justice'. Huhne responded by announcing his resignation as Secretary of State for Energy and Climate Change in order to 'avoid distraction' from his official duties. In a short statement outside his London flat, Huhne said the CPS decision was 'deeply regrettable' and brazenly asserted: 'I am innocent of these charges and I intend to fight this in the courts and I am confident that a jury will agree.'

He resolved to remain as the Member of Parliament for Eastleigh and to continue to serve his constituents.

Like Charles Clarke, Jacqui Smith and Liam Fox, for all the pressure he was under and the personal turmoil the affair had caused, Huhne did not want to resign from the Cabinet. However, he felt he was left with no option:

I didn't think it was possible to be charged with a criminal offence and go on being Secretary of State. In theory it is possible, because obviously you could argue that you're innocent until you're proven guilty; but in practice, the relationship with your colleagues is such that I think that would be very, very difficult.

Indeed, Clegg and the Prime Minister had talked to Huhne about what would happen in the circumstances of a charge being brought against him. They had made it clear what Huhne would have to do in those circumstances. In effect, he had no choice.

By the time he resigned, some of his family relationships had begun to repair. Reports that none of his children were speaking to him were untrue and his daughter contacted one newspaper to put them right. Even so, his youngest child had been particularly affected by the *Sunday Times* stories, which had been launched the day before his A level exams began.

It was often commented on around Westminster that Huhne seemed completely untroubled by events and that he continued as if nothing had happened or was happening. It was a remarkably confident performance by any standards. He gave an appearance of such authority that few thought there was much chance of a conviction, almost up to the point when he pleaded guilty. His sudden guilty plea came as a shock to most of Westminster and the media.

So how did it come about in the way it did? Huhne's legal team had told him in no uncertain terms that, assuming that this was a normal process and given that the star prosecution witness, Constance Briscoe, had been abandoned as she was no longer considered by the prosecution to be a reliable witness, when they made an application to dismiss the charges it was almost certain to be successful. Indeed, Briscoe was later found guilty and jailed for sixteen months on three counts of intending to pervert the course of justice for lying in a police witness statement about her friendship with Pryce and about her role as Pryce's intermediary with journalists in the attempt to 'bring down' Huhne, as well as altering a copy of her statement to cover up her dishonesty.

Their confidence was strengthened by the fact that the allegations related to such an old offence. None of the signed statements given by Huhne and Pryce at the time of the original speeding offence about who was driving still existed; the police were reliant on second-hand electronic records of who had claimed what. Huhne's advisors were absolutely convinced the case would be dismissed – and so was he.

Huhne also felt that there was a certain degree of irony that the same Director of Public Prosecutions, Keir Starmer, had dismissed his request to reinvestigate allegations of voicemail hacking at the *News of the World*, even though Huhne believes he set out the allegations and the evidence to back it up in great detail to Starmer, Sir Paul Stevenson and John Yates at the Metropolitan Police. Huhne feels some bitterness about his treatment from Starmer, believing that the DPP, who has a duty to have regard to public opinion, did not do so in relation to newspaper phone hacking, but did when newspapers were having a good run at a Cabinet minister in May 2011.

For all the confidence of Huhne's legal team, when the judge in his case later decided that, whatever the strength or weakness of the prosecution case, in his view it had to go to a jury, Huhne's resistance was over. Having fought the allegations for two years, Huhne knew that a drawn-out court case would be immensely damaging for his family. 'I think it would have been truly horrendous and I did not want to be in that position,' he says.

> I had very much the examples of Jonathan Aitken and Jeffrey Archer to mind: both of them had perjured themselves in court, which is a far more serious offence than the one of which I was accused. I personally preferred – both for the reasons of not dragging my family through any further proceedings, and because I did not want to perjure myself – to step back.

Huhne finally made the decision with his solicitor very late in the process and it was a choice he agonised over. He was torn because, surprisingly, he still felt there was a real possibility, given what he believed to be the weakness of the prosecution case, that if he went through the whole court process, the jury might acquit him. But he also had to weigh up the benefits of winning against the dangers of going through a bloody confrontation with his ex-wife and perjuring himself in court, even if he had already lied to the public about his guilt during interviews. Huhne decided it was not worth the risk.

It was the least worst option in the circumstances, in Huhne's judgement. He also hoped that it would make it easier for Pryce's court case. His hopes of clinging onto his political career had now vanished, but by now he was prepared for that loss. Although losing the job of Secretary of State was a bitter blow, Huhne comforted himself that he had spent most of his career doing other things. He knew that there was a life outside politics – and that there were lots of things he would not sacrifice for a political career. That was the point at which he decided that he wasn't prepared to go any further. He pleaded guilty.

In the final analysis, Huhne's final decision on the court case was made with the same ruthless robotic calculation that had always been part of his political career. It had allowed him to rise high, but also brought him to earth with a deafening thud.

THE SENTENCE

Huhne got a sentence of eight months and, as a first-time offender, the eight months were reduced to four. In addition, he was eligible, at the discretion of the governor of the prison, to be let out on tag after half of that four-month sentence. So he served around two months in prison, with a small part of this time in HMP Wandsworth, a classic 1851 listed building, and the rest in an open prison, where he was classified as a 'no risk'.

He says there were no particularly low points for the former MP in prison.

> I knew I had to spend two months in prison – nine weeks – and you get through it. The worst part of the penalty in this whole process was losing a job that I loved. I'd particularly been passionate about it because I'd been responsible for Lib Dem policy on climate change and renewable energy when I was in opposition. It was one of the issues I'd particularly invested a lot of time in and it was one of the things that made me get out of bed in the morning. So losing the

Secretary of State job was the biggest part of the penalty. The second biggest part of the penalty was obviously the fallout for the family and all the public attention. Prison came quite a long way down the list of what was least pleasant about all the things that were visited on me.

Prison was not easy or pleasant, even an open prison. But as ever, Huhne was thinking ahead, beyond prison, to the difficulties that a criminal conviction would cause him. 'If you're a professional,' he says,

> in a white-collar job, that's the thing that has all sorts of consequences, even if I'd had a suspended sentence. The reality is that my political career would still have been ended. The reality of it would still be that it would be extremely difficult to get house insurance. The reality of it is all the consequences which flow from being convicted. So prison is one half of this whole process but if you're a high-profile convict then a lot of the other parts are actually, in my view, just as testing.

Losing his job was a terrible punishment for Huhne and the impact has left a deep impression. It says a great deal that Huhne regards this as the worst punishment he suffered, even above the damage the saga had inflicted on his family. The extent of the ructions caused within his family was revealed in excruciating detail during his court case, when a series of text messages between Huhne and his youngest son, Peter, then eighteen years old, were read out.

Following the revelations of Huhne's affair and the publicity surrounding it, Huhne's contact with Peter appeared to have completely broken down. By Christmas of 2010, Huhne was resorting to wishing his son a happy Christmas by text message. Huhne wrote: 'Happy Christmas. Love you, Dad', to which his son responded, 'Well I hate you, so fuck off.' A few days later, Huhne sent Peter another message to tell him how proud he was of him winning a place at Oxford, which he signed off again by telling Peter that he loved him. Peter replied by telling Huhne: 'Leave me alone, you have no place in my life and no right to be proud. It's irritating that you don't seem to take the point. You are such an autistic piece of shit. Don't contact me again, you make me feel sick.' Five months later, Peter responded to another of Huhne's attempts to make contact in the following terms: 'Don't text me you fat piece of shit.'

THE AFTERMATH

Although many of the crises detailed in this book have shared similar characteristics, the impact on the people at the centre of the storm has been very different in each case.

Much of the difference in terms of the lasting personal legacy is due to the individual's character and temperament. This is where Huhne differs from the others in the book. He, like Kipling, looks upon triumph and disaster as the twin impostors that they are. He has never been persuaded that his successes were uniquely due to his own talents or, equally, his failures due to his vices.

He has a strong view about success and failure in our society. He believes they are surprisingly random and that fate is shaped largely by chance events. One of his favourite movies is *Sliding Doors* starring Gwyneth Paltrow, which has two entirely different endings depending on whether or not the heroine manages to get on the tube train just before the doors close. He believes life is like that: there are these small moments which can have very dramatic and different effects.

'Life in politics,' he says, 'but also in business, is full of felicities and infelicities. I have quite a fatalistic view of how things happen.' It came from a life-changing early experience in India when Mrs Gandhi threw out the Western correspondents. Huhne travelled around India during her period of emergency rule, trying to assess the strength of the opposition. Huhne's experience of an immensely poorer and less fortunate society, where he witnessed terrible illnesses on a daily basis, such as an eight-year old child with an enormously swollen leg from elephantiasis and people needlessly dying from tuberculosis, brought him the conclusion that there's little a person can do to control their own destiny. He says,

> No matter how much you may do things and get lucky, or do things and get unlucky, the reality is there is a great stream that is carrying many of us along and that the room for individual movement is limited. It's there, but it's limited, and I think that if you take that view, which I have done for a very long time, then triumph and disaster are the same in the end.

By and large, his political friends have stuck by him. Most people have been pleasant, with a couple of exceptions. As many of this book's subjects have found, there are always a few fair-weather friends in politics, and at a point of crisis people usually find out who they are. Huhne believes that only one colleague behaved genuinely badly towards him, but refuses to say who.

The future will probably be challenging for Huhne. But, having been a high profile figure and as a former Cabinet minister, he will have a range of potential options. He won't be rushed into making rash decisions about what to do next, but he is assessing a number of offers and has already taken up several. He wants to put together a portfolio involving some university teaching, some journalism (he already writes regularly for *The Guardian*), some business and some *pro bono* campaigning on issues that are close to his heart. He has, for example, accepted a two-day-a-week role as European chairman of US-based Zilkha Biomass Energy (ZBE).

There are relationships that have been patched up and others that still need more time to heal, but for Huhne it's hard to know how much of the fallout is to do with the particularly public circumstances of his crisis and to what extent it is typical of break-ups, which are never easy at any time.

He has no plans at the moment to get engaged or to marry Carina Trimingham; Huhne says the couple are 'happy as we are at the moment'. Trimingham has embarked on a new career studying law and they intend to see how that goes.

After a tumultuous few years and an extraordinary set of circumstances, Huhne's life is undoubtedly getting back on track. Throughout his ordeal he had the bravado to think he could win until the very last moment, yet other than not falling in love with Trimingham he does not believe he could have done anything differently in the last five years. The speeding-points episode he had stored up for himself all those years earlier was always a potential

Achilles' heel that could be used to bring him down. Once he had risked the wrath of his wife by leaving her for another woman, and once his wife had taken the momentous decision to gain revenge by destroying his career, there was no decision he could have made that would have delivered a different course of events. He feels an injustice, even anger about what happened to him, and occasionally allows this to get the better of him, for example when he blamed his prosecution on Constance Briscoe in an article for *The Guardian*, to the extent of comparing himself implicitly to the victims of the Stafford hospital scandal by virtue of being the 'victim' of a profession (barristers) turning a blind eye to their misgivings about one of their own (Briscoe). But by and large, he accepts his fate with a stoicism that Kipling might have applauded at least for now.

CHAPTER 4

VINCE CABLE GOES TO WAR

"Can I be very frank with you ... I have a nuclear option, it's like fighting a war. They know I have nuclear weapons, but I don't have any conventional weapons. If they push me too far then I can walk out of the government and bring the government down and they know that."

– Vince Cable

As a keen ballroom dancer, Vince Cable had long expressed his desire to appear on the BBC's *Strictly Come Dancing* and he finally got his wish in December 2010, only to be beaten to the Christmas Special Crown by celebrity actor and singer John Barrowman.

But only days before the programme was broadcast, a scandal had erupted around Cable, the aftershocks of which would batter the Conservative–Liberal Democrat coalition government for most of the next two years. Yet none of the stress that he should have been feeling was evident whilst he danced the foxtrot with partner Erin Boag, because the Christmas Day one-off special had been recorded several weeks earlier.

For years, Cable had built a reputation for his nimble political footwork, allowing him to build a powerful position inside his party and among the wider public despite his forthright views. It was perhaps only someone of Cable's standing and authority within his party who could have presented the then leader of the Liberal Democrats, Charles Kennedy, with a letter signed by eleven out of the twenty-three frontbenchers, including himself, expressing a lack of confidence in Kennedy's leadership of the Liberal Democrats.

Cable's stock rose still further when he became acting leader, after Sir Menzies Campbell was forced to resign in October 2007 following another Liberal Democrat putsch. He may have regretted ruling himself out of the race for leader early on, as his performance as acting leader was regarded as outstanding by both commentators and many Liberal Democrat MPs.

Having been Chief Economist for Royal Dutch Shell, he was in a good position to understand the forces at work in the wider UK economy. He won plaudits for his repeated warnings about the high level of personal debt in Britain sustained by a housing bubble. He was also a significant voice of criticism during the Northern Rock crisis, calling for nationalisation of the bank, often outflanking both shadow Chancellor George Osborne and Chancellor Alistair Darling – both of whom at times looked flat-footed and indecisive by comparison with the significantly older man. At the time he became a voice of both warning and authority as the financial crisis unfolded.

During this period, Cable's authority both in the country and within his own party peaked to the extent that the Liberal Democrat 2010 general election campaign initially focused as much on Vince Cable as on the less well-known leader of his party, Nick Clegg. Although Clegg's profile shot to stratospheric levels during the campaign, thanks largely to the first leaders' televised debate, the relationship between the two men has continued to be cool and problematic, with Cable believing that he could at any time call upon his power base to destabilise Clegg should he ever need to do so.

Never short of confidence either in his own ability or influence, Cable was thought to be a pivotal figure in the dramatic days between the 2010 general election and the formation of the coalition government. Despite being side-lined by Clegg during the negotiations over coalition with the Conservative Party in early May 2010, he is believed to have made overtures to senior Labour politicians in the hope of providing an alternative to the Conservative–Liberal Democrat partnership favoured by Clegg. It was these unauthorised manoeuvrings that gave Cable experience of the press camping outside his house. The attention got so bad that at one point he stayed with his daughter in a different part of London in order to avoid the paparazzi outside his own house.

With the coup against Kennedy, the financial crisis, and the general election campaign, Cable had been near the centre of the political action on a number of occasions – but he had never been at the epicentre of the storm himself. The closest he probably came was an incident in Labour politics in Glasgow in the 1970s, something that has left its mark to this day. At the time, the political scene in Glasgow Labour politics was said to be somewhat like Tammany Hall, the New York political machine that ran the city for the Democratic Party. The Labour Party in Glasgow was run by a tight-knit group and was very working class and strongly sectarian.

As an ambitious young Labour politician, Cable would want to work his way through this quagmire of patronage and politics.

For a time, all appeared to be going well. Identified as a potential talent by the leader of the Labour group, he was chosen to fight the parliamentary seat of Hillhead in 1970, the last Conservative seat in Glasgow, but lost. In the council elections of the following year he was parachuted into the safe Labour seat of Maryhill in the north of Glasgow.

Once elected, Cable was a diligent councillor, serving the local population well in spite of his relative inexperience. He applied the same conscientious approach to his duties on the council's planning committee. Having identified problems in a planning application relating to a large pub in the city, he announced his intention to vote against the proposal – but he soon discovered that within the ranks of the Glasgow Labour Party there were some rather powerful power brokers that nobody wanted to cross.

The next thing Cable knew, he was getting a late-night phone call. He was advised in no uncertain terms that voting against this planning application would be 'terribly unwise'. He also received a personal call from the applicant, a man who had won a fortune on the pools and who now both ran the local pubs and was a backer of the local Labour Party. Having regarded the tone of these contacts as threatening, the young rising star stood up in a local party meeting the following weekend to express his dismay that he had been propositioned. Although there were only fifteen to twenty people present, his remarks landed Cable in hot water, and he was sued for libel. Cable, an impecunious young man with a young family to support, felt the pressure and was desperately worried.

For several months Cable went through what was a horrible and highly pressurised experience for a young man. Fortunately for him and his family, he had the services of a very good lawyer (who was a supporter of the SNP as it turned out), who effectively got him out of trouble.

Cable also had a brief but uncomfortable time as a parliamentary candidate in York, where his support for David Owen's policy on Trident missiles replacing the old Polaris system led to a schism in the local party and generated several days of uncomfortable headlines in the local press.

Neither of these events in Glasgow or York was a significant national political event let alone scandal, but they demonstrate a trait in Cable's character that has run through his political life. Confident in his opinions and integrity, he speaks his mind without fear or favour, although perhaps without always thinking through all the possible consequences. Indeed, he continued to say and do largely what he wanted in the early months as Secretary of State for Business in the new government, despite an attempt by Nick Clegg to bring him into line both during the coalition negotiations and afterwards.

There were constant rumours of his unhappiness working in a Conservative-led government and Cable was never slow off the mark to criticise his Conservative colleagues. A senior Liberal Democrat colleague recalls that this was partly down to his state of mind at the time: 'I don't think Vince was very happy after the coalition was formed. He wasn't part of the negotiation team, hadn't really bought into it, and was very much more in favour of linking up with Labour. We speculated that he would be the first to resign.' Indeed, he told the *Sunday Telegraph*'s political editor, Patrick Hennessy, 'People sometimes ask me, "Are you having

fun?" No! It's hard work and it's tough, but it's important.' The
message to Hennessy seemed to be that he was there under duress
and against his better judgement, because there was a job to do.
Better to be in the tent but preferably on his terms.

It was essentially Cable's bravado that got him into trouble with
the Murdochs and BSkyB. But to understand why, it is important
to understand the background to the BSkyB bid. On 12 May 2010,
Cable was appointed by the Prime Minister, David Cameron, as
Secretary of State for Business, Innovation and Skills. As a Liberal
Democrat he couldn't be Chancellor, and Clegg wouldn't make
him Chief Secretary to the Treasury, partly due to his poor relationship with George Osborne and partly because Clegg wanted
his own right-hand man David Laws there. The BIS appointment
was unquestionably second-best in Cable's own mind but still an
important and influential economic department inherited from no
less a big beast than Lord Mandelson.

In his capacity as Business Secretary, Cable held certain back-
stop powers to regulate company mergers under the Enterprise
Act 2002, enabling him to block or delay mergers in certain cases
on 'public interest grounds'. However, on 15 June 2010, shortly
after the coalition government was formed and Cable took office,
one of the year's most controversial takeover bids was announced:
the bid by Rupert Murdoch's News Corporation to purchase all the
remaining shares in BSkyB, the hugely valuable satellite broadcast-
ing company and owner of the Sky TV channels.

Encouraged by the arrival of the new government, senior News
Corporation management had been led to believe that their desire
to take full control of BSkyB would be looked upon favourably – at

least by senior people in the Conservative Party. James Murdoch stated at the Leveson Inquiry that he had deliberately waited until after the election, to avoid BSkyB becoming a political football. But he was also well aware that with a Conservative government the political climate towards a takeover would change.

Murdoch's impression of the new government's attitude to the bid was further strengthened following a conversation with the new Secretary of State in which Cable told him that he saw few problems with the takeover. Indeed, the OFT failed to see an issue and did not consider the transaction likely to raise substantive competition issues. Officials were also of the view that the bid did not pose serious concerns.

The Secretary of State's power to intervene on public interest grounds is also an exceptional one and his or her role is to act in a 'quasi-judicial' manner. Cable was well aware that this required him to conduct an examination of the merits of the case with an open mind, that the process was highly transparent, that any intervention should be based on robust evidence, and that all public interest decisions had to be published with detailed reasons and were open to legal challenge. Whatever his private views towards the Murdochs or News Corporation, Cable understood that, were he to ignore evidence and act in a prejudicial manner, it would leave him vulnerable to the embarrassing prospect of any subsequent decision by him to block the merger being overturned in the courts.

Between the announcement of the bid and the formal notification to the European Commission in early November, Cable received numerous submissions on whether to intervene on public interest grounds. He did not discourage these submissions and consulted with Liberal Democrat colleagues with policy experience in the area.

As more substantive representations started to come in, Cable began to believe that there were genuine concerns about the merger and that the case for intervention should be explored very thoroughly before reaching conclusions. By late summer, it was obvious that Cable was looking for reasons to intervene in the deal. He had decided he would intervene and the department's job was to find him the legal justification, which it duly did.

The formal notification of the bid by News Corporation for the remainder of BSkyB to the European Commission came on 3 November 2010. The following day Cable issued an intervention notice regarding the bid. The effect of this was to require Ofcom to provide a report on public interest issues by 31 December 2010.

As far as Cable was concerned there was little more to be done on the issue until the report from Ofcom returned to his department. On Friday 3 December, Cable held one of his regular MP's surgeries at his Twickenham constituency office in south-west London. Levels of tension in the Twickenham constituency office were unusually high that day. A group of protestors had arrived from central London to target Cable's constituency office under the banner of the student protests against higher tuition fees. At the time there were enormous student protests on the streets of central London, particularly targeting Liberal Democrats who had 'sold out' their opposition to a rise in tuition fees during the coalition negotiations. Indeed, they'd even failed to argue their case during the intensive sessions with the Conservatives.

Cable thought the group were connected to anarchists who had been largely responsible for the violence and vandalism that had marred the large student protests in central London. The protestors were aggressive, threatening staff and residents and banging on the door of Cable's constituency office in an attempt to force their way in. Cable confronted the group himself before his staff phoned 999 and the police.

By the time the police had arrived and then dealt with the protestors, all the local residents who had come to talk to the their MP about housing and other local issues had disappeared with the exception of two women, presenting themselves as local mothers, who steadfastly remained. Cable, who had just finished an interview and was expecting to go home, still worrying about how to deal with the rioters and the police, found it odd that the two women were still sitting there, wanting their meeting. His staff later confirmed to him that the behaviour of the two women was indeed 'peculiar', and later investigations revealed that they had secured the appointment using false addresses.

The women continued the deception throughout the subsequent MP's surgery interview, professing to be local mums upset by George Osborne, who had made some comments in his party conference speech about child benefit. The women told Cable they wanted to know what he thought about Osborne's remarks. Partly because of the tension of the earlier events of the afternoon, Cable obliged and then started to open up significantly beyond the issue at hand.

As is now well known, the two 'local mothers' subsequently turned out to be reporters for the *Daily Telegraph*. Sting reporter one turned out to be Laura Roberts, a pretty blonde Oxford graduate from west London. Then aged twenty-nine, she had joined the *Daily Telegraph* after working for the *Daily Mail* and *The Scotsman*. Sting reporter two was Holly Watt, then twenty-eight, and like her colleague, an attractive and confident Oxbridge graduate. These were two upwardly mobile, aspiring journalists; indeed, Watt was nominated for 'Scoop of the Year' in 2008 and played an important role in the *Telegraph*'s coverage of the MPs' expenses scandal. She has since become the *Telegraph*'s Whitehall editor.

It has been suggested in some quarters that Cable was rather taken with the two young women, although he denies having any recollection of them, other than that they were young. 'Various people have tried to spin a story how these were seductively beautiful women, but I have no recollection what they looked like and they had the same impact on my local office colleagues', he maintains. Whatever the truth, Cable was without doubt quick to provide these two young women with more macho language than normal. Never one to hold back his views, perhaps after the antagonism with the protestors and the adrenalin surging, Cable was feeling bold. Cable later told the Leveson Inquiry that he:

> talked about a 'big battle' going on over immigration caps, and 'big arguments' on banks, tax thresholds and civil liberties. I used the word 'war' several times. These comments show how this high level of tension had spilled over into the language I used throughout the conversation, and not just when discussing one particular topic.

But even for someone happy to stir the pot on issues with colleagues, his language on this occasion was striking. Cable weighed in on his coalition partners, saying, 'There is a constant battle going on behind the scenes. We have a big argument going on about tax and that is party political, because I am arguing with Nick Clegg for a tough approach and our Conservative friends don't want to do that.' Rather unkindly, he said, 'Cameron is being attacked by his own people for being a Liberal … He and Osborne are hated by their own party faithful.'

Rather than feeling bound by collective responsibility, particularly in the context of a coalition formed against the backdrop of growing financial crisis in Europe, Cable made clear that he was prepared to bring the government down if he didn't get his way:

Can I be very frank with you … I have a nuclear option, it's like fighting a war. They know I have nuclear weapons, but I don't have any conventional weapons. If they push me too far then I can walk out of the government and bring the government down and they know that.

He also claimed, as part of the broader political fight he was waging, to have 'declared war on the Murdoch empire' and that the whole of the 'Murdoch empire' was 'under attack':

I am picking my fights, some of which you may have seen, some of which you may [sic] haven't seen. And I don't know if you have been following what has been happening with the Murdoch press, where I have declared war on Mr Murdoch and I think we are going to win … he has minority shares and he wants a majority – and a majority control would give them a massive stake. I have blocked it using the powers that I have got and they are legal powers that I have got. I can't politicise it but from the people that know what is happening this is a big, big thing. His whole empire is now under attack … So there are things like that we do in government, that we can't do … All we can do in opposition is protest.

Later, Cable claimed in oral evidence to the Leveson Inquiry that he was also motivated to use the language he did in order to demonstrate that he was not going to be intimidated by News International's intensive lobbying of his Liberal Democrat colleagues and attempts to politicise the BSkyB bid process. Cable was aware from what his party colleagues were telling him that News Corporation representatives had been approaching several of them in a way he judged to be inappropriate. The reports suggested that News Corporation representatives were either trying to influence his views or seeking material which might be used to challenge any adverse ruling he might make following the completion of the Ofcom report.

His colleagues expressed alarm about whether this whole affair was going to lead to retribution against the Liberal Democrats through News International newspapers. As it happened, evidence to support these reports was borne out in an article by Toby Helm in *The Observer* on 23 July 2011. Cable felt the article added a sense of Liberal Democrats being under siege from a well-organised News International operation. Coming from a party that had hitherto been at best ignored by News International, this was a new and somewhat unsettling experience. Cable contests therefore his references to a 'war on Murdoch' were to make the point, rather theatrically, that he had no intention of being intimidated by a powerful media group.[1]

Cable then gave no further thought to his conversation with the two female constituents for several weeks. Late on 20 December, whilst at home in London, he took a late-night call from Jonny Oates, senior Liberal Democrat press officer, telling Cable someone had bugged the constituency surgery conversation on 3 December. Cable felt the impact immediately: 'I was obviously rather shaken by this … you just feel, "Oh my god what's going on?" I felt alarmed.'

The Business Secretary had forgotten about the conversation on 3 December amidst the pressure of all the other events going on as Secretary of State, so he was prompted by Jonny Oates to see if he could recall anything at all so that a sensible response could be prepared. Cable simply couldn't remember the events at first and initially it did not occur to him that the conversations being suggested had taken place. Oates was forced to keep pressing him to remember whether anyone had come to his surgery who could have been an undercover reporter. It was only gradually that the memories came back and he 'vaguely remembered' those two concerned mothers.

---

1   It is interesting that in the report of his inquiry, Lord Justice Leveson concluded that this explanation could not be used to excuse Cable's remarks. Although context could explain Cable's comments, Leveson believed it did not excuse them given his responsibilities:

> He did not pretend otherwise, either at the time or to the Inquiry, recognising that his words had given rise to an appearance of bias … It is, however, important to underline that if what he said had not been recorded by a journalist but had, in fact, been heard by a constituent (as he believed was the case), it is certainly possible that what he said could have returned to impact on the bid after he had decided it: his constituent might then have gone to the press.

Oates – now head of office for Nick Clegg – reassured Cable that he was not the only Liberal Democrat to have been bugged. Oates, typically calm in his demeanour, assured Cable that although his remarks were embarrassing, the situation wasn't a complete disaster. Oates asked Cable to tell him everything he could remember so they could put out a statement. It was the press officer's job to try to put the episode in context and to explain to the public, via the media, how exactly it had happened so that some form of defence or interpretation of Cable's use of language could be put forward. In order to do that, Oates had to try to piece together what exactly had been going on. The two men talked through events for some time and then put out a statement in which Cable essentially apologised and made clear that he had never had any intention to bring down the government. The statement also made clear Cable and the Lib Dems' view that the way the information had been obtained was deplorable.

At this point, Cable was under the impression that it was only his boast about having a nuclear option and leaving the coalition was being reported. That night, the *Daily Telegraph* reported on its front page for the next day's edition Cable's comments during the undercover interview about holding a 'nuclear option' and his belief that he could at any stage bring down the government by resigning. But it did not carry his comments about declaring war on the entire Murdoch empire. This was merely the end of the first round of his impending storm. Indeed, at this point, he did not even remember making the comments about the Murdochs and BSkyB. Soon the story about nuclear options and bringing the Government down was forgotten as Cable's 'war on the Murdoch empire' took centre stage.

The statement prepared by Oates was issued in response to the *Telegraph* splash, but it crucially made it clear that Cable, whilst expressing his regret at his comments, had no intention of resigning:

> Naturally I am embarrassed by these comments and I regret them.
> I have no intention of leaving the government. I am proud of what
> it is achieving and will continue to play my full part in delivering
> the priorities I and my party believe in, which are enshrined in the
> coalition agreement.

Cable let out a huge sigh of relief as the story didn't attract a huge amount of attention. Reading the papers that morning Cable felt bad about his loose talk, but he and his team felt the matter had been largely diffused. There was no sign of photographers or camera crews following Cable around until later – a sign that media interest was still low.

Later that morning Cable attended Cabinet. In light of the way Cable had spoken and many of his digs over the years at senior Conservatives, he must have been surprised and delighted by the response he got. He still felt embarrassed, but the Cabinet were collegiate and laughed about what had happened. The subject did come up during the Cabinet meeting, but it was treated in a light-hearted way, with a great deal of laughter and ribbing of Cable about it. Afterwards, the Foreign Secretary, William Hague, gave him moral support suggesting, 'Don't worry, we all think the same about the *Daily Telegraph* as you do.' Although he was embarrassed about what had happened he felt no ill feeling from his Conservative Cabinet colleagues.

Conservative Cabinet members were friendly and treated it as a one-off episode: unfortunate, but something that could have happened to anybody. Had there been no further revelations, the whole episode would have gone no further and been forgotten very quickly.

Following Cabinet, and having digested the coverage in the morning papers and seeing how the story was being covered by the rolling news channels, Cable felt the worst was now over. That afternoon, between 2 and 3 p.m., the Prime Minister and his deputy held a pre-Christmas press conference together. Cameron revealed that Cable had been apologetic at Cabinet and Clegg said he was 'right to be embarrassed' by the *Telegraph* revelations. Clegg appeared to draw a line under the affair by finishing an answer with 'end of story'.

The story, however, was about to get a second wind. The European Commission announced that it had unconditionally cleared the News Corporation takeover of BSkyB on competition grounds. This made the so-far-unreleased part of the transcript all the more explosive.

Whilst the PM and his deputy were holding a press conference, Cable had taken his private office of about sixteen people for a late lunch at the Cinnamon Club in Great Smith Street, one of the finest Indian restaurants in London. Cable was able to relax and enjoy the expensive curry dishes and fine wine list, believing a difficult day was just about over. Unfortunately, the rest of the transcript had been leaked to the BBC's business editor, Robert Peston, who at around 3 p.m. disclosed Cable's comments about 'declaring war on the Murdoch empire' on the BBC News channel.

How Peston got the story is fascinating if a little murky. The *Telegraph* had deliberately held back the most damaging part of the taped comments about Murdoch and the BSkyB deal, believing it would probably cost Cable his job. Telegraph Media Group had made its opposition to a News Corporation takeover of the rest of the BSkyB shares absolutely clear. In October 2010, the *Telegraph*'s chief executive, Murdoch MacLennan, signed a letter (along with senior executives of the BBC, Channel 4, the *Daily Mail* and Trinity Mirror) asking Cable to consider blocking the takeover. It also knew that Cable had privately been carefully studying how it might be possible to either slow the deal down or stop it going through.

On the basis of the old maxim 'the enemy of my enemy is my friend', the Telegraph Group was keen to see Cable kept *in situ* whilst decisions were made on the deal, knowing that Cable was anything but a friend to Murdoch. It did not publish the information, despite posting on its website a notice saying it had published the full transcript. There was no indication that anything had been removed from the transcript by the newspaper.

The BBC's Robert Peston claimed 'a whistleblower who is upset that the *Telegraph* chose to omit these remarks' leaked them to him. Peston's connections in the business and media world were well known, as was his knack of unearthing high-quality news stories – often breaking them live on air. For many, he had become a go-to man to break a business or financial story.

But penetrating the inner sanctum of the Telegraph Group and causing it huge embarrassment is quite something, even by his own high standards for sniffing out stories. The *Telegraph* took it very seriously and called in corporate investigations firm, Kroll Associates, to seek out the source. Allegedly, News Corp had let it be known that helping its bid for a full takeover of BSkyB would enhance career prospects. Kroll Associates interviewed existing and former *Telegraph* employees, and examined email and phone records, but were (despite suspicions) reported to be unable to prove which disgruntled employee had decided to blow the whistle on the *Telegraph's* decision not to publish the Cable comments on Murdoch.

The leak however was undoubtedly of commercial benefit to News Corporation, the parent company of News International, in relation to the News Corporation takeover bid for BSkyB.

As lunch at the Cinnamon Club continued, Cable was informed about Peston's disclosures by a member of his team who had kept her BlackBerry on. Cable immediately abandoned his colleagues to their end-of-year lunch as the real storm finally hit. Suddenly, he felt completely pole-axed by events as all the details of the conversation came flooding back. The rest of the afternoon was a blur, but Cable recalls feeling 'absolutely dreadful' as the realisation hit home.

Events were moving incredibly quickly, much more quickly than Cable knew at the time. News Corp had released a statement at 4 p.m. declaring itself 'shocked and dismayed by reports of Mr Cable's comments. They raise serious questions about fairness and due process.' There was real concern within Government about legal action being taken. In fact, News Corp was really only interested in removing Cable and finding a more sympathetic ear for its plans. Once they knew about Cable's comments they were determined to remove him from the decision-making process.

Across Whitehall, frenetic activity had been unleashed as a quick solution was required. Jeremy Heywood, the permanent secretary at No. 10, suggested the option of transferring responsibility for media competition issues to the Department for Culture, Media and Sport. Heywood was quickly deployed, dealing with the nuts and bolts of the solution and Chancellor George Osborne was brought in to advise and agree the solution.

Although the press were speculating that Cable was about to lose his job, particularly when Andrew Mitchell was seen arriving at Downing Street, there was never really any prospect of him being sacked, with all the reverberations for the coalition that it would entail. The main issue was about handing over responsibility for BSkyB to another Minister because the decision itself had become compromised. The decision was largely settled upon shortly after a 4 p.m. meeting in Downing Street attended by Cameron, Osborne, Heywood, Ed Llewellyn and senior Downing Street political advisers.

Cameron did not want to sack Cable as he was providing a 'valuable contribution to the coalition government'. George Osborne felt what Cable had said did not deserve a resignation and also said, at least in public, that he thought Cable was doing a good job as Business Secretary. But he was more frank about the dangers that sacking Cable or forcing him to resign might pose to the unity of the coalition: 'Frankly, I also had concerns about the impact of such a resignation on the coalition and the unity of the government.' It seems that Cable did have a unique standing within the coalition government after all. He had judged himself unsackable – and been proved right.

At the time, this was hardly lost on Tory backbenchers, who insisted Vince Cable would have been sacked in such circumstances had he been a Conservative. Senior backbencher John Whittingdale, who chairs the Commons Culture, Media and Sport Select Committee, said the Business Secretary would almost certainly have gone if he had not been a Lib Dem. The differing treatment meted out to Liberal Democrats in government has continued to be a running sore with Conservative front- and backbenchers ever since. The Labour Party for its part issued a statement strongly suggesting that Cable should be sacked.

Following the Prime Minister's meeting with his advisers, Cameron called a meeting of 'The Quad' – himself, Nick Clegg, George Osborne and Danny Alexander – in Downing Street. There was much speculation in the media and on rolling news blogs that the purpose of this meeting was to discuss Cable's future. However, the talks were about agreeing and deploying the plan to move responsibility across Whitehall departments, rather than whether Cable would need to be fired. Cable was asked to see Nick Clegg immediately after his meeting with Cameron and the rest of the Quad. It was not a happy experience for him to be summoned, in light of the pair's difficult relationship. It was, as Cable admits, 'a tricky conversation on a very tricky day'. It is interesting that following that short meeting, Cable did not have a great deal of interaction with Clegg, although the Deputy Prime Minister made it clear that he was in favour of Cable continuing in his job.

Cable went straight from Clegg to a phone call with the Prime Minister. The tenor of both conversations was similar. There was a serious problem caused by Cable's indiscretion that had to be dealt with, but in his conversation with Cable Cameron focused more on the task of what the government should say in its public statement rather than tearing into him. Cable speaks surprising fondly of the Prime Minister:

> Cameron has always been very courteous. He's not a Rottweiler; we now know there was an awful lot going on but that wasn't clear [to me] at the time. He was obviously very concerned but he wasn't being angry or aggressive – he saw we had got a big problem, and that we've got to release a statement on what's going to happen.

Cable agreed that the tenor of the press statement should be apologetic and agreed the move of responsibilities that 'the Quad' had rubber stamped. The speed of the decision-making was quite spectacular and suggests that the No. 10 machine, at least at the time, was not quite as defunct as some have since suggested.

At 5.45 p.m., 10 Downing Street issued a statement criticising Cable heavily and failing to offer explicit support for his position as Business Secretary. So strongly worded was the statement that it suggested to one informed commentator, Adam Boulton of Sky News, that Cable wasn't out of the woods yet. The Downing Street statement began:

> Following comments made by Vince Cable to the *Daily Telegraph*, the Prime Minister has decided that he will play no further part in the decision over News Corporation's proposed takeover of BSkyB. In addition, all responsibility for competition and policy issues relating to media, broadcasting, digital and telecoms sectors will be transferred immediately to the Secretary of State for Culture, Media and Sport. This includes full responsibility for Ofcom's

activities in these areas. The Prime Minister is clear that Mr Cable's comments were totally unacceptable and inappropriate.

Shortly afterwards, Cable issued his own statement expressing his deep regret and accepting the decision of both the Prime Minister and Deputy Prime Minister to move responsibility for BSkyB across government. It was deeply embarrassing for an old hand like Cable but he knew he had caused massive embarrassment for the government.

Lord Justice Leveson would later conclude in his report that Cable's comments had left the government facing a media storm and under enormous pressure to act quickly. He was right: the media storm would only have gathered strength if decisive action had not been taken. News Corp were understandably deeply concerned by Dr Cable's words and a solution which restored confidence in the decision making process was urgently required. There were sound reasons, including important political ones, not to remove Dr Cable from office, but it was essential to ensure he had nothing more to do with the BSkyB bidding process before it became tainted irreversibly.

After his conversations with Clegg and Cameron, Cable returned to his supportive private office somewhat exhausted by the events of the past two hours. But despite the media circus developing around him, Cable had to sit down with officials and closest aides to manage the transfer of responsibilities for BSkyB out of his department. His special adviser, Katie Waring, was dealing both reactively and proactively with the press. She was making sure the statement was properly dispersed to the media and explaining that

Cable would not be resigning – something he was keen that she should emphasise. Having secured the support of his party leader and the Prime Minister at the top of the coalition government, Cable's team, guided by Oates and the Downing Street press office, were now trying to do what they could to calm the situation, or at least remove most of the heat from it.

It was by then late afternoon, and Cable decided to leave his press team and civil servants to it and go home. He normally went home on the train or bus, but his office felt that it wasn't a good idea because the press were surrounding the building. Press attention had substantially increased since Peston's revelations. As expected, the press pack were waiting for Cable when he finally arrived at his London home.

Whilst the trouble around Cable grew during the afternoon, he called his wife and told her what was happening. She immediately travelled up from their New Forest farm to London to be by his side. It was just as well, because over 21–24 December the press remained determinedly camped outside Cable's house morning, noon and night.

Cable and his wife found it very difficult to live under the microscope for those four days. It was a bitter winter and thick snow was on the ground at the time. Indeed, despite their ordeal, the Cables actually felt slightly sorry for the journalists and photographers who were making their lives hell. For the first two days, the Cables had managed to plot an escape route through their garage which the journalists didn't spot. Eventually, even this was found and the couple were forced to use the main gate and run the gauntlet.

The constant intrusion in these four days had an enormous effect on Cable. Even as a front line politician, he found it very difficult to deal with. He was obviously aware of the huge and constant media coverage, but because he found the coverage so distressing he felt he simply had to disengage. Although he knew he was in the headlines every day, he could not and would not look. He could not see the point of putting himself through the daily torture of reading the newspapers. He had said what he'd said and could do nothing apart from go to ground and ride it out.

Such disengagement appears to be a coping mechanism deployed at the worst point of a scandal or crisis by the person at its centre. This is perhaps unsurprising when someone's life appears to be out of their immediate control. This is something that powerful, influential people at the peak of their political trade have difficulty in accepting. For many, there appears to be a choice between detachment or being driven to a state of emotional exhaustion.

Cable also had feelings of resentment and anger because he felt wronged and that only part of the story was out there. He was unable to give the full story of BSkyB during the ongoing media storm. He would have liked to have gone on the offensive and said much more at the time, but was advised for reasons of crisis management not to do so:

It was because it was in such a difficult environment and nobody knew the whole history of the BSkyB bid. I knew the whole story but I wasn't able to talk about it and I got very strong advice not to talk about it and just wrap the thing away and just try and get back to life as normal.

He'd agreed with his department to keep a low profile and stay away from the office for those last days in the run-up to Christmas in the hope that it would blow over. There wasn't very much going on anyway because it was approaching the quiet Christmas period. The view from his department was to keep his head down, give as few opportunities to the press as possible to 'doorstep' him and get on with a backlog of paperwork. Even so, he found concentrating on his work very difficult.

Cable now relied on his family to support him and to restore his deflated spirits. Cable was thoroughly depressed by events and needed the love and support of his family. In 'the goldfish bowl', as he described it, he now had intense conversations with his wife and daughter about what he should do next, including whether he should, in fact, resign.

The thing that seems to have caused Cable the most distress was an article in *The Sun* on 23 December. The previous day, his wife had volunteered to go out to the shops to ensure they had enough provisions to see them through at least the next few days, whilst he continued to keep a low profile. It was a particularly cold and unpleasant day and Cable had been forced to run the gauntlet of the encamped press hordes every time he went in and out of his own front door. *The Sun* then wrote, according to Cable, a story accusing him of using his wife as a human shield. It infuriated him, as he felt it was 'a particularly vicious piece, really, really nasty stuff'. For the embattled Cabinet minister, it was the low point – the press attacking him was felt to be fair game, something where he felt he was resilient enough to cope with personal criticisms, but when his wife was dragged into it, it hit him particularly hard.

It is a theme that many of the people at the centre of the storm feel strongly. Criticism of what they have done is fair game – although they often feel aggrieved at its partiality – but criticism of or contact with their family is quite another matter altogether.

Despite the battering at the centre of the political storm and the low point he had reached, after a few days Cable began to develop a thick skin against the criticism and to recover his centre of gravity. Fortunately, he and his wife had booked to go to rural Perthshire for a break and once they had headed off things calmed down. Christmas and some distance from London came as a respite at just the right time.

However, Cable was still considering his future when he reached Scotland with his wife. Once there he rang around his friends and advisers to seek their counsel, including Norman Lamb, Ed Davey, Steve Webb, David Heath and Norman Baker, to discuss whether he should resign. The reaction was unanimous, that it would be the wrong thing to do and he should not. Cable felt at this point he had got over his real low point and wanted to speak to his friends and colleagues and canvass their political judgement. It was not at this stage an emotional cry for help, but he did want reassurance that he was doing the right thing by staying put.

The general view was that Cable should not get things out of perspective, that he should let the storm die down and then get on with the job. Not a single Liberal Democrat parliamentary colleague took the view that the matter was a particularly terrible embarrassment that wouldn't eventually blow over. Not one suggested that he should resign.

THE AFTERMATH

For the next three to six months, Cable was dogged by constant references in the press portraying him as the villain of the piece who had got it wrong over BSkyB, before the full picture about widespread illegal phone hacking at the Murdoch-owned *News of the World* began to emerge in July 2011, and in particular, the revelation that private investigators acting on the paper's behalf had accessed the voicemails of the murdered teenager, Milly Dowler. As Cable recalls:

> The whole period for three months afterwards, there was maybe even six months of constant references in the press. They'd all got it wrong, their stories were all about these two beautiful women and they'd interpreted it in completely the wrong way. Nobody under-stood the context until the hacking scandal emerged and the full story then emerged in all its gory detail. Until that happened, I was in a sense the bad guy who'd done something wrong.

Even for someone usually so sure of his abilities and opinions, Cable felt his confidence was damaged by the whole affair. Even though his ordeal was relatively brief by comparison to others' in this book, such an unpleasant and unsettling experience is in his view, 'bound to' knock a politician's self-confidence. In the New Year, he faced the typical series of events that a Secretary of State has to deal with. At the first departmental oral questions in the House of Commons, he found the Labour benches 'up for it' and keen to make hay following his indiscretions. He endured an uncomfortable time.

However, whilst his opponents in official opposition might have been expected to revel in his discomfort, on the flipside, Cable remembers receiving some unexpected acts of kindness from people at Westminster, sometimes surprisingly so:

> People are very different in public than they are in private. All the people that I met round Parliament were very kind and sympathetic and actually one or two of them, David Blunkett actually, in the middle of it gave me a personal call on the theme 'don't let the bastards grind you down, we've all been there and had this nonsense'.

Cable has already recalled that his lowest personal point during the whole saga was when tabloid newspapers started to drag his close family into it, printing a picture of his wife running errands for him whilst their house was surrounded by photographers and journalists. Yet having survived their time at the centre of the storm, Cable believes that such ordeals can actually strengthen politicians' family relationships. If anything, the knowledge that: 'I think it sort of solidifies relationships these crises actually. I think it's had a beneficial effect. I knew my family were there and were very supportive.'

Fortunately, Cable's constituents didn't turn against him after finding their local MP at the centre of the leading national political scandal. His reputation as a hard-working local MP endured and he found that the frenetic interest of the national media didn't permeate down to ordinary people:

> I wandered round Twickenham and people were kind of friendly and supportive. I have a good reputation as a local MP and that wasn't

dented. I hadn't committed a crime or even had an affair, it was this mysterious thing in the media that nobody could understand.

For all the drama, column inches and hours of news coverage devoted to political scandals, the indifference of the public on an occasion such as this perhaps provides a reminder to those in the political 'bubble', and those at the centre of the storm, to keep such matters in perspective.

On 30 May 2012, Cable got his day in court and told the Leveson Inquiry that he had heard of 'veiled threats' that the Liberal Democrats would be targeted if he had found against News Corporation and blocked its bid for BSkyB:

> I had heard directly and indirectly from colleagues that there had been veiled threats that if I made the wrong decision from their point of view of the company, my party would be – I think somebody used the phrase 'done over' in the News International press, and I took those things seriously, I was very concerned. I had myself tried to deal with the process entirely properly and impartially, and I discovered that this was happening in the background. I frankly stored up my anger at what was taking place, but in that very special and tense situation, I rather offloaded my feelings.

Looking back, even if his confidence was knocked in the medium term, Cable feels no long-term damage was done to his career. Although his reputation as a straight-talking sage was damaged, having been made to look foolish by two female journalists, he feels the much more serious scandal that followed over phone

hacking, and the evidence of News Corporation's aggressive lobbying tactics that emerged at the Leveson Inquiry showed that he was
'right all along' about BSkyB and the Murdochs. By May 2011, five
months after the scandal broke, the *Daily Telegraph* was censured
by the Press Complaints Commission for the 'subterfuge' Watt and
Roberts used to target almost all Lib Dem ministers serving in the
coalition government at the time.

When I interviewed him for this book, Cable told me that
the experience had made him more wary and more guarded, and
that was not necessarily a bad thing. 'Part of being ministerial is that
you can't shout your mouth off the whole time, even in private', he
admitted. As time has passed and memories of the episode have
faded, partly as a result of the weight and intensity of the political
scandals that have followed it, Cable has returned to his old tricks
somewhat and not infrequently shares his trenchant assessments
of his Conservative colleagues and their policies with the national
media. For the time being, however, his ambitions to lead the
Liberal Democrats are firmly stalled. Whilst this may owe much to
the remarkable political recovery of Nick Clegg, one suspects that
Cable's scandal damaged his chances of gaining momentum when
Clegg was at his weakest.

CHAPTER 5

JEREMY HUNT LOSES CONTROL

The eldest son of an admiral, a former pupil of the elite private school Charterhouse, and a contemporary of both Boris Johnson and David Cameron at Oxford, Jeremy Hunt was expected to rise quickly through the ranks after his election to Parliament for South West Surrey in 2005. Indeed, one political columnist suggested that you could hear Hunt's ambition squeaking as he walked.

According to a well-known tale, at the end of his time at Oxford, Hunt had a conversation with one his fellow students, Mark Field, about where these two talented young men would end up, which the pair signed off with 'See you at Westminster.' Field has been the MP for the Cities of London and Westminster since 2001.

Whilst Field may have beaten his friend to Westminster, once Hunt arrived, his rise through the ranks was rapid. He was promoted to the Conservative front bench as shadow Minister for the Disabled just six months after becoming an MP. In July 2007, he joined the shadow Cabinet as shadow Secretary of State for Culture, Media and Sport. He was perhaps the biggest winner from the 2005 intake of around fifty new MPs.

Hunt held onto his Culture, Media and Sport portfolio following the wrangling for posts that took place as part of the coalition negotiations in May 2010. In his first few months as Secretary of State, Hunt, who had involved himself in a succession of entrepreneurial business ventures before entering

politics, eventually earning millions of pounds from the success
of Hotcourses, the directory publishing company he founded,
took a generally pro-business and pro-entrepreneurship stance
on much of his work.

In opposition, Hunt had warned in speeches that major international players and the big US networks were being driven away
from investing in British media by regulations, and called for
deregulation in the creative media industries akin to the 'Big Bang'
which had revolutionised the City in 1986, making it the major
financial centre of the world.

Hunt's deregulatory stance led him to express sympathy for
News Corporation's intended bid for the shares it did not already
own in BSkyB, the owner of the Sky TV subscription channels.
Hunt told the *Financial Times* shortly after taking office that
he didn't see News Corp's bid as having much of an impact in
reality: 'It seems to me that News Corp do control Sky already,
so it isn't clear to me that in terms of media plurality there is a
substantive change.'

But despite being the Secretary of State for Media, the BSkyB
bid was outside his jurisdiction, falling, as did other mergers, under
the responsibilities of the Secretary of State for Business.

Hunt added that he wouldn't want to 'second guess' what the
regulators might decide on the issue. Privately, his views were
stronger. On the day News Corp's bid for BSkyB was cleared by
European regulators, Hunt texted the Chancellor, George Osborne:
'Could we chat about Murdoch Sky bid? Am seriously worried we
are going to screw this up.'

Out of the blue on 21 December 2010, Hunt would appear to have got his wish when responsibility for the bid was suddenly transferred to him from the Department for Business. Following Vince Cable's unfortunate blundering over his claims to have declared 'war on the Murdoch empire', the government had little option but to take the matter out of Cable's hands.

Having ruled out the prospect of Cable leaving either the government or his role as Business Secretary, the neatest solution appeared to be the transfer of responsibility for media mergers from the Business to the Culture Secretary. Osborne texted Hunt at 4.58 p.m. that afternoon, as the Cable scandal broke across the rolling news channels: 'I hope you like our solution.'

It was to become the biggest dose of bad luck Hunt's career had ever been dealt. Even that might be an understatement of an experience Hunt likens to having 'the whole world think you're guilty of a murder that you know that you didn't commit'. Any joy Hunt may have taken from having responsibility for the BSkyB bid lasted about a nanosecond. The issue was politically explosive and led Hunt to recall Tony Blair's observation in his memoirs that in politics you should not make enemies on purpose because you'll make enough of them anyway.

Politics sat right at the heart of the controversy over the BSkyB bid and it deeply divided left and right in British politics. Labour still bore the scars from the Wapping dispute in the 1980s and the Murdoch papers' support of Mrs Thatcher. *The Sun*, in particular, had ruthlessly exposed Neil Kinnock to ridicule in the 1992 general election and helped deliver victory to John Major. As the paper boldly, and probably accurately, claimed itself, it was 'THE SUN WOT WON IT'.

After *The Sun*'s switch back to support the Conservatives in 2009 in the middle of the Labour Party conference, directly after the Prime Minister's speech and thus timed to inflict maximum damage on Gordon Brown, the Murdoch papers' staunch support for Tony Blair and the New Labour was quickly forgotten within the party's ranks.

For the left of politics in general, Rupert Murdoch is almost on a par with Margaret Thatcher as a hate figure. Much like the late Prime Minister, Murdoch had inflicted heavy defeats on Labour, both at general elections and in famously breaking the union strikes at Wapping. The left believed that Hunt was now guilty by association: to them he was on the side of the devil that was Murdoch. It would make rational argument on the issue of BSkyB very difficult. In a matter of minutes Hunt had moved from relative anonymity to the left's Public Enemy No. 1.

Once Blair had finally been deposed by Brown after several aborted attempts, Cameron saw his opportunity to make a move on Murdoch. Planning had been taking place before 2007 and Cameron's closest confidants regularly discussed how they might win back Murdoch and his newspapers – but with Blair still Prime Minister it was unlikely. But meetings were held informally without minutes – if there was ever to be some cosying up to the Murdochs in the future, there was to be no way to infer any bargains were made. Getting closer to News International carried huge political risks even in 2007.

The loose plan developed to use whatever connections were available to woo Rupert Murdoch's key British lieutenants, including James Murdoch and Rebekah Brooks (née Wade) and to employ Andy Coulson, the former *News of the World* editor. George Osborne was keen on Coulson, both because of his considerable ability in tabloid journalism and also perhaps because of his impeccable connections within News International.

It is probably coincidental that Coulson joined Cameron's Conservative leadership team operation in July 2007, the same month that Gordon Brown became Labour Party leader. But the the intent was clear. The crucial issue was that Rupert Murdoch was not entirely convinced by Cameron's personal credentials or his policies as a prospective Prime Minister. In 2007, Murdoch had not completely given up hope that Brown might turn out to be a good premier.

Cameron and his team therefore focused on Rupert's son, James Murdoch, who was now running a good swathe of the Murdoch empire and was of a similar age and outlook to the Leader of the Opposition. The Conservative team made warm noises about Murdoch's views on the BBC and BSkyB and, more widely, media policy. This stopped well short of making any copper-bottomed promises on a BSkyB takeover, but James Murdoch and his team were convinced that Cameron was open to the idea. Jeremy Hunt's comments in opposition were part of that cause for optimism.

Coulson's closeness to Rebekah Brooks was well known, as was hers directly to Rupert Murdoch. Cameron and Osborne had opened a direct line to the top of News Corporation through Coulson and, as he had on previous occasions when *The Sun* changed its political allegiance, there is no doubt that Murdoch personally sanctioned the switch of the newspaper's support, albeit with a slightly heavy heart.

THE SKIRMISHES BEGIN

When Hunt's new decision-making powers were announced, the skirmishing began almost immediately. Labour had spent some time trawling the archives and were quick to pick up his previously supportive comments on the BSkyB bid. The then shadow Business Secretary, John Denham, wrote to the Cabinet Secretary, Sir Gus O'Donnell, quoting Hunt's various remarks expressing sympathy for the News Corporation bid and suggested that Hunt was not a fit person to be in charge of the bid. As the Cable affair had made clear, given the quasi-judicial nature of the Secretary of State's role in media mergers, the office holder would need to be able to show they had acted with impartiality. Denham suggested that the 'prejudicial statements' Hunt had previously made in favour of the BSkyB bid rendered him equally unfit to preside over it.

That evening, it was revealed that Hunt had held a private meeting with James Murdoch on 28 June 2010, shortly after the announcement of the News Corp bid, at which no civil servants were present. A DCMS spokesman described the meeting as 'an informal first meeting between Jeremy Hunt as Secretary of State and James Murdoch'. Hunt had also attended a dinner hosted by News Corp on 20 May, within weeks of coming into office, with his special adviser Adam Smith, following a speech James Murdoch made at University College London arguing for robust legislation to protect copyright. *The Guardian* also reported that civil servants took no minutes of a second meeting on 21 July 2010 between Hunt and BSkyB's chief executive, Jeremy Darroch.

On 23 December, Labour MP and witch-finder general Tom Watson wrote to Gus O'Donnell describing Hunt as 'knee-deep in News Corp'. Watson had made it his personal mission to destroy the Murdochs' power base in the UK over continuing allegations of phone hacking at their British newspapers. Fortunately for Hunt, the pressure that was building was relieved by parliamentary Christmas recess. This meant that the pressure of Urgent Questions, Parliamentary Statements and Departmental DCMS Oral Questions was gone until mid-January. It gave Hunt and the government the time and breathing space to prepare its defences.

HOW HUNT TRIED TO DEAL WITH IT...

Whatever Hunt's own favourable views on the BSkyB bid, he knew that he had been handed by Cable what, in rugby terms, is known as a 'hospital pass'. From the outset, he knew he would be under intense scrutiny and would have to do things strictly by the book and take the proper legal advice at each and every point where necessary. The politics were only made more fraught by the growing phone-hacking scandal. Hunt therefore spent most of January 2011 ensuring the process was clear to all involved and taking advice.

At the end of the third week of January, Andy Coulson, the former editor of News International's *News of the World* Sunday

newspaper who had become the Conservative Party's, and later
the government's, Director of Communications, was forced to
resign following allegations of his alleged knowledge of phone
hacking at the *News of the World*. Coulson was later found guilty
by an Old Bailey jury of conspiracy to hack phones and faces
a retrial on a charge of buying royal telephone directories from
police officers. But the impact of Coulson's resignation made the
whole BSkyB issue completely toxic.

When a Cabinet minister is required to act in a 'quasi-judicial'
manner, he or she has limited room for manoeuvre in their decision-making, whatever their personal views. Now that the News
International issue was fast becoming the most controversial in
British politics, Hunt had absolutely none. Every action and decision
he took would be scrutinised in forensic detail. Another gaffe on the
issue like the one Cable had made would have been disastrous for
the government's reputation for competence, and provided its opponents with a field day. Hunt needed to proceed with the greatest care.

In late January, he issued a statement saying that, based on the
evidence from Ofcom, the media regulator, he considered that
the News Corporation/BSkyB merger had the potential to oper-
ate against the public interest in media plurality and he therefore
intended to refer it to the Competition Commission for detailed
scrutiny. However, before doing this he would take more time
to consider a proposal from News Corporation to spin off Sky
News, its free-to-air news channel, to a separate, more independent company in order to mitigate any increased influence that
Murdoch's News Corporation would enjoy over Britain's news
consumption as a result of the deal. Hunt also asked the Office

of Fair Trading and Ofcom to begin discussions with News Corp about the Sky News plan.

After a period of negotiation, Hunt insisted that News Corp amended its Sky News proposals to meet the concerns of the regulators; otherwise he would refer the merger to the Competition Commission. News Corp duly made revisions, improving its offer by agreeing to the appointment of an independent chairman not affiliated to the Murdoch family or their companies. News Corporation would also guarantee the funding of the newly independent Sky News for ten years.

In Hunt's eyes, the proposal would guarantee Sky News's independence, the secured funding supporting the channel in much the same way that the television licence fee supports the delivery of news by the BBC. The deal was to be so tight as to make the new Sky News as sure of their cash flow over the ten-year period as any company could hope to be.

Having checked the proposal with the two regulators, Hunt was able to give the provisional green light for News Corporation's bid by 3 March 2011. He was careful to explain his involvement in the process in an interview of that month, stating, 'It was not for me to make suggestions as to what would be an appropriate remedy. I was very careful in this process not to end up getting in direct negotiations with News Corporation.'

After a number of initiatives, delays, proposals and consultations in the following months, Hunt finally gave News Corp the go-ahead to acquire the remainder of BSkyB on 30 June 2011, subject to a short consultation period. He was keen to get the matter cleared up before the parliamentary recess on 19 July. Hunt felt he had forced News Corp to strengthen the undertakings regarding the independence of Sky News, even though he had been advised that the deal could have gone ahead without it.

HOWEVER...

Two weeks before Parliament broke up for the summer recess, a bombshell struck. On 7 July, News International, News Corporation's British arm, announced that the *News of the World* was to close after the next Sunday edition following the emergence of significant evidence to support allegations of phone hacking. Hunt did not want to suspend consideration of the BSkyB bid as he believed the hacking issue was not relevant to his decision, but he pushed back the decision in order to consider the estimated 140,000 responses to the consultation that had been received.

With political anger and public interest about the role of the Murdochs and News International newspapers in phone hacking reaching fever pitch, the implications potentially ran right to the top of the government. The intensity of Cameron's team's efforts to ingratiate themselves with the Murdochs were bound to raise questions about what they had known about phone hacking and other illicit or unethical activities, and whether they had been prepared to support the commercial ambitions of a rotten media empire (as it was now increasingly being depicted) in exchange for the support of its newspapers.

The Prime Minister himself decided he needed to lance the boil. Cameron now indicated on 11 July his opinion that News

Corp should abandon the bid for BSkyB and focus on clearing up the mess created by phone-hacking allegations. A few hours later, Hunt announced to Parliament that he would refer the bid to the Competition Commission after all. Two days later, as it became engulfed by the crisis, the previously impregnable News Corp withdrew its bid for BSkyB amidst further revelations of phone hacking.

The Prime Minister nonetheless came under heavy pressure following revelations about the involvement of News International staff in phone hacking whilst Andy Coulson was editor of the *News of the World*. Revelations about George Osborne's sixteen meetings since the 2010 election with News International executives and Hunt's two meetings with James Murdoch only made matters worse. The impression was being given of government collusion with News International. The Prime Minister's response was to announce on 20 July an independent public inquiry into 'the culture, practices and ethics of the press', to be led by a judge, Lord Justice Sir Brian Leveson.

As far as Hunt was concerned, although there was significant coverage around phone hacking, the announcement of the new inquiry and Leveson's appointment to chair it seemed to take the pressure off him. As the months passed and the inquiry started its work hearing from the victims of phone hacking, Hunt himself felt fairly relaxed.

ALL HELL BREAKS LOOSE

Although the frenzy around phone hacking had broken out in the summer of 2011, it was not until April of the following year that all hell broke loose for Hunt. On the afternoon of Monday 23rd, out of nowhere, Hunt got an email from a contact in the media telling him that something 'very big' was about to be exposed about him.

Hunt was puzzled and surprised. As he searched his memory, he couldn't for the life of him think of any smoking guns he might have left lying around. Whatever the story was and whenever it was coming, there were no press camped outside his house when he arrived home that evening, even though James Murdoch was appearing before the Leveson Inquiry the next day. Hunt, now an experienced frontbencher, didn't lose any sleep over what he had been told.

Outwardly at least, Hunt never panicked throughout the whole protracted crisis. He is admirably even-tempered by nature, but in addition, much of his life had left him well attuned to the intrinsic snakes-and-ladders element of politics and well equipped to deal with the difficulties. Having been Head Boy at Charterhouse and later elected President of the Oxford University Conservative Association whilst studying PPE, he would have been no stranger to political attacks from a relatively early age.

When James Murdoch gave evidence to the Leveson Inquiry the following morning, Hunt was quite happy with how it went, although he told his aides and confidants that he saw a 'bumpy ride' ahead in the days and weeks to come.

Indeed, any satisfaction Hunt may have had with Murdoch's verbal evidence before the Leveson Inquiry was shattered when a dossier of emails running to 163 pages was published on the order of the inquiry. The emails revealed secret contacts over the bid, apparently raising doubts about Hunt's impartiality. The dossier appeared to show that Hunt's office had given News Corporation's public affairs director, Frédéric Michel, commercially confidential inside information on ministerial thinking over the company's bid for BSkyB, including detailed information on Ofcom's latest views and repeated suggestions that Hunt wanted the bid to succeed.

Michel quickly issued a statement clarifying that his records of conversations in which he had referred to Hunt personally in fact referred to conversations between himself and Adam Smith, Hunt's special adviser, and not Hunt himself. Michel's statement initially did not get much media traction until late in the day and then only as a result of Hunt's team being tipped off about its existence by a BBC journalist. As the bombshell of the Michel emails exploded around Hunt, he gained the impression by the evening that there was a kind of expectation in the Westminster village that he was 'going to be toast'.

When Hunt himself read Frédéric Michel's statement clarifying that the News Corp contacts were not with him but with his long-standing special adviser, Adam Smith, Hunt realised that with the Labour opposition and the media pack seeking blood, Smith would be in trouble – even though after reading the emails he didn't believe Smith would have said the things reported. Whilst Hunt felt sorry for Smith, as the Michel material was clearly exaggerated, he recognised his adviser was going to be 'dumped in it'.

As the day-long evidence session with James Murdoch drew to a close, Hunt rushed to a private meeting with David Cameron and the Cabinet Secretary, Sir Jeremy Heywood, at which he assured them that he had not been aware that his special adviser had been systematically leaking information and advice to News Corp about its bid for BSkyB. It was agreed at the meeting that Hunt would release a statement effectively pleading for time and announcing that he had written to Lord Justice Leveson asking to bring his appearance before the inquiry forward so that he could present his evidence:

> Now is not a time for kneejerk reactions. We've heard one side of the story today but some of the evidence reported meetings and conversations that simply didn't happen. Rather than jump on a political bandwagon, we need to hear what Lord Justice Leveson himself thinks after he's heard all the evidence.

Amidst the frenzy of revelations, Hunt sought to get across to the public that he wanted to manage the bid in a fair way. He suggested that his number one priority was to give the public confidence in the integrity of process, always asking for advice from independent regulators and following that advice to the letter. Getting the ball thrown into Lord Justice Leveson's court was essential in conveying that message. He appealed to every Englishman's sense of fairness: he just wanted his day in court to prove he had been objective and fair in his approach.

If nothing else, it was good politics – he needed to buy time, particularly as the Labour leadership felt Hunt's scalp was almost guaranteed and felt the public was with them in seeking to collect it. Driven on by a media frenzy of 'guilty unless proven innocent beyond all reasonable doubt', Harriet Harman called for Hunt's resignation within an hour of the 163 pages of documents being posted on the Leveson Inquiry website. Harman later admitted that she had not even read the full documents. Labour leader Ed Miliband followed suit and called for Hunt to be sacked, saying he had been 'standing up for the interests of the Murdochs' rather than those of the British people. Miliband accused Hunt of 'acting as a back channel for the Murdochs', challenging Cameron to fire Hunt if he didn't resign.

Armed with Michel's clarification and his confidence in his own handling of the affair, Hunt did not feel his position to be under any great threat and initially didn't even feel Smith would necessarily have to resign. At about 6.30 p.m. that evening, Hunt sent Smith to buy a bottle of wine and he and his team had a drink to cheer Smith up before going home. Nonetheless, Smith felt compelled to offer his resignation.

Hunt's wife called to warn him that the press were already outside their London home. The presence of photographers was quite frightening, particularly for his young family. Luckily, Hunt's parents were staying with the family at the time, so they had some emotional support. When he got home, there were about a dozen press and media already in attendance.

Hunt's father, who was in his eighties and not in the best of health (he would pass away in October 2013), was very worried about his son's reputation. As a naval officer, integrity and honour were extremely important to him, and his son was being accused of lacking both. Despite doing his best to hide his worry and concern, Hunt knew his father was feeling the pressure on his behalf and was very upset by it.

Nobody would want to put their elderly father through such an ordeal. Indeed, Hunt Senior was concerned right to the end of his life about the fortunes of his son. Even though he was terminally ill, their last conversation ended with Hunt's father wishing him 'good luck', knowing his son had a big parliamentary occasion the following day.

The press remained camped outside Hunt's house except when it rained; then they would sit in their cars and get ready to leap out. For those at the centre of the media storm, the gaze of the waiting press must feel like a constant threat, but Hunt noticed that in the evenings, once the press had realised he would not be re-emerging, they didn't tend to stick around. For nearly all the central players in these dramas, once they are safely home the press might stay for an hour or two outside but then they will usually evaporate gradually into the night.

Throughout the evening Sue Beeby, Hunt's trusted media adviser who had returned early from maternity leave to assist, and Lisa Hunter, another aide, were dealing with the press, trying to get more of the facts into the public domain, initially without much success.

Hunt does not remember receiving calls from No. 10 particularly, but he later recalled that the Prime Minister was with him from the beginning, and that if Cameron felt someone had acted honourably, he would stick by them:

> Right from the start, he was there beside me and I knew that he would be with me all the way. He is not someone who would change his mind on that. He takes a view of 'Is there an issue here?', 'Has that person behaved honourably and decently?' and if satisfied by the answers he supports them.

Hunt believed that the Prime Minister's support was crucial, as others took their lead from it. Other Cameron ministers featured in this book who have been through scandals and crises, notably Liam Fox and Andrew Mitchell, tend to concur with Hunt's assessment. Either way, if the Prime Minister's support helped Hunt survive, it didn't do the same for Mitchell and Fox. Prime ministerial support is an essential prerequisite for an embattled Cabinet minister to survive, but it appears to be rare for the Downing Street machine to leap into action to protect someone. Behind the scenes, the minister might receive a message of moral support, but for the real work of battling through the storm, he and his team are on their own.

Hunt's first five years at Westminster had not been without their problems and misfortunes. He was the subject of attacks in the media over comments he had made about the Hillsborough tragedy, where he wrongly suggested that the events were related to hooliganism and subsequently issued an apology. He had also been investigated by the Parliamentary Standards Commissioner for a breach of the expenses rules, eventually repaying over £10,000, something his Liberal Democrat opponent attacked him for ferociously. He was also familiar with the stresses of running a business.

But the intensity of the BSkyB crisis made him realise for the first time the potential impact his political work could have on his family. There were several moments when Hunt really worried about the pressure on those closest to him. There was a realisation that things were no longer affecting only him. 'Politicians are quite egocentric and certainly I had not appreciated that before this whole thing happened. Your good name has an impact on your wife when she goes out for coffee with her friends, or when she goes to work – whether you like it or not.

Hunt spent the Tuesday evening following the Michel bombshell with his family, explaining what was happening. However frightening they may have found it with the press camped outside their front door, they rallied round him, and continued to be a source of strength for Hunt throughout the whole process. One wonders whether Hunt, or any politician, could survive a protracted storm if the focus was on their family.

Hunt would need all the support he could get. The following morning's newspaper headlines were devastating: the growing storm around him dominated the front pages. *The Guardian*, which had led the outcry over phone hacking, had a large picture of a smiling Hunt underneath the headline 'Minister for Murdoch'. The staunchly Labour-supporting *Mirror* led with 'Murdoch's Stooges: Cabinet minister illegally tipped off Sky about £8 billion deal … and PM "caught lying"'. The free commuter paper *Metro* had a caption on the front page saying 'Knives out for Hunt: minister faces calls to quit over Murdoch links', whilst *The Independent*'s front-page headline was 'Murdoch's revenge', with a caption saying 'Culture Secretary urged to resign after explosive emails show his office briefed News Corp on £7.5bn BSkyB bid' underneath pictures of James Murdoch, Cameron and Hunt.

Headlines like these project a version of the story into homes and workplaces around the country that immediately takes hold in the minds of the readers. But are they always accurate? Separating fact and fiction can be an enormous problem during the worst of a political storm – both for the participant and for the media. The lines can become blurred between the actual events and other parties' interpretations of those events. Sometimes the atmosphere created by the media can be extraordinarily powerful and compelling, over-whelming all those actually involved in the events themselves. These stories can sometimes become self-regenerating and sustaining. All that can be done in these circumstances is to go to ground and wait for an opportunity once events have calmed down.

Nor was the sense of the enormity of the crisis confined to the left. The *Daily Mail* featured a full-page close-up picture of the embattled Hunt, with the headline 'Revenge of the Murdochs: Nine months on from hacking scandal, Culture Secretary faces calls to quit as News Corp releases devastating emails revealing his "absolutely illegal" help for BSkyB bid', whilst the *Daily Telegraph* headline read 'Absolutely illegal: emails reveal collusion between Culture Secretary and Murdoch's News Corp empire as it was trying to take over BSkyB'. Even News International's own *Times* ran with the headline 'Hunt in the frame over handling of BSkyB deal', although its bestselling newspaper, *The Sun*, did not mention the issue on its front page.

Hunt might have expected some awful headlines but he hoped that those close colleagues who knew him well would stand by him. In his moment of deep crisis, when his future career hung in the balance, he now found out who his real friends were. These colleagues fell into three groups; those who did what he expected; those who did less and those who went well beyond what he expected.

Whilst Hunt had called for the public to await judgement until after Leveson, he hoped that politically experienced colleagues would understand what was going on and get behind his attempts to survive the onslaught. Hunt hasn't forgotten which group each of his 'friends' fell into at the time. But what he needed most, as is often the case in the middle of a political crisis, was people who were willing to offer public support. Those who made that effort in Hunt's hour of need are remembered with gratitude.

Hunt recalls, 'Your true friends are the ones who will actually say things publicly, and that's what makes the difference.' He recalls fellow ministers such as Andrew Mitchell and Nick Herbert as being among those prepared to battle, publicly and privately, to save him. He recalls that the support from colleagues, and from his political and parliamentary aides, was crucial to his survival during the darkest hours of his political career.

He also remembers a Liberal Democrat MP, Duncan Hames, who, unexpectedly gave Hunt his public support by saying he had 'no questions about Jeremy Hunt's integrity'. To an embattled Conservative minister, one MP from another party speaking up on their behalf was worth ten of his own side. Indeed, one of the positive things to emerge from the crisis was that in the heat of battle, Hunt feels he formed friendships that he hopes will last a lifetime.

As usual, Hunt woke at 6 a.m. the day after the James Murdoch testimony and Frédéric Michel's statement and went for a run. There were no photographers there at that point but by the time he got back the press were all waiting. The assembled media were pretty astonished to find him coming back from a run when they'd assumed that he was tucked up in bed asleep. But they got their first shot of the day, which was all they required.

Indeed, Hunt's relationship with the journalists who doorstepped him outside his Pimlico home was slightly surreal. The poachers and the target had two completely different understandings of the situation they were involved in. The journalists did not even see it as a contest; they were all convinced that Hunt was going to resign. They thought it was only a matter of time and they were competing among themselves as to who could deliver the *coup de grâce*. Hunt, on the other hand, shortly after the event, claimed that he remained completely confident that that wouldn't happen and that when the facts came out people would understand.

Some of this is undoubtedly post-rationalisation of events. Hunt now admits he had seriously considered his predicament overnight and was still giving it further thought that morning. He was evidently unsure when he went into the Department for Culture, Media and Sport early that morning whether he would survive the day. He wasn't helped when the DCMS Permanent Secretary, Jonathan Stevens, told him that he thought the number, extent, depth and tone of contacts between Michel and Smith suggested by the emails of Fred Michel 'went beyond what was acceptable'.

The second floor of DCMS, located at the time just off Trafalgar Square, where ministers and their private offices were based, was not without similarities to *Night of the Living Dead* early that Wednesday morning. The place was rudderless as the Permanent Secretary appeared to wander around aimlessly with a tragic smile on his lips. Adam Smith looked as if he had had the blood drained from his veins overnight as he waited for the axe to fall, whilst Hunt's two press advisers did their best to lighten the mood with a combination of sympathy for Smith and gallows humour. Hunt, too, was not his usual tiggerish self; instead, he was unusually withdrawn, pale and uncomfortable.

At the time, with a large slice of understatement, Hunt referred to 25 April 2012 as 'a difficult day'. Now he describes it as 'the worst single day in my political career without question'. He was taking frequent calls from No. 10 as the choreography of the day was worked out. The Labour Party was known to be pressing for an Urgent Question on the floor of the House, which would put further pressure on his position. The plan was to wait until the last minute to see if it was likely to be granted and, if so, try to get on the front foot with a statement.

No. 10 expected the Commons Speaker, John Bercow, to be unhelpful to the government. Telephone tag continued between Hunt and Downing Street as the clock ran down to 10.30 a.m., at which point the decision would be taken away from them and they would be informed whether or not an Urgent Question had been granted. With minutes to go, the Speaker was informed that Hunt would make a statement to the House.

Hunt now had to prepare the most important and difficult statement of his career, and at the same time he had to deal with his loyal friend Adam Smith's resignation, which had become necessary to buy the time needed to get the truth of what had really happened into play. Hunt and the very able Smith were extremely close colleagues and neither the discussion nor the parting was easy. Hunt had hoped it wouldn't prove necessary, but overnight the contents of Smith's conversations with Michel had been allowed to sink in. When Smith repeated his offer to resign in a short meeting, Hunt, having talked with No. 10, accepted it.

The collective view of those around Hunt, including the Prime Minister's office, was that Smith should go. In his head, if not his heart, Hunt agreed with the decision. They all understood that politics is a profession in which perception is sometimes as important as reality, and there was a perception that some of the conversations that Adam Smith had had were damaging. Smith accepted that there were texts sent in which he used inappropriate language. Put it all together and the conclusion was that it would be difficult to find any other option than Smith resigning.

Hunt felt terribly guilty because Smith was 'an incredibly loyal, decent guy'. He questioned himself on whether he should follow Smith. As he recalls, 'I basically realised that something had gone wrong on my watch and even though I didn't authorise it, I wasn't aware of it, I had some responsibility for it.'

At least in retrospect, he justifies his determination to stay on as a result of the calculation that if he had resigned, whether or not the truth eventually came out, the public would permanently be left with the overriding impression that News Corporation's bid for BSkyB had been corruptly run by the government, with Hunt himself bearing much of the guilt. Hunt felt that 'for Adam's sake as well as my sake I needed to fight to make the case that this deal was handled impartially'. Within the DCMS, those on both sides of the divide between politicians and civil servants believed that, as a department, they had handled the BSkyB bid honourably, so they were keen to ensure that the case was properly explained to the world.

As he went through his time at the centre of the storm, Hunt began to recognise something new. 'The thing that I realised going through that political process was that my integrity mattered far more to me than any political prospects.'

Adam Smith's resignation was announced at around 11 a.m. that morning. A statement was issued in which Smith effectively took the rap and bought Hunt more time. Whilst he may not have recognised all that Fred Michel had said in his witness statements about their conversations, Smith had realised he 'went too far' and it was contrary to the requirements set by Hunt and the Permanent Secretary. He therefore stepped down as Hunt's special adviser.

Whilst Smith's statement was being circulated, Hunt's parliamentary allies were working furiously in the House of Commons to organise backbenchers to support him in his own forthcoming statement. Whatever Hunt's confidence that the truth of the matter would be enough to save him, his allies felt that if the statement went badly the game was up and he would be forced to resign by the end of the day. His political allies found his civil service team somewhat blinded by the glare of events and shell-shocked by the departure of Smith, who, apart from Hunt himself, was the bedrock of the whole team. A clear plan was needed to ensure Hunt survived the rest of the day.

With the assistance of a whip, his parliamentary aides gathered together backbenchers to brief them on the day's events and how to protect their colleague. Backbenchers were briefed that the full truth was not out in public, but would only be known once Hunt had been before the Leveson Inquiry. They were asked to play their part in the attempt to ensure that Hunt got the chance of a fair hearing.

Unlike some other ministers, Hunt had plenty of goodwill in the bank, having taken the time to hold numerous meetings and coffees with backbenchers over the previous year, many of them from the crucial 2010 intake. Now was the time to draw it down. A battery of helpful questions was prepared and circulated. Backbenchers were specifically asked to let the House know what they themselves knew about Hunt's upstanding character and that he was a decent and honourable person.

Hunt was due to give his statement immediately after Prime Minister's Questions. Having had to deal with the difficult discussions with Smith over the latter's resignation, he was still frantically writing his statement in the car on the way to the Commons. The paparazzi were waiting for him as he left the department and when the doors of the car park finally opened, Hunt's party was greeted with a wall of paparazzi taking photographs. The noise and flashes of light were of an intensity he had never encountered before in his life.

Hunt's decision to make big departmental savings and to stop having government cars then backfired as the driver, from a taxi firm, was quite nervous as the car made its way through. Inexplicably, instead of turning left to Parliament, he turned right. When Hunt asked him why he had done this, he turned off into a cul-de-sac to do a U-turn. However, the paparazzi realised where they were and flooded across the road. They were completely surrounding the car, like bees to a honey pot.

Hunt's car eventually drove out, but still had to get through bumper-to-bumper traffic around Trafalgar Square. The paparazzi followed them on the journey, with the cameras glued to the windows. At the same time, the clock was ticking. The driver's nervousness nearly made Hunt late for PMQs, which was inevitably going to focus on him.

At Prime Minister's Questions, under hostile questioning from Ed Miliband, the Prime Minister made clear his full support and explained that Hunt would give a full account of himself both to the Commons and to the Leveson Inquiry. It was a clear signal to the opposition and, more importantly, backbenchers that he was going to fight to keep Hunt.

At 12.30 p.m., after PMQs, Hunt got up to make his own statement. It was a difficult statement and he was nervous, but he could feel the strength of support from the backbenchers on his own side. Hunt acknowledged that the volume of communications was not appropriate in a quasi-judicial process and that his special adviser had overstepped the mark. But he was anxious to dispel the accusation that the revelations of the volume of texts and conversations between his special adviser, Adam Smith, and News Corp was evidence of a 'back channel' through which News Corporation was able to influence his decisions.

Hunt insisted that he had only seen the transcripts of these communications on the previous day and that they had not influenced his decisions in any way at all, not least because he had insisted on hearing the advice of independent regulators at every stage of the process. He concluded the statement by restating his total confidence that when the Leveson Inquiry heard his evidence, the public would see that he had conducted the bid process with scrupulous fairness throughout.

The Labour benches accused Hunt of using his special adviser as a human shield, throwing him to the wolves to deflect attention away from his own close relationship with Rupert Murdoch's News Corp. In her response to Hunt's statement, Harriet Harman called on him to resign again.

Hunt went on the counterattack at the start of the debate, following his statement and Harman's response. He started by wanting to 'stick it' to Labour, and remind them of what they had done in respect of the Murdochs whilst they were in power. However, this only resulted in him being shouted down by the Labour benches. Hunt felt he learned an important lesson on that occasion for any future political crises or difficulties: only counterattack after first responding to the questions asked about your own behaviour.

Hunt had survived the day of the statement. His and his allies' main goal had been for him to make it through until he had the opportunity to give his own account of events at the Leveson Inquiry.

Having survived the Commons, Hunt now had to get ready for his appearance before Leveson. Few colleagues were able to give advice in how to deal with a judicial inquiry, because few of his generation had faced one. There was quite a bit of 'feeling his way' on this for Hunt. One of the main things he learned during the whole crisis and the subsequent Leveson process was that when someone is making their case, they need to be robust throughout.

It has already been noted how, despite the extensive political machinery of the major parties and 10 Downing Street, embattled ministers find themselves to a large extent on their own in dealing with scandals and crises. But this was even more so in Hunt's case. Because of the Leveson Inquiry, Hunt had to cut off his contact with the Prime Minister on all matters relating to BSkyB and News Corporation after his statement to the Commons.

Unfortunately for Hunt, Lord Justice Leveson refused to bring forward his appearance before the inquiry, leaving the prospect of others going before him and causing further problems whilst Hunt faced a lengthy wait to defend himself. The press continued to pursue Hunt at his home and he remembers the moment when he finally weakened.

Having been extraordinarily strong, despite what he would describe as character assassination from the media and the left, Hunt still had a big wobble. It was on one particular day and, as with Jacqui Smith and Vince Cable, it involved running the gauntlet of cameras outside the house:

> I didn't want to walk outside the front door of my house. I had a whole horde of photographers there and I was putting on my overcoat to go to work and I thought, 'I really don't want to do this.' That's quite a scary thing to be afraid of … walking out of your own front door.

It was and is entirely understandable. There are few in politics, or indeed any walk of life, who could have borne the sheer intensity of the attention over such a lengthy period of time. There was no let-up, as, with Rupert Murdoch due to appear at the Leveson Inquiry on Thursday 26 April, Labour leader Ed Miliband went on the attack on BBC Radio 4's *Today* programme.

Hunt, he implied, was only still in his job because he was acting as a firewall between the scandal and No. 10. He suggested that if Hunt went, the questions would move onto the relationship and conversations with Rebekah Brooks and Rupert Murdoch. He finished with a flourish: 'Does this matter for politics? I say it does matter because what matters is that you govern in the interests of the British people, not in [the interests of] a few rich, powerful people who have access to you.'

The claims were made with some substance, as a close inspection of Cameron's relationship with Brooks, Coulson and others would have been somewhat uncomfortable for the Prime Minister. However, Miliband also claimed that it was not credible to say Adam Smith acted as a lone wolf in repeatedly briefing News Corp on how the Culture Secretary wanted to help the company in its bid for BSkyB: he must have had Hunt's knowledge and support.

Perhaps worse for Hunt, Jonathan Stephens, the Permanent Secretary at his own department, the DCMS, appeared before the Public Accounts Committee. Stephens's appearance did nothing to calm the febrile atmosphere and almost landed Hunt in trouble once again. Under questioning, Stephens declined ten times to confirm Hunt's version of his role in the BSkyB affair. Stephens told the Select Committee that he would neither confirm nor deny his alleged role in allowing Adam Smith, Hunt's special adviser, to speak to James Murdoch's office. Later, the DCMS issued a statement saying Stephens was 'content' with Smith's role. This followed Hunt's claim in Parliament on Wednesday that Stephens had 'agreed' that Smith would be the point of contact with News Corp.

A few coalition colleagues were less sympathetic to Hunt's position. Bernard Jenkin, the Conservative chair of the Public Administration Select Committee (PASC), called on David Cameron to refer Hunt's case to the independent adviser on the ministerial code, Sir Alex Allan. Later, on *Question Time*, Deputy Lib Dem leader Simon Hughes broke ranks and also called for Hunt to be referred for investigation by Allan.

Hunt's predicament soon proved the source of tensions within the coalition, with Nick Clegg taking advantage of the Conservatives' difficulties to put the boot in. He urged Cameron to refer Hunt to the independent adviser on the ministerial code and took the extraordinary step of personally urging Hunt to refer himself. The Deputy Prime Minister told Hunt that the row over his relationship with BSkyB was hugely damaging to the coalition government as a whole and needed to be resolved urgently.

These concerns were magnified when Clegg repeatedly tried and failed during increasingly anguished conversations to persuade the Prime Minister of the need to refer the case to Allan. Clegg could not understand the Prime Minister's reluctance to refer the case, given his insistence that the independent adviser would find no evidence of the ministerial code having been broken by the relationship between Hunt's office, the News Corp lobbyist Fred Michel, and the Murdochs. Cameron rebuffed Clegg, arguing, 'Why are you bothering? ... Nobody's interested.'

Clegg claimed that this was a matter of politics rather than any personal animus towards Hunt. A source said:

> Nick Clegg values Jeremy Hunt as a collaborative colleague in the coalition. That is not the issue. This was about the Liberal Democrats being unable to support what we felt was the politically unsustainable decision not to refer. When it became clear that they wouldn't help themselves, Nick wasn't going to expend political capital defending them.

Clegg's behaviour left a nasty taste in the mouth of many Conservative backbenchers. Whilst they had initially taken to the battlefield to defend their man, it was felt the Liberal Democrats had behaved like untrustworthy mercenaries, riding away from their flank to open it to the enemy, rather than loyal coalition partners. They point to the fact that many senior Conservative MPs could have had a field day over the David Laws expenses scandal or Chris Huhne but they held firm.

Although such calls for referral to the adviser on the ministerial code may now seem simple and innocuous, they were extremely unhelpful. There was a feeling that this referral would only stoke up more difficulties and provide another hurdle for Hunt to jump over. In response, Downing Street publicly refused to say whether Hunt would be referred for investigation over breaches of the ministerial code until after his Leveson evidence. The line was that it did not make sense to cut across one judicial inquiry with another inquiry, a reasonable enough position under the circumstances.

The extent of the problems Hunt faced is illustrated by the Prime Minister being forced to go before the Commons to answer an Urgent Question as to why he had decided not to refer Hunt in response to the allegations that Hunt had breached the ministerial code over his handling of the News Corp bid for BSkyB. It was the first time in ten years that a Speaker had ordered a Prime Minister to come to the Commons.

The pressure increased on Hunt yet further when Lord Justice Leveson said he would not judge whether the Culture Secretary had breached the ministerial code over his and his former special adviser's handling of Rupert Murdoch's £8 billion bid for BSkyB. Leveson was not prepared to stray an inch from his terms of reference. This cast doubt on the Prime Minister and Hunt's own earlier position that Leveson was the right place for the truth to come out and criticisms to be made.

It remained to be seen if the Labour Party or the media could force the issue to a conclusion. They were determined to try and, as May 2012 continued, the pressure built. Labour again called for Hunt to resign following the disclosure of an email to the Leveson Inquiry by the former News International chief executive Rebekah Brooks that appeared to show that he had sought private advice from News Corporation over how Downing Street should respond to the phone-hacking scandal.

In the email, from Fred Michel to Rebekah Brooks, Michel warned, days before *The Guardian* revealed in July 2011 that murdered teenager Milly Dowler's voicemail had been targeted by the *News of the World*, that 'JH [Jeremy Hunt] is now starting to looking into phone hacking/practices more thoroughly' and he 'has asked me to advise him privately in the coming weeks and guide his and No. 10's positioning'.

The email suggested Hunt had sought to avoid a public inquiry into phone hacking. If that wasn't bad enough, Michel wrote to Brooks in the same email that Hunt was poised to make an 'extremely helpful' statement about the company's proposed acquisition of BSkyB, saying that the takeover would be approved regardless of phone-hacking allegations.

Although Michel had already admitted that his contact with Hunt was in fact with Hunt's adviser, Adam Smith, it didn't stop Labour going on the warpath again. Ed Miliband told the media it beggared belief that Hunt remained in his job, and that the accumulation of evidence about his links with Rupert Murdoch's company when he was considering its bid for BSkyB made his position untenable.

The problem with Michel's correspondence, however exaggerated it was, was that there was always a grain of truth in it, which made it more difficult to simply dismiss. In this case, as with the others, Michel had not spoken with Hunt, but it would be true to say that Hunt did not feel phone hacking should play any part in the decision he was making regarding BSkyB.

Chris Bryant, a campaigning MP on the issue of phone hacking, increased the pressure by suggesting a criminal offence may have been committed if News International had been handed information about the previous year's BSkyB bid by Hunt's office. The point he made was a good one: that everything Michel predicted would be said by Hunt in Parliament was in fact said. News International did have information about what the Secretary of State was going to say before he said it, and also before commercial operators did. Bryant believed that was a criminal offence.

Thankfully for Hunt, on 24 May, Michel gave evidence to the Leveson Inquiry reiterating his earlier statement that although he had written hundreds of emails to James Murdoch claiming to have had briefings, feedback and 'strong', 'long' conversations with Hunt throughout the thirteen-month passage of the bid, these conversations had in fact been with Adam Smith, not Hunt. He provided a detailed explanation of the references to 'Hunt', 'JH', 'he' and 'Jeremy' as summaries of what he had been told by Adam Smith in his written witness statement.

However, that same day, Adam Smith also appeared before the Leveson Inquiry. Under persistent questioning, he repeated that Hunt had always said there wasn't a problem with the Murdoch bid. In a document shown to the inquiry, Hunt had expressed to the Prime Minister his view that if the Murdoch bid was blocked 'our media sector would suffer for years'.

Hunt had also been dropped back in it by the former head of the civil service Lord O'Donnell's statement to the Leveson Inquiry that Hunt should have known if his special adviser was giving feedback to News Corporation. O'Donnell was clear that ministers and secretaries of state should know exactly what their special advisers were doing, particularly in relation to quasi-judicial decisions.

Smith had sent 257 text messages to Michel during the course of News Corp's BSkyB bid in 2010 and 2011. In his evidence, he had said that senior figures in the Department for Culture, Media and Sport, including Hunt, were all 'generally aware' of his activities and had not expressed concern with the way he was dealing with Mr Michel. It led to another outbreak of Harriet Harman calling for Hunt's head and the Prime Minister going on TV to express his full confidence in his Culture Secretary.

To add insult to injury and in the middle of the storm, *The Guardian* reported that Hunt had failed to declare thousands of pounds of donations from media and arts companies which had sponsored a series of networking events before the 2010 general election. Hunt was forced to amend his entry in the House of Commons register of members' interests after what aides described as a 'miscommunication' with his deputy, Ed Vaizey.

On 31 May 2012, it was finally Hunt's turn to appear before Leveson. He had spent weeks preparing to give evidence, cancelling numerous meetings and engagements to accommodate the need for meetings and practice. He was completely calm on the day, though one wrong answer could have meant the end of his Cabinet career. Hunt knew he could have been gone by the end of the day, as he did not know how the public would interpret what he said – or how the media would interpret it.

He went from his department to the House of Commons to pick up parliamentary aides and they travelled to the Royal Courts, discussing the day ahead, interrupted only by the thud of photographers hitting the car windows to take pictures as the courts came into view. As Hunt left the car to enter the building in full view of waiting TV cameras, a wall of noise from anti-Murdoch protesters erupted.

Hunt gave evidence for nearly six hours and apart from a hesitant first hour, it went remarkably well. A bit of fine-tuning in the first break and a No. 10 announcement to divert attention meant that Hunt emerged with his reputation intact. Within minutes of him finishing his six-hour stint, No. 10 announced David Cameron would not be referring Hunt's handling of the bid to his independent adviser on the ministerial code, a decision branded as 'disgraceful' by the Labour deputy leader, Harriet Harman.

It was revealed during the course of Hunt's evidence that he had been in direct text contact with James Murdoch whilst he had quasi-judicial responsibility for News Corporation's BSkyB takeover bid. Hunt admitted that with the benefit of hindsight, the private communication was wrong. 'I think probably now I wouldn't take the same view, and I would just avoid all text messages,' he said. But Hunt had survived his Leveson appearance and even *The Guardian* declared his position safe the following day – at least until a reshuffle. He was, though, in their view, 'severely damaged'.

Leveson was a big personal test for Hunt, one that tried all his political and personal skills to the limit. Five and a half hours is a very long time to be questioned under oath. Most importantly, he was asked about things that had happened over a year ago and was expected to provide detailed answers. A person in that situation can say 'I don't know' to a question once or twice, but he can't do it consistently. Hunt spent a lot of time in the build-up going through papers, reminding himself of the chronology, re-familiarising himself with legal documents that had been exchanged, finding out what had happened on what date, and reading documents he had never even seen before. He wanted to make sure that he was on top of things. His preparation was exhaustive.

But if he thought that surviving his Leveson appearance put an end to the matter, he was wrong. Although Nick Clegg showed signs of coming round to supporting Hunt's role in News Corporation's aborted bid for BSkyB, saying he had given a 'full, good and convincing account' of his actions, the Liberal Democrats were soon considering a Labour parliamentary motion calling for Hunt to be referred to an inquiry for breaches of the ministerial code. Not for the first time, Conservative MPs were furious. Labour's motion was rejected by 290 votes to 252, but the government's eighty-plus majority more than halved to thirty-eight in the vote after the Liberal Democrats abstained. Enraged Tory MPs accused the Liberal Democrats of 'treachery'. One senior Tory said at the time: 'It was typical Lib Dems – a high moral tone and low politics.'

Hunt recalls that Labour 'played the man, not the ball' with its parliamentary motion. It was unpleasant, but by this point he was not surprised. During the course of the debate he was forced to suffer the further indignity of having Chris Bryant, something of a parliamentary thespian, describe him as having 'lied to Parliament', an accusation normally considered to be so fundamental a breach of parliamentary protocols as to result in the accuser being removed from the House of Commons.

However, when several Conservative MPs got up to protest against Bryant's use of unparliamentary language, Speaker John Bercow allowed his comment to stand, declaring opaquely that 'I am simply saying that on the advice that I have taken, nothing disorderly has occurred'. Only a few months later, Speaker Bercow would have the Labour MP Paul Flynn thrown out of the Chamber and fined for suggesting far less directly that the Defence Secretary had lied over military deaths in Afghanistan. But only on this occasion, Bercow was content to stand by and allow Bryant to repeatedly call Hunt a liar.

Hunt wasn't surprised by Bryant's behaviour, as he is well known for hyperbole and regarded as a bit of an attention-seeker. But he was wounded by the Speaker's behaviour, by the intimation that somehow there was some implicit acceptance that Bryant had a point. Whilst Hunt had on previous occasions been forced to correct the record following statements and questions in the House when he had made an error, something that ministers are bound to do on occasion, and often on the basis of information provided to them by others, it was entirely different to deliberately lying to Parliament.

Behind the scenes, Speaker Bercow had already been extremely unhelpful to Hunt. Bercow had wanted to have all the Leveson evidence released and published for parliamentary use before Hunt's appearance at the Royal Courts. It would have finished him

off, as it would have meant that the press would have a field day
going through all the material without Hunt being able to defend
his actions. Hunt felt that the fair thing was to allow his account
to be heard and tested in court, to allow him to defend himself as
part of a judicial process and under the cross-examination of a QC.
Bercow did not, apparently, see this as desirable. It led to a tense
and difficult meeting between the two men in the Speaker's office.
In a heated discussion the pair could not agree and the outcome
was settled only when Leveson himself intervened and ruled that
the judicial process should not be disturbed.

Hunt now contents himself that the Leveson Inquiry vindicated
him despite the behaviour of people such as Harman, Speaker
Bercow and Chris Bryant. He says,

> The moment I knew that my name was cleared was when we had
> the parliamentary statement after the publication of Leveson. My
> name did not appear once in Ed Miliband's response to the Prime
> Minister. So this was the man who had said to the Prime Minister,
> 'He should go, he should go,' and yet no mention whatsoever. It
> meant that Labour had realised that what Leveson had said was
> conclusive and that the matter was closed.

THE AFTERMATH

The peak of Hunt's storm lasted for almost two months, but the
issue of the BSkyB bid would have been one of the dominant issues
facing Hunt for almost a year and a half. Aside from the days and

weeks leading up to Leveson, and his appearance before the House of Commons after the resignation of Smith, Hunt recalls being happy to get on with his desk job for most of the time, and many of his priorities carried on as normal. In terms of building his political profile, he had to opt out of things like the BBC's *Question Time*. But most of his priorities, such as super-fast broadband and the Olympics, carried on as normal.

Whatever people's views on Hunt, the Murdochs, phone hacking and the BSkyB bid, his political survival in the face of such a toxic crisis, which surrounded him for almost eighteen months, is a testament to his temperament and his resilience. Nor did he allow the media storm affecting him and his closest staff to come to the detriment of his duties as Secretary of State: his signature priority, the delivery of the London Olympics, was regarded by many as one of the greatest national successes in living memory.

Reflecting on the crisis now, Hunt is admirably philosophical, describing the affair as 'a curious period'. Despite becoming a hate figure for the left, which still continues to this day, Hunt comforts himself with something David Aaronovitch wrote at the time. 'He posed the question "Should Jeremy Hunt resign?" The answer was "Yes!" Then he asked, "Who is Jeremy Hunt?" "Err, we don't know." It made me realise the bile isn't personal,' says Hunt.

Unlike Cable's BSkyB troubles, Hunt's crisis did not dent his confidence in his own ability. Indeed, following his surprise promotion to Health Secretary before the Leveson Inquiry had even reported, he rapidly established himself as an active and effective Secretary of State in the policy area often thought of as the third rail of British politics.

If anything, he has developed a harder edge and a thicker skin as a result of his ordeal at the centre of the storm: 'You definitely emerge much stronger. You learn where your bottom lines are, on a personal level. You learn the things that really matter to you.' At the time, the then Chief Whip, Patrick McLoughlin, told him that he had been blooded and that it would stand him in good stead in his future Cabinet career.

Hunt himself believes that politics is a long game and people should remember that, if you're lucky enough to hold on to your seat, it could be a 25-year career. 'Therefore', he says, 'there are those people who behave with integrity and those people who don't ... and I think that the mistake people make is ... they go for short-term political advantage whilst forgetting that actually, in the end, a parliamentary reputation is built up over very many years.'

Although there were people who let him down during his crisis, he bears no bitterness; that is the nature of politics. Instead, he prefers to think about the people who stood up for him, because that is what you really remember.

One of the things that kept him going in his darkest hour was a private letter from someone he had never met: former Archbishop George Carey. The letter contained kind and reassuring words that Hunt should 'stay firm' and that 'more people like you are needed in public life'. To Hunt, this small act of kindness meant a great deal.

In the long run, the crisis perhaps helped Hunt deepen his political perspective. He used to joke with his special adviser that sometimes an issue would crop up, and they would say, 'Well, I'm not going to have to resign over it, so let's not worry about it.' After what happened, it now takes a lot to drive Hunt off course from his political priorities as Secretary of State for Health.

But perhaps his biggest lesson from the whole affair was personal and character-related. The BSkyB episode has brought a fundamental change in Hunt: he claims he no longer plans his political career, because it's a waste of time. One minute Hunt was the rising star, a successful Culture Secretary with the Olympics on his CV, then suddenly, through an unexpected twist of fate, his whole career and personal reputation were in the balance – all through being accused of something he had not done. It certainly provides a reminder of the randomness and uncertainty of a life in politics.

CHAPTER 6

CHARLES CLARKE FROM HERO TO ZERO IN UNDER A YEAR

"The Brown camp was perpetually about undermining Tony [Blair] in every respect. I was a Tony colleague and they were undermining me all the time in terms of background and press briefings 100 per cent. There were half a dozen of them who were doing that perpetually."

— Charles Clarke

T he events which led to Charles Clarke's downfall were of a different nature to the other crises and scandals in this book. It was neither a personal issue nor a big policy failure. It was to a large extent an administration issue, where the government made mistakes, which then led to a political challenge from the Conservative opposition and media. The only question was, in those circumstances, whether the Prime Minister and his senior advisers would cave in to a noisy challenge or whether they would not. Clarke believed – wrongly, as it turned out – that Blair would not buckle.

Clarke's personal style may well have inadvertently made things worse, as he was intellectually combative with his colleagues and, some would argue, arrogant. Politicians who have been faced with a similar set of circumstances to Clarke have survived their moment

of crisis, and in some cases even prospered. Peculiar circumstances
and personality traits meant that Clarke did not.

Whilst he would admit to making mistakes and agree to a certain
degree of arrogance, even Clarke was taken aback by the unrelenting nature of the in-fighting at the very top of government. He
experienced what he came to see as a fifth column in government,
directed aggressively by Gordon Brown and his minions against
Blair's ongoing leadership. Whilst errors made Clarke vulnerable,
it was the in-fighting that finished his career.

As Damian McBride's memoir *Power Trip* makes clear, there were
two centres of power in Blair's government, which grew to be equal
and opposite in strength; by 2006 they had reached such dimen-
sions that progress in thinking and policy was severely hampered
on a daily basis – some would say rendered almost impossible. It is
now well known that whilst the official government was run from
No. 10, at the same time the unofficial one was running next door.
As one of Blair's most prominent and forthright allies, Clarke was
in the line of fire.

The fact that he was ultimately unceremoniously sacked from
his job, by a Prime Minister to whom he was a close ally and who
in any case found such things terribly difficult, is unusual in many
ways and must surely be seen as part of the bitter internal wars of
New Labour.

Charles Clarke was probably always destined to go into politics.
His father, Richard Clarke, otherwise known as 'Otto', was a

permanent secretary and his mother a civil servant. Otto had joined the Labour Party and become a local councillor and author for the Fabians in the 1930s. His son was quick to go into left-wing student politics at Cambridge and became president of the NUS. Soon after finishing there he became a Labour councillor in Hackney and in 1980 started working for Neil Kinnock, eventually becoming what would now be termed a special adviser, or 'Spad' for short.

To begin with, Clarke's position was a part-time one, funded partly by an education charity, but he went full-time when Kinnock became leader of the Labour Party and of Her Majesty's Opposition. He stuck with Kinnock until the latter lost in 1992, and Clarke himself went on to become a Member of Parliament in 1997. Despite brief dalliances into other areas, politics was in his blood and he enjoyed it immensely.

With such a highly political background, Clarke was bound to have flirted with numerous political dramas of variable significance over the years. Indeed, as president of the NUS, he saw the union's travel and printing companies go bankrupt, causing redundancies and deep unhappiness among students. It all led to a resolution of no confidence in Clarke tabled before the NUS conference. He fought the motion and only just held on.

It was a very sharp experience – both the event itself and the political side effects. It taught him a valuable lesson: that real leadership meant being straightforward and taking arguments head-on; there was never any point in trying to run away from them. His desire to tackle issues in this way, according to colleagues in the Labour Party, made him frequently prickly and difficult.

A different type of issue arose in the early 1980s when Clarke
was a councillor in the London borough of Hackney. The council
joined a protest against the Thatcher government's policy of capping
the amounts of money that could be raised from local taxation in
an attempt to stop unrestrained spending by so-called 'loony left'
local authorities. The Labour campaign's main tactic was to refuse
to set any budget at all for the financial year 1985–86, requiring the
government to intervene directly in providing local services – or to
concede defeat.

As chairman of housing and vice-chairman of economic development, Clarke favoured setting a rate but Hackney councillors were
deeply divided. With the council composed of fifty-nine Labour
members and one Tory, the Labour group was divided 29–30 on
setting a rate or not. The council therefore split 30–30.

In 1985, this was a deeply emotive issue to those on the left,
and made for a highly charged dispute where councillors had to be
escorted into the chamber by the police on the night of the rate-
setting meeting. Clarke was a key player in the council hierarchy
and he spoke in favour of setting a rate. Using his experience of
student politics, he set out the case in a straightforward and robust
way. Not doing so, argued Clarke at the meeting, would potentially
leave the council unable to do what they as Labour councillors
were seeking to do: deliver services to local people. Those present,
Clarke argued, could not evade responsibility for the implications
of their actions. His stance on the issue and direct manner caused
deep anger in his group.

Clarke readily admits that some people find him arrogant.
Throughout his career, he generally thought his political positions

through and, having done so, was prepared to take up strong positions to defend them and then carry them through. Although he didn't set out to make enemies for the sake of it, he regards antagonism as an almost inevitable by-product of being effective in politics:

> It depends how confident you are in your own judgement … you
> have to be clear and set out your case and if you are interested
> in changing politics then you will find that you make enemies.
> That's the nature of the game and I think politicians who cave in
> are weak.

Clarke also had the opportunity to learn from the many crises that Neil Kinnock faced as Leader of the Opposition. The former Labour leader was forced to take up a series of unpopular positions within his party, whether dealing with the trade unions or the militants in Liverpool. As a result, Kinnock faced bile and hatred from a large minority on the left of British politics.

Clarke watched this from close quarters and admired Kinnock for both his resolve and his response to the pressure. It proved a significant education on how to deal with pressure and how to stand up for what was necessary.

In Kinnock, Clarke saw someone who would not give in to people who put him under pressure, including when deeply unpleasant hostility was directed at him personally. That was true within some sections of the Labour Party and with the trade union movement, who opposed his drive for modernisation of the party. It is interesting to note that, of Kinnock's opponents, Clarke remembers the late Tony Benn, who later in his political career assumed the mantle of elder statesman and became something of a national treasure, as 'one of the most unpleasant of politicians in his generation'. However, Kinnock would not let it affect him.

In reality Neil Kinnock's biggest struggle was not with people such as Tony Benn, his party or the trade unions, but with the 'constant grinding down from the right-wing media'. The criticism was admittedly very aggressive at that time, and there is no doubt that it was designed to undermine Kinnock's efforts to look electable. Clarke observed the constant and unrelenting nature of the negativity Kinnock faced from the media and felt it led to 'the erosion of one's soul'. Pressure from opponents was one thing, but character assassination from the media was felt to be 'insidious' and bound to get under a leader's skin.

The unpleasantness of the campaign against Neil Kinnock is often commented on because of its virulence, and is often laid at the door of the Murdoch or right-wing press. Yet it should be remembered that only five years after Kinnock's defeat in 1992, another opposition leader, William Hague, would face a very similar stream of derision from the very same newspapers and journalists. It would be fair to say that the media can be equally dismissive and disagreeable to any party leader.

Many politicians who have been through political crisis believe that constant media criticism takes the edge off their performance and undermines the spirit. In this book we will see what it did to Jacqui Smith and her family, to Andrew Mitchell, Vince Cable and others. What really got under Clarke's skin, however, was when he perceived that lies were being written about him in the newspapers. The papers also published extremely offensive cartoons about him in physically unpleasant ways, but this didn't bother him. As he recalls, 'The person of the cartoon was a caricature that you could take or leave. As a caricature it's a point of view and I never minded that, but the lies that people see in the paper I found undermining.'

Clarke's sensitivities and those of his former boss, Kinnock, were remarkably similar.

THE HOME OFFICE

Before Clarke arrived at the Home Office he spent time as Tony Blair's Education Secretary. Again, it was a challenging brief with several important and controversial issues to deal with. The scale of the policy decisions to be made makes for daunting reading: what to do about private and faith schools, so much disliked by the left? How to deal with student finance for students aged sixteen to nineteen? More difficult again were teachers' pay and performance-related pay, which meant problems with the unions. Most controversial of all was his introduction of university top-up fees – a rather remarkable achievement for a Labour secretary of state. This was not something that would have had wide support in the Labour Party; indeed, its manifesto had specifically pledged to rule it out.

All very serious issues for a secretary of state, but in Labour's early years of government things were clearer: the party was still pleased to be in government, there was a direction of travel which was well set out and the whole government was unified in its delivery. Despite the outcry over top-up fees Clarke, in his usual robust way, argued his case and remarkably emerged unscathed from what was a very tricky battle with Gordon Brown, the left of the Labour Party and the unions.

Having battled students, his council colleagues in Hackney, Militant and the teaching unions, Clarke was appointed Home Secretary in December 2004, following the resignation of David Blunkett. There are unlikely to have been many politicians better prepared to do battle in the 'politician's graveyard' that was the Home Office at that time, a department later described as 'unfit for purpose' by Clarke's successor, John Reid. It was not only a troubled department but a big one, and Home Secretary was a very big job for Clarke to take on.

In fact, Clarke has never agreed with Reid's assessment of the Home Office or with the widely held belief around Westminster that it was trouble for all home secretaries. He saw it as a challenge, where there was a lot to change but certainly nothing to fear. Even after the events that caused the demise of his Cabinet career, he would still not agree that it was inevitable he would fail.

The most immediate difficulty Clarke faced was the attitude he encountered at the Home Office. The first thing that the permanent secretary, Sir John Gieve, said to him was, 'We are a department of disasters, so there's a prison breakout, there's a terrorist attack, there's a policeman shot and we then have to pick up the mess.' There is little doubt that this had applied to the department under a whole string of Home Secretaries, from Willie Whitelaw right through to David Blunkett. But this was not what Clarke expected or wanted to hear from his permanent secretary.

From the beginning, Clarke regarded this attitude as unacceptable. Such events – prison breakouts, policemen injured or killed

– may not be predictable, but they were foreseeable. The job of the Home Secretary – and indeed the entire department – was to minimise the chances of those events taking place, to try to prevent them and ensure that there was a process in hand that could deal with the crises if and when they arose. As Home Secretary, he wanted to create a framework that would enable him both to predict the risks the department was likely to experience and to deal with them in the most effective way. Clarke felt Sir John was not the right man to have alongside him to undertake the reforms and planning necessary to deliver a robust Home Office. The tensions between the two men were to develop early and the relationship remained problematic. This friction became more important for Clarke as the foreign nationals prisoner crisis unfolded.

The fact that the Home Office could work well was demonstrated by the response to the July 2005 terrorist attacks in London. The reactions of the police and the other emergency services were excellent, which resulted from thorough training and planning for that kind of disaster. It was fortunate (or well foreseen) that a thorough exercise replicating the response of the emergency services to a terrorist incident had recently taken place at Bank station. To Clarke, it demonstrated that the Home Office was indeed 'fit for purpose' when it came to dealing with real issues of importance.

When news of the 7/7 attack filtered through, a Cabinet meeting was underway, chaired by John Prescott, the Deputy Prime Minister. Tony Blair was in Gleneagles at the G8 summit. Clarke received a note saying that there was something going on in the underground. Initially it was thought to be some kind of electrical explosion, but shortly afterwards it became clear that it was much worse than that. Clarke asked Prescott to conclude Cabinet and immediately called a COBRA meeting for half an hour later.

There were two COBRA meetings that morning. Andy Hayman, the Metropolitan Police's Assistant Commissioner for Specialist Operations attended the second, presenting what he thought to be the facts about what had happened. Hayman was right that there were four attacks but, at that point, nobody knew if there would be more. The Madrid explosions in 2004 had been followed immediately by others and the police didn't yet have a clear picture of the developing situation. The security services were involved immediately and they were clear there had been no previous indication of what might happen.

The immediate issue was how the government would handle the transport system, and the question of whether the public transport system in London should be closed down or not. Alistair Darling, who was then Transport Secretary, and Clarke had to resolve it quickly; the public would have been unforgiving if they had kept it open and there had been further attacks in which people were killed. Darling and Clarke agreed to close down the public transport system.

As is the role of the Home Secretary in such circumstances, Clarke had to make a hastily constructed statement outside Downing Street to inform the public what had happened and give reassurance. It was followed by a statement to Parliament. The occasion was laced with tension. It is rarely the case for a secretary of state giving a statement to be late coming into the House, but Clarke was still getting information at the last minute and he wanted to give the House the fullest possible explanation. In the circumstances, the House was suspended, but the Speaker, Michael Martin, and the House were generous. Clarke delivered his handwritten statement, bringing people up to date with events.

He then called together the leaders of the various faith communities in the early afternoon, because there were fears concerning a major backlash against Muslim communities. Through COBRA there was a clear system of communications and a rapid press conference of all the uniformed services demonstrating their capacity to handle the immediate situation and possible further attacks. The biggest nightmare was a further attack, which of course there was a fortnight later, although thankfully without success. Clarke was in close contact with Blair in Gleneagles, telling him to go ahead with the G8, as they were on top of the situation in London.

Clarke was in control in London and John Prescott was in support. Blair then returned to London later that afternoon and assumed control, convening a further COBRA meeting on arrival. But by then it had become a relatively mechanistic process to make sure casualties were being dealt with effectively and to explain what was going on.

Unsurprisingly, 7/7 was one of the most intense experiences Clarke has had in his whole life. For the few hours until Blair returned from Gleneagles, he effectively led the government in its response to the worst ever attack on British soil. But he feels he was good at doing it, had the right support and handled the pressure well. Having been put to the test in some of the gravest and most difficult of circumstances a government can face, Clarke likes to think he got it right.

For the vast majority of the population things returned to normal quite quickly, within a couple of days. Meanwhile the government was desperately trying to find out if there was any plan for another attack. There was frenzied activity and forensic work was being undertaken by the intelligence services to unearth potential plots. For Clarke, it took over his life completely for a short time. He was unable to do anything else for three days. The same happened with the second set of attempted attacks that followed a fortnight after 7/7.

Clarke had to work long hours to stay on top of the situation, putting in several long nights. His normal working pattern was to work from 8 a.m. to about midnight on Monday to Thursday but to try to keep Friday to Sunday in his Norwich constituency – even as Home Secretary. He was particularly concerned to take time with his family, so he worked much less at the weekends. His handling of the 7/7 bombings and their aftermath suggest a Home Secretary in command of his brief, prepared to put in the hours and competent under pressure. Yet within a year he had lost his job.

Clarke knew the immigration system was a terrible mess. Indeed, it was well known throughout the department from the permanent secretary down the chain of command. Things were so bad that when the job of Head of the Immigration and Nationality Directorate became available, few wanted to apply for it. It ended up going to Lin Homer, the chief executive of Birmingham Council. But it served as a warning to Clarke that people were beginning to see just how big the mess was.

His job was to try to fix poor performance and to put the infrastructure in place to respond to future problems. As Home

Secretary he was at the centre of a big department where all kinds of terrible events could unfold. The Home Office was not a department all about terrorist threats, by any means: challenges ranged from the rights of people to defend their personal property, as was raised by the infamous case of the Norfolk farmer, Tony Martin, who had shot dead a burglar in his home, to changes in the judicial system that were said to undermine Magna Carta. At the same time, people expected their Home Secretary to be a reassuring presence, in control, whether it was an issue about policing, crime, justice or terrorism.

Clarke knew that he could never achieve a situation where there would be no disasters. Disasters would happen, so the question was how to deal with them and Clarke was conscious of making sure the right preparation was undertaken, bringing people together to make sure they were ready.

Between his appointment in December 2004 and the general election in 2005, Clarke had become clear that the changes and reforms needed to the Home Office would take a whole parliament to achieve. He told Blair that he wanted to take on the job and wished to be reappointed to the Home Office for the entire parliament in order to see through the reforms. He told Blair it would be very difficult and challenging work. There would be all kinds of storms and crises, since the reforms needed to take on entrenched vested interests. One of the big regrets Clarke still harbours today is that he didn't get to finish the job.

The key issues for Clarke included much-needed reforms to the police, migration and the penal system – some of which were carried through before his departure but by no means all. He gave a thoughtful and lengthy speech on 19 September 2005 entitled 'Where Next for Penal Policy? Following the terrorist attacks, the speech signalled that the Home Office was back to 'business as usual' on the major reform agenda: the content of his speech was widely regarded as a progressive programme of reform and had support across a broad cross-section of interested parties.

Although it didn't feature in the speech itself, the genesis of the foreign prisoners crisis lay in that event. Douglas Hurd, who had presided as chairman at the event, brought matters to a conclusion and Clarke was approached from the audience and asked if he was aware of the number of foreign prisoners in British prisons. Clarke, although aware in general terms of the issue, said no, he did not know the exact figures. It immediately set alarm bells ringing and Clarke returned to the Home Office to ask officials for the figures. He was shocked to be told that the number was around 10,000 out of a total population of around 80,000.

Clarke's instinctively thought to himself, 'This is ridiculous. Why are they here? Who are they? What are they doing in our prisons? What's going on?' He set about a process of analysing these questions within the department. He asked his officials for an action plan with short-, medium- and long-term options for reducing the numbers of foreign prisoners in the prison population. Clarke's urgent call for action resulted in an increase in resources devoted to the issue, a serious attempt to get more effective international agreements and better communication and working relationships between the prison estate and the Immigration and Nationality Directorate (IND). At a Home Affairs Select Committee hearing on 25 October 2005, Clarke confirmed that he was addressing the issue.

Of course, he could have taken a different approach and tried to play things down. By taking urgent action he was moving a difficult political issue up the nation's agenda, potentially helping to create the crisis for his personal position that followed. By trying to find the truth about foreign prisoners and publicly mentioning it to the Home Affairs Select Committee he made the issue 'a live one'. If he had kept completely schtum, it might never have developed into the crisis it became.

But Clarke's bullish personality would never have allowed this to happen. He believed that if you want reform, you have to look at the details of what is happening. If you found problems you naturally needed to find and implement solutions and reform. But he knew any serious attempt at reform or change made the reformer vulnerable to political attack. He accepted that his political philosophy meant that he could never have the quiet life as a minister. Taking people on was in his blood.

On 26 October 2005, the foreign national prisoners issue moved to arena of the Public Accounts Committee, during the course of a hearing about the removal of asylum seekers. During the evidence session an exchange took place between Richard Bacon MP, one of the committee's most effective members, and Clarke's permanent secretary, Sir John Gieve. Bacon asked about the number of failed asylum seekers who had been released from prison because their removal could not be arranged.

Officials thought the number of foreign prisoners who had been released to be around 500, but Bacon wanted a more detailed answer, containing the number of criminals released who were failed asylum seekers. The question of numbers led in turn to further questions, such as where the released foreign prisoners were, what types of crimes they had committed and what sentences they had served. The exchange, at the time, did not move matters forward much, but the request for more detailed information was to unleash further, more difficult, problems for Clarke.

Gieve promised a written note to the committee containing the information, which was duly received on 14 November. In the submission it was reported that the department knew of 403 foreign nationals who were released from prison without deportation proceedings being completed. It turned out that the department didn't have the information that Bacon had requested about offences and nationalities but it 'thought' that none would have been convicted of serious offences. As it turned out, the figures were wrong. Even Clarke acknowledged that it revealed 'a completely ridiculous' state of affairs.

In retrospect, Clarke realises this was the crucial point at which he could have made a difference had he realised what the situation was on the statistical data. He had a structural problem in the department with the collection of detailed figures for which the Permanent Secretary had provided no solution. This was not the support Clarke was looking for and highlighted their poor working relationship.

Gieve left the Home Office in December 2005. Clarke wished that he had gone in June or July 2005; but in the event his departure took place a full six months later. His evidence to the PAC turned out to have toxic ramifications for Clarke. Gieve later told the Home Affairs Select Committee that he had not alerted ministers to the seriousness of the situation because he was 'unaware of the scale of the problem' himself.

For all of Gieve's later admissions, it was Clarke who, in December of 2005, had the embarrassment of being forced to warn the Prime Minister, Tony Blair, that hundreds of foreign prisoners had been freed without the required investigation into whether or not they should be deported.

In essence, there were two separate issues that became entangled – some would say deliberately – in bringing Clarke down. The first was the large number of foreign national prisoners (or 'FNPs' as they became known in political and bureaucratic parlance) held in the prison system and how best to deal with the situation. This Clarke had reacted to quickly, putting plans in place to reduce the numbers. The second issue was that a number of FNPs had been and were being released from prison at the end of their term but not considered for deportation as they should have been. On this, Clarke was blindsided, as ministers had not been told that some foreign prisoners were being released without being considered for deportation. Even the Home Office's senior officials were not aware of the seriousness of that situation.

It was not until late-March 2006 that ministers were finally made aware of the gravity of the issue. On 30 March a submission from officials was finally sent to Clarke which set out the situation and its scale in detail. Clarke was on a plane (rather ironically, in light of later concerns about immigration matters) on his way to Bulgaria and Romania to negotiate their accession to the EU.

On his return to the UK, Clarke now made a big mistake. He took the issue of foreign prisoner information seriously and was pleased it was coming into the open because he believed he could mobilise public support for his actions. However, he failed to make an immediate statement in person to the House of Commons. Instead, he issued a written statement, because he still hadn't grasped the political explosiveness of the issue. David Davis, the opposition home affairs spokesperson, was on Clarke's tail and working very effectively, portraying him as not caring enough about the issue.

Davis kept asking questions that the Home Office couldn't answer because it didn't keep count of the number of foreign prisoners. The Home Office was forced to admit that it didn't keep the data, for example, on how many foreign prisoners there were or how many were murderers or what the nationalities were. The department, and by extension Clarke, looked incompetent.

Clarke's decision to issue a written statement rather than address the House of Commons was a disaster. It went against his own 'rule number one', which is that as Home Secretary you must aim to give the people of the country confidence that you know what you're doing. Clarke's handling of the situation gave exactly the opposite impression, despite him having set up a special unit with the police to identify each released foreign prisoner and their full circumstances. Even when the Prime Minister asked Clarke for the data, he could not provide it. The answers just couldn't come quickly enough.

In retrospect, it is likely Clarke could have paid more attention to the numbers and that it was a symptom of the lack of grip of the issue. This was why the issue became a scandal: he simply wasn't aware that people were not being referred for consideration for deportation until very late in the process. Unfortunately, it wasn't until Easter that the bulb came on and he realised the issue had turned into a major storm.

In late April, with a local elections campaign underway, things got politically rough for the New Labour government. The government's popularity had taken a lasting hit from the widespread public anger and mistrust over the Iraq War, and the foreign prisoners issue was now another major thorn in its side. As the full extent of the mishandling of events became clear, Clarke offered Tony Blair his resignation on 25 April 2006. The offer was fairly mechanistic: with characteristic self-confidence, he advised Blair not to accept it. He believed strongly that his departure would solve nothing, and Blair, at that moment, agreed. Nonetheless, Clarke also believed that the Prime Minister should have the option of a Cabinet minister's resignation if a major problem arose on their watch, and he confirmed in a radio interview the following morning that he had offered that choice.

Clarke's admission gave his own enemies in the Labour Party and outside the feeling that a scalp was near, and merely added to his difficulty. He had calculated that Blair was unlikely to accept his resignation and would offer him support, thus buying time to fix the problem. As we have already seen, a party leader's personal support is almost essential if ministers or frontbenchers are to get through huge difficulties.

But Clarke had miscalculated. Blair's support was at best luke-warm and it gave the Brown camp a signal to move on a key Blair ally in Cabinet. They saw it as a scalp worth having – as, of course, did Clarke's official opposite number, David Davis. It is long accepted as normal practice that opposition parties should try to force the sacking or resignation of government ministers, although some consider the deliberate attempt to cut down the careers of ministers, regardless of their personal merits, to be one of the more distasteful and negative aspects of modern politics.

Clarke was widely considered to be a 'Blairite' on policy and enjoyed a good working relationship with Tony Blair. But why was there such particularly bad blood between Clarke and Brown?

Clarke's supporters believe Brown was a weak man who surrounded himself with bullies who used their position to damage his enemies. They argue that, when Prime Minister, he chose a Cabinet of people who would never challenge him. Brown found it very difficult to accept any rivals who would challenge him intellectually – anyone, in effect, he could not bully into agreeing with him. He disliked Clarke because the latter had always been prepared to stand up to him on policy and strategic decisions.

Brown had never forgotten what had happened on tuition fees. He had fought a terrific rearguard action against fees, but Clarke teamed up with Blair to force it through, though it was only with some difficulty and a last-minute acceptance from Brown that they managed to carry the day. When Clarke got into serious trouble in March 2006, Brown, who was already planning a move against Blair, could see the advantages.

For Clarke, there was no question about what was happening – and his reckoning has since been confirmed by the memoirs of Brown's former spin doctor Damian McBride. As Clarke recalls it:

> The Brown camp was perpetually about undermining Tony in every respect. I was a Tony colleague and they were undermining me all the time in terms of background and press briefing. There were half a dozen of them who were doing that perpetually. That's what they

did the whole time, but I regarded that as part of normal life. I don't approve of it, I think it's disgusting, it's a form of politics that ought to be excoriated.

According to Clarke, others in the Labour Party just had to accept it was going on. 'We were all grown up, we all knew what they were doing,' he says.

On a whole string of issues being put through Parliament, Brown's camp actively undermined Clarke, which made operating a huge department with life-and-death responsibilities incredibly difficult. Brown's camp were not motivated by the policy itself, or by the interests of the government, but were almost entirely focused on undermining Blair's operation. New Labour had a separate 'state within a state' in its midst that answered to its own leader.

With these forces at play behind the scenes, in public Clarke was the Home Secretary who didn't know the data, and as the issue kept growing he looked more incompetent. Nonetheless, if the issue had been simply one of data on foreign prisoners, he would quite likely have survived. However, 2006 had been a difficult local election campaign for Tony Blair, and the issue had resonated against Labour candidates on the doorstep. Worse for Blair, he knew another Brown push to force his resignation as Prime Minister was coming.

The Blair–Brown fault line in the Labour Party had been widening since 2005. Brown's clique had been growing restless, pushing Blair for a date when he would quit as Prime Minister and looking for reasons to push him. By the first week of May, Blair was suffering the aftermath of a tricky Prime Minister's Questions and looking ahead to the local government elections, the results of which were expected to be disastrous. A reshuffle was already planned for the Friday.

In the local elections held on 4 May 2006, Labour suffered its worst result for more than twenty years, coming in third. Two issues were blamed for the severity of Labour's woes: the foreign national prisoners scandal (as suggested by the popular media), and John Prescott's affair. On the back of a putative local election result and with another Brown attack under preparation, there had to be a scapegoat.

Blair's advisers told him that he had to act to see off Brown, that Clarke's position was unsustainable in the long-term and that he should therefore take action to cut him adrift. He would look more in control and head off Brown. In fact, the Labour result by Saturday looked less bad than many people had expected. Had it not been for the suspected Brown move against Blair, Clarke might have survived; certainly the compelling need to sack him may not have been so keenly felt. Blair effectively decided to give up Clarke to protect his position against Brown.

So the PM decided very late that Clarke would be his 'sacrificial victim' in his reshuffle. Only a few days earlier – indeed, as late as after PMQs on the Wednesday – Blair had assured Clarke that he would keep him on. The two had always maintained a good professional working relationship, and Blair's assurance made the outcome later that week more surprising to Clarke. Why would he want to sack one of his key and senior supporters in Cabinet?

When Blair told Clarke of his decision to sack him, on 5 May, he said the pressure was so great he would have to make a change. 'It is just something I have to do' was Blair's refrain. Clarke, understandably, did not want to go. He felt angry with Blair, and thought the

PM was making a mistake, but he had little choice but to accept the decision. However, he refused to do so until the pair had completed two lengthy conversations the night before the announcement was made. These conversations offer an insight into how difficult Blair found reshuffles.

An angry Clarke argued fiercely against Blair's move to sack him and made sure the Prime Minister was aware of all the ramifications of his decision. Clarke told Blair that sacking one of his senior supporters in the Cabinet would just make Brown's attempted 'putsch' easier to complete. As talks progressed, Blair could be said to have buckled, and instead of a straight sacking a negotiation began about other Cabinet positions. Clarke was offered the defence job 'as well as any other Cabinet post apart from Foreign Secretary or Chancellor'.

Clarke's pride stopped him accepting the offer of an alternative portfolio. Blair's decision effectively to sack him from the role of Home Secretary was more than a symbolic point: it was a declaration of Clarke's failure in that role. Rightly or not, Clarke felt it to be a statement by Blair of a lack of confidence in him, which would make it impossible for him to carry through other jobs.

However, one suspects that the real issue for Clarke was having to stomach a demotion. People around Blair, such as Peter Mandelson and Jonathan Powell, told Clarke they were suggesting that he should be Foreign Secretary – a position he would have accepted. This conveys an impression that pride and a degree of arrogance were in play as much as anything to do with any perceived failure at the Home Office rendering Clarke incapable of holding another Cabinet brief.

Clarke attended a dinner at Chequers a week or so after he was sacked from the Cabinet. Blair told him that evening that he had wanted him to be Foreign Secretary in the reshuffle and that he had been planning to do it. However, even if Blair had wanted to appoint Clarke, it is likely that Brown would have blocked it. This would help explain what was considered at the time to be the almost inexplicable appointment of Margaret Beckett to the post.

There was no resignation letter from Clarke. Others in the department offered to resign to save him, including the newly appointed Lin Homer, but he felt that would have been completely unfair as he had made a number of mistakes himself and was ready to take responsibility.

The media laid into Clarke mercilessly. He remembers it as 'appalling' but found nothing new in that. Clarke found himself in the eye of the storm for a few months; under Kinnock, he recalls, 'we had seven or eight years of complete crap'. He never accepted the treatment meted out to him as just, but like so many other politicians he felt that there was little choice but to live with it. There was no point speaking his mind about media intrusion, inaccuracy or anything else because none of the media would report it fairly, if at all, and it wouldn't get him anywhere. Even if they did, it would just make him sound like another carping politician.

Despite the media attention, the parliamentary drama, Clarke never felt the same pressure over foreign prisoners that he felt with the July bombings. He feels the pressure during 7/7 involved potentially life-or-death decisions about real events and a potential future attack. These were fundamentally important matters of substance. The foreign national prisoners scandal, he felt, didn't affect anybody's life in a real sense. It might have done in the future, and people could make arguments about individuals committing crimes against people. But Clarke believes the prospect was fairly remote. For him it was a Westminster-bubble story that led to him being sacked.

Strangely, Clarke also did nothing to try to bolster his position with colleagues on the back benches. He gave his parliamentary private secretary and special advisers no instructions and the Whips' Office did nothing to assist. Whereas other subjects in this book arranged for their supporters to be positively galvanised during their darkest hours, Clarke left himself totally at the mercy of others: the Prime Minister, Brown's clique, the media and opposition forces. Clarke felt the main thing was to try to sort out the situation on the numbers and give out all the information out they could. It was another error.

Had he sought support, he might have been able to stop backbench 'colleagues' such as Ken Purchase going on Sky News and BBC Radio 4's *World at One* to say that Clarke should go. Purchase told the BBC, 'There's no excuse for management failures: it's so clear the warnings were given last summer, even late last autumn, to ministers; they failed to activate a review and a change in the way work was carried out.' Many Labour MPs felt the whole affair had been handled incompetently and Charles Clarke would have to take the rap for it. Clarke and his team should have been trying to block these moves by Labour MPs as best they could.

Unlike in other cases in this book, the crisis did not have a significant impact on Clarke's family. Clarke's personal circumstances were
quite different to those of others featured here. His wife was not
based in London during the working week and nor were his children.
It lent a measure of protection from the intrusion and inconvenience
from the media. With the pressure faced by Clarke at work and with
his career hanging in the balance, it would have been understandable
if his family had noticed a change in behaviour. However, Clarke
doesn't believe it was ever discussed, although perhaps they just
wanted to be supportive.

However strong the family were, they still hated the intensity
of the pressure that he was under and the horrible things that
were being said in the media. It was particularly difficult for the
children, but they were already somewhat battle-hardened, having
been through a difficult period when Clarke was Education
Secretary. Clarke's children were thirteen and sixteen at the
time of his battles at Education and were subject to teasing and
remarks from their teachers, rather than by other children. He
later found that teachers were sometimes giving his children a
harder time then was fair, and con stantly talking down to them.
Unfortunately, the children didn't tell him about it until a long
time afterwards.

It is fortunate for Clarke that he has for many years been
able to compartmentalise his work and home life. His wife still
comments on his ability to do so. Clarke regards this as an important skill in modern politicians. As he describes it himself, it is
part of ensuring that 'you are not the person who you read about
in the papers'.

THE AFTERMATH

Clarke lost his seat in Norwich South at the 2010 general election after being a thorn in Gordon Brown's side and a major critic of his premiership. Perhaps it was payback for all the effort Brown and his team made to undermine Clarke when Secretary of State both at Education and the Home Office. But it is equally likely that Clarke just loved to expound on his views of where the government was going wrong. He has never been one to mince his words.

Clarke knew that Brown would never appoint him to his Cabinet in 2007. But even after Brown's departure and the election of one of his younger acolytes, Ed Miliband, to the Labour leadership, Clarke, despite his long public service, has not been elevated to the House of Lords to sit alongside many other former Home Secretaries. It suggests the bitterness of the Brown–Blair feud still skulks just below the surface.

Clarke still believes Blair made a terrible mistake for his government by sacking him. He now says,

> It was a mistake for me but that's OK. It was a mistake for him, as he said to me himself: he'd effectively removed his key allies in Peter Mandelson, David Blunkett and myself from the government, and left Gordon's people completely untouched. He didn't need to do it in my case.

Likewise, Blair – among many of Clarke's friends – has told him he made a terrible mistake by going to the backbenches rather than accepting one of the other Cabinet positions he could have taken instead. But Clarke has convinced himself he did the right thing in turning the lower-ranking Cabinet jobs down. One wonders whether he actually believes it. He could have been Defence Secretary in a Blair government. It would have been a demotion of sorts, but not a big one. There would have been policy issues for him on renewing Trident, and Clarke believes he would have immediately walked into a situation where there were tensions between what he thought and what the government thought. Nonetheless, Trident could easily have been kicked into the long grass by agreement, as it has been by the coalition government to a large extent.

Even today, it doesn't take a great deal to get Clarke thinking about the departments and what he might have accepted and achieved had he taken the job. It suggests a man who feels he was cut off in his prime and has significant regrets.

CHAPTER 7

<u>JACQUI SMITH ON THE HOME FRONT</u>

"Yes, I did find it enormously embarrassing and I still feel slightly embarrassed. Sometimes when I'm out with Richard now I think to myself that people are looking at us, thinking, 'He's the one who watched the pornography.'"

– Jacqui Smith

The crisis that forced Jacqui Smith out of the Cabinet – and later out of the House of Commons – was part good old-fashioned scandal involving sex, and part bad luck. When the worst collective crisis to face the political class in living memory, the scandal over MPs' expenses, hit, Smith became its poster girl, one of its most notorious individual cases. Yet in a controversy in which individual claims ran into the hundreds of thousands of pounds, what lay at the heart of Smith's downfall was a bill for a mere £10. Smith serves as an uncomfortable example for all politicians of how a Cabinet minister can be brought down for purely personal rather than political reasons. The story itself is sad, unedifying, but also compelling.

Jacqui Smith is a very strong woman, who felt she could person-ally have withstood more or less everything that politics could throw at her. But when the political crisis started to wreak havoc on her family and her home life, a woman who had risen rapidly up the ranks of the Labour Party to one of the highest offices of state in Britain was at times left unable to get out of bed. The episode left deep scars, not only for her but also for her husband and children.

Smith's time at the centre of a political storm provides a troubling insight into the traumatic personal impact on those caught up in political scandals.

Jacqui Smith was appointed as Britain's first female Home Secretary on 28 June 2007, in the new Prime Minister Gordon Brown's first reshuffle. It was a bold move and one that caught the eye of press waiting to devour the details of the ups and downs of the ministerial career ladder.

Smith had little time to enjoy her promotion from Chief Whip, however: she had barely managed to park her feet under her desk in the Home Office before she was faced with every Home Secretary's worst nightmare – a major bomb plot. She had walked into the Home Office on that Thursday afternoon to begin her induction from the civil servants and was woken on Friday morning by her private secretary telling her that the police had foiled a major terrorist car bomb in Haymarket.

The car bomb had been targeting a night club in central London with a Mercedes packed with sixty litres of petrol, gas cylinders and nails. Had it exploded, the bomb would have caused carnage. Police carried out a controlled explosion and made the car safe, but her early-morning call was still a remarkable baptism of fire for the new Home Secretary.

Normally the incoming minister would have had a formal induction with the police and security services, but events were such that Smith met them all *in situ* in the course of a few days, with one bomb plot foiled in London and another attempted at Glasgow Airport on the Saturday afternoon, when a dark green Jeep Cherokee, loaded with propane canisters, was driven into the glass doors of the Glasgow International Airport terminal and set ablaze. It was the first terrorist attack to take place in Scotland since the Lockerbie bombing in 1988.

Thankfully, no members of the public were hurt, but Smith was immediately faced with a series of activities: collecting the information; chairing the government's COBRA emergency planning committee; and briefing European ministers, her official opposition counterpart, David Davis, and the Liberal Democrats' then home affairs spokesman, Nick Clegg. It was an immersive induction into what it was going to be like to be Home Secretary in the new era of terrorism.

Smith had to make a strong first impression in order to prove to the public that she was up to the job of defending British citizens and keeping them safe. Despite her very recent elevation, she performed her role of reassuring and informing the public well and it helped to get her off to a good start in the post. Smith says now that it was 'quite ironic that people said, "Oh you were very calm," – as if what they expected the first female Home Secretary to do was to rush up and down the street going, "Oh, I can't manage it, it's too difficult!"'

Smith was known by her colleagues at Westminster as a reasonably calm sort of person. But more importantly in such exceptional circumstances, she was surrounded by the right expertise. Although her immediate predecessor as Home Secretary, John Reid, had described the Home Office as not fit for purpose, Smith discovered she could count on the great strength of the infrastructure and of the counterterrorism team when she needed it.

Nor should it be overlooked that Smith was a very experienced politician when she arrived at the Home Office. She had been a minister for ten years, at Education, Health, the Department of Trade and Industry, and Education again. She knew the structure of government and how it worked. Had she (or indeed anyone else) had to face this terrorist threat in the first day of her first ministerial job, her performance may not have been so assured.

The worst moment for Smith was the Glasgow attack on the Saturday afternoon. Having had the incident in London over the course of Thursday night and in the early hours of Friday morning, Smith had been at her desk all day on Saturday when the Jeep hit the front of Glasgow Airport just before 4 p.m. Although it was assumed within the Home Office and security services that the Glasgow attack was the work of the same terrorist cell, Smith's mind soon turned to the possibility of further devastating attacks that the government knew nothing about and were therefore unable to prevent.

As Charles Clarke had discovered at the time of the 7/7 attacks, in such circumstances a Home Secretary's thoughts move quickly to questions of scale: are more terrorist groups or cells involved? Is this a one-off incident, or are we on the brink or a whole series of attacks? It is often what Home Secretaries can't foresee that worries them more than what is in front of them, because they feel an enormous responsibility for the protection and reassurance of the public when they take on the role. Smith was no different.

In some respects, a terrorist incident was straightforward to deal with compared to the political problems that were piling up in the Home Office, however. ID cards, proposals to extend the time criminal suspects could be held without charge from twenty-eight to forty-two days, arguments about the reclassification of cannabis and many other controversial issues were on Smith's agenda. If that wasn't enough, the controversial Damian Green debacle dropped into the middle of it all.

Green, the Conservative MP and then shadow Immigration Minister, was arrested by the Metropolitan Police at his constituency home in November 2008 and held for nine hours on suspicion of conspiracy to commit misconduct in a public office, charges relating to the unauthorised disclosure of confidential material from within the Home Office. The material disclosed to Green was claimed to have severely embarrassed the government by highlighting failures over immigration and other matters.

The police investigation, launched at the instigation of the Permanent Secretary at the Home Office, David Normington, involved Green's constituency and House of Commons offices being searched, as well as his London and Ashford homes. In the process, the police removed official documents and bank statements, a computer hard drive and a mobile telephone, and searched personal items such as love letters written to his wife some twenty years earlier. The arrest and detention of a senior opposition MP in these circumstances caused a huge and long-running furore.

The Green affair was yet another huge headache amidst the political problems to be solved, but Smith was by now an old hand. She had more than enough experience from other departments.

However, none of the dramas from her ministerial work could prepare Smith for what was about to hit when the MPs' expenses scandal happened. The challenges were totally different. She had never had any personal issues or problems that impinged on her work. As Home Secretary she was well supported in her day-to-day role – there were tasks and events that were extremely challenging and difficult, but thanks to the support she received, both at home and at work, she was able to focus almost entirely on these issues from the moment she was awake to the moment she fell asleep. The effect was that, during office hours, Smith was effectively distanced from her own personal and family life – however much she may have wished otherwise.

Smith's family life provided a strong personal foundation for her political career. Although she employed her husband, Richard Timney, as her parliamentary researcher and constituency office manager, she felt she could deal with any political problems as she went along so long as they were kept separate from life in the family home. It made events so much more difficult for her when a personal problem arose.

Unlike the other subjects of this book, Smith is a woman and a mother. Timney had given up his job in order to support Smith even before she became a Member of Parliament. After she was elected, in addition to his work in her constituency office, making sure everything happened as it should locally, Timney also assumed the primary role in parenting the couple's two teenage boys for much of the week. Although Smith would contend she was still a 'proper mum', when it came to the minutiae of the family routine, her husband tended to it. This enabled Smith to focus on her Westminster role and put in the time and effort required to rise through the ranks.

Smith says,

> I was extremely well supported and did not have to worry about all of those things that were going on in the constituency or with the family, so I could focus on how questions like 'How are we going to deal with this terrorist attack?' 'How am I going to sell ID cards?' 'How am I going to cope with the police having a march and calling me all the names under the sun?' All of those things you're more able to cope with because everything else in your personal life is sorted out.

Despite her solid home life and ministerial experience, Smith did have concerns about how prepared any minister was for running a major department. This was later reported by some newspapers as Smith feeling she couldn't do the job, but that was never the case. In an interview with Iain Dale in *Total Politics* she told him, 'I hope I did a good job [as Home Secretary], but if I did it was more by luck than any kind of development of those skills, and every single time I was appointed to a ministerial job I thought that.'

What Smith was trying to relate was that it is very hard, if not quite impossible, to prepare someone for ministerial life, and that there is more that could be done to give those appointed more time to learn the ropes and have enough time to reflect or have an induction before getting underway. Because these basic training and development structures do not really exist, being a successful minister, as she saw it, was due to individual effort rather than any particular help available.

Fortunately for Smith, she at least had a clear view on entering the Home Office of what she wanted to achieve, of where she wanted people to focus their efforts and of her own personal style of leadership. After all the shake-up and reorganisation under John Reid, with whole parts of the department being spun off to form the new Ministry of Justice, Smith wanted a period of time in which she could rebuild people's morale and belief in the importance of their work. She wanted the department to get its confidence back and be clear about the positive objectives she wanted to set and deliver.

Despite the various political controversies and dramas, from June 2007 until early 2009, Smith's tenure as Home Secretary appeared to be going fairly well. Then the first wave of trouble hit. On 8 February the *Mail on Sunday* reported that Smith had claimed £116,000 in Commons expenses for a second home whilst effectively lodging with her sister Sara. The second home was the £300,000 detached house in her Redditch constituency in the Midlands where her husband and two young children lived.

The initial story didn't hit Smith particularly hard; she was convinced that she had not done anything wrong (and, indeed, she still is). It was not her sister's flat, as first suggested: it was a house that Smith and her sister had shared since 1997. The only break had been whilst Smith had been on maternity leave – but for all intents and purposes they had lived together for years.

The papers portrayed Smith as renting only a room in her sister's house, suggesting therefore that her 'second home' could not be in Redditch and that she was abusing parliamentary expenses for personal gain. Smith contests strongly that 'it wasn't a case of "I've got my room at the back and I've got a shelf in the fridge with my name on it". Even the Parliamentary Commissioner for Standards, after he'd undertaken an investigation, accepted that it was my home.'

Smith wasn't a joint tenant or mortgage holder; she simply paid rent to her sister. In addition, she paid her share of the bills. Smith believed that her arrangements fully abided by the rules of the House of Commons and that she had a long-standing approval from the Fees Office. She had even got permission in writing.

If the initial story was not the bombshell that perhaps the Conservative Party and *Mail on Sunday* had hoped, this did not stop it from preventing a furious backlash against Smith. Taxpayers' groups called it 'morally reprehensible'. *The Sun* weighed in, under a 'Reported for Sleaze' headline, with allegations that Smith had 'claimed £152,000 in expenses in 2006/7 on top of her £142,000 salary' and since 2001 had taken a total of £782,000 in expenses. David Cameron also suggested that 'Smith may have questions to answer' about her expenses claims and that the revelations 'did not look good'. Political blood was in the water and opposition politicians and the media were sensing a kill.

Smith first got an inkling of the story on the Friday before it broke in the *Mail on Sunday*. Even to this day she can remember exactly where she was. Her first reaction was, 'What are they on about?' She had checked the arrangements with the House of Commons Fees Office and been given a clean bill of health. Her special adviser broke the news to her and she responded that all was OK because she had checked it out and been told it was all above board. It left her cross and frustrated that people would probably get the wrong end of the stick, but she didn't think it was career-threatening by any means. At this stage the MPs expenses scandal had not broken, so Smith would not have seen the damage it could do.

The story had arisen from a neighbour of Smith's, Mrs Jessica Taplin, who lived five or six doors down the road from her. Taplin believed that she had counted up the number of days that the police were outside Smith's house in London and that it demonstrated that it could not be her main home. She first contacted David Cameron's office and was pointed towards the *Mail on Sunday*.

Despite the media outcry, John Lyon, the Parliamentary Commissioner for Standards, initially dismissed the need for an inquiry as there was 'not sufficient evidence'. He then changed his mind following a letter of complaint from Mrs Taplin on 16 February, writing to Smith on 17 February informing her of his decision to investigate.

At this stage the outcry was not affecting Smith's work, as she believed it would all be sorted out by the Commissioner and that as she was in the right there wasn't much to worry about. The real bombshell that knocked Smith off her feet was delivered by the *Sunday Express* on Sunday 29 March. It reported that Jacqui Smith had submitted a £10 bill for two adult pornographic movies enjoyed by her husband.

Smith was in her car on the way back from Birmingham to Redditch to a meeting with some Equitable Life policy holders when she heard about the *Sunday Express*'s scoop. Her special adviser phoned and asked, 'Have you spoken to Richard yet?' Smith had not. Her adviser insisted that Smith do so as soon as possible and then ring her back.

There followed a fraught conversation between Smith and her husband. Timney told her that they had submitted a receipt and it had got two pornographic pay-per-view films on it. Naturally, Smith wanted to know how it could possibly have happened. Unfortunately for Timney and Smith, it had been included on a bill for their total phone, internet and TV package. Smith concluded the conversation with her husband by saying that she would have to resign. She managed to pull herself together in the minutes that followed and headed into the Equitable Life meeting.

Smith immediately knew the scale of difficulty in trying to ride out the storm that would break around her. Having coped well with the second-home expenses, this was of an entirely different order and her instinctive reaction demonstrated that she understood that. Of all the difficulties that Cabinet ministers in this book have got themselves into, this is perhaps the most embarrassing and the one the public would have least sympathy with. It portrayed Smith and her husband (and their relationship) in the worst possible light and was never likely to generate any sympathy for them.

Smith finished her meeting, cancelled her next one and went home. With her job soon to be hanging by a thread, she and her husband went through exactly what had happened. There were false rumours that the films had been accessed by one of Smith and

Timney's children. As a matter of fact, the children would know better. When the scandal broke, their son told Timney, 'God, Dad, don't you know about the internet?' It is an ironic twist that one of the reasons Timney did not use the internet to access pornography was because his laptop was provided to him by the House of Commons in his capacity as a Member of Parliament's staff, and he didn't want to embarrass the Home Secretary.

Timney was forced to make the most embarrassing and excruciating apology in front of the gates of the couple's Redditch home. His statement to the cameras lasted all of twenty seconds, but one cannot imagine how difficult that must have been for someone who was not in public life but simply became caught up in it because of who his wife was.

Unlike the original story about her 'second home' expenses, Smith now found this new revelation incredibly difficult and traumatic. In the Home Secretary's office there is a desk with all the newspapers laid out daily. Things were so bad that officials took the unusual step of removing all the newspapers from Smith's sight. Her emotions were so raw that she simply could not bear to read them; indeed, she felt that if she had read everything written about her she would not have been able to function.

Smith's civil servants rallied round and were supportive and protective – even more so than ever – after the events unfolded. This may have partly been because she was a woman and partly because of the nature of the case. The press, of course, thought it was a fantastic story – with good reason. Even Smith knew it: 'I bet people thought, "Oh, he's a bit weak because she's the Home Secretary, he's at home like some sad little loser watching a porno whilst she's working … and what's more she's got this on the taxpayer." Every element of it was awful.' There were very few straws to clutch at. It was reported that an angry Smith decreed that Timney would be sleeping on the sofa. But the truth is that this was briefed by her special adviser, who said it as a way of suggesting that Smith was angry at him. In fact, she wasn't angry at him for watching the pornographic films. She was angry with her husband mainly because he had got the expenses claim wrong:

> He isn't some porn addict and funnily enough he hasn't watched an awful lot since, but that wasn't what I was angry about: we could have a discussion about that. What I was angry about was that we'd been so idiotic as to use this receipt where you claim an amount for your TV connection and phone package. He chose the one bill for the whole year to put which listed everything. Incidentally it also had two films that the kids had watched, *Surf's Up* and *Ocean's Twelve*!

With the embarrassment of events and the press reaction, Smith was now contemplating an imminent resignation. The problem was that it was the Friday before a major weekend meeting of the G20 at the Excel Centre in London. Smith knew how important the G20 meeting was to Brown, who wanted to be seen leading the world through the financial crisis. One of her special advisers told her that the Prime Minister would not appreciate her resigning at that point, thereby diverting attention away from his big moment.

In the meantime, Smith found colleagues were being supportive. On the Sunday night and the Monday morning she received an enormous number of kind text messages and phone calls. Smith also remembers, though, the people who didn't support her – those who wanted to keep their heads down, to steer clear of her and the nature of her crisis. Some may have been concerned about anyone looking too closely at their own receipts.

Smith's husband felt there were people who could and should have done more to support her and did not. He feels quite bitter about it. She herself is not but says it occasionally crosses her mind when she encounters certain former colleagues and friends: 'Where were you when I needed help?' The most prominent example of such a person is Labour's long-standing deputy leader and most vocal feminist, Harriet Harman, who wasn't as kind as she could have been. As deputy leader, Harman did an interview with the *Today* programme in October 2009 after the Commissioner's Report had been published. John Humphrys suggested Jacqui Smith should not be allowed to stand again and used the word 'dishonesty'. It still rankles with Smith today that Harman did not try to defend her colleague, and didn't point out that the Commissioner had found that she hadn't been dishonest.

Smith found that those in the Labour Party who were most vociferous about how awful the media is tended to be the same people who believed every word said about her, including many things that weren't true. She still gets cross today about some people who 'seem always to be banging on about how you can't believe anything you read in the newspapers'. Yet it appeared there was an exception for what they had written about her.

But she had the unswerving support of the Prime Minister, Gordon Brown, whom she remembers as being 'incredibly kind', not a description always applied to Brown by those who have worked in proximity to him. He called her to reassure her, issued a supportive statement from Downing Street and ordered a 'protective shield' to be put up around her. Brown was also demonstrably supportive when he saw Smith publicly on the Monday after the story broke (30 March) on Horse Guards Parade. The PM, the Foreign Secretary and the Home Secretary were there to greet arriving dignitaries. Brown gave Smith a big kiss to ensure the world knew he was on her side. With this level of support, Smith accepted it wasn't good timing to slap in her resignation, and carried on.

Carrying on, though, was actually an even greater punishment than stepping down. Lyon now announced a second investigation into the claims for pornographic films, and Smith herself had to undertake a public apology. Resignation would have brought some peace and quiet, some respite from the awful coverage that continued.

It was a 'horrible experience' for Smith and her family, with very little laughter and only the odd piece of gallows humour. The family in Redditch was under siege for a time from journalists outside the house. The children had to leave and return for school by the back gate, with huge numbers of people at the front of the house waiting for pictures or a few words. There was little privacy to be had. Even now, the experience continues to leave its mark: 'Yes, I did find it enormously embarrassing and I still feel slightly embarrassed. Sometimes when I'm out with Richard now I think to myself, it will just cross my mind, that people are looking at us thinking, "He's the one who watched the pornography."'

The children would not talk about the situation at the time, though Smith and Timney tried to discuss what was happening. In

fact, the children tried to be protective towards their parents, trying
to take the pressure off them, saying they were OK. Smith's youngest was too young to understand it all, but he suffered from being
teased at school. He came home and cried after one incident, when
another child had said, 'Oh, your dad's at home watching a porno.'
For a twelve-year-old it was hard to have your father attacked in
this way, even if you didn't quite understand all of it.

Smith's older son had a strong group of friends who were very
supportive of him, and he was older and at that time more robust as
a character. But even he has changed as a result of what happened.
The interest in politics that he displayed in his early youth is now
gone. The 'pack of wolves' mentality really struck him, the going
through the bins for titbits of information and the intrusion of the
press into the lives of friends and neighbours.

The media went to Smith's friends, neighbours, even to her uncle,
a vicar, to ask if Smith had been in touch for spiritual advice. They
tracked down friends through the Friends Reunited website and
contacted people she had been at school with. Smith's entire life
story became open season. She hadn't realised the extent to which
the press would trawl through her entire life and people she knew
and friends she had made.

Because of the subject matter, this made things much worse. 'I
felt awful,' she says, 'as if I had to apologise to everybody for what
was going on. The people that I worried about, more than my kids
almost, was my mum and dad. You feel very responsible for your
kids and what your parents are finding out about you.' The worry
reached the extent that it was hard to get up every morning in
London and check how many people were outside. Once she had

managed that, Smith faced 'having to take a deep breath to go out and walk through them. It's quite wearing on you; it takes quite a lot to do.'

She had times when she just sat down and cried. One of her lowest points came just before she resigned when she'd just been on a Cabinet away day. The following morning, coinciding with the DPP deciding not to prosecute Damian Green, the papers had pictures of Smith looking at her worst all over the front page, coupled with commentary suggesting she was under the cosh. That day was a low point. She mistakenly looked at the papers in bed, and this time it really shook her to the core. She was left feeling so shattered emotionally she could not get out of bed.

The other low point came after her resignation, when John Lyon reported in October. One would have thought that this was because the ongoing pressure to prove her case had been emotionally debilitating for Smith, with the investigation lasting six months. But in fact, she had never felt under pressure over her housing claims, confident as she was that she was in the right. This is why the final ruling made such an impact on her. Smith thought she had proved her case to Lyon and that everything was going to be fine. When it turned out not to be all right, the shock was acute.

Smith had spent hours and hours sitting with Lyon explaining in tiny detail where she had slept every night for four years and going through her diary. This, of course, was at the same time that Smith was Home Secretary and trying to stay on top of an enormous workload. She admits that it must have affected her work and that she wasn't able to be as focused as she would have wanted as the investigation ate into the time she could devote to her main job.

She says now, 'It didn't only take up my time. It took up a hell of a lot of time for example of my special advisers, who supported me a lot during it.'

The impact of the scandals that had hit her meant she was already pulling her punches in the Home Office with regard to fighting certain fights. The effort to fight a case across government departments needs a lot of energy and commitment, as well as persuasive skill. But weighed down by fighting off the scandals, she backed off from the struggle of trying to skirmish on too many fronts, and that meant things such as police accountability were simply left to fester for the next government.

The constant interest in her expenses also had an impact on how she was able to perform the public aspects of her role, which, as she noted, are of particular importance in the job of Home Secretary. As Liam Fox found in the days and weeks leading up to his resignation, the scandal crowded out anything Smith wanted to say about her responsibilities. She particularly remembers going on the *Today* programme to discuss burglary and other crime-related matters, to be faced with only one question on burglary and all the other questions relating to expenses.

Despite everything, Smith truly loved her job and would not have resigned but for one reason – her family. Yes, she had gone through terrible embarrassment and struggled to focus on her job at times; yes, she had the media intruding into her life; yes, she couldn't get out of bed on occasions; but still she felt she could have brazened it out in the end. It wasn't that Smith couldn't take any more: it was the pressure on her family that told in the end. The burden was making them ill.

The pressure on Richard, her husband, was particularly intense, because he was at the centre of it all. Whilst it's normal for someone in the public eye to have to lie low from time to time, for a previously unknown, ordinary man, not being able to go out of the house is extremely difficult. He had become a prisoner in his own home, and the embarrassment of the films had made him even more reclusive. Like Smith herself, Timney found it increasingly hard to function in his role as constituency lynchpin and family organiser. Smith knew that she could only function at Westminster if Timney took the strain at home and in the constituency. The unrelenting pressure had had an enormous impact on him and he simply couldn't continue with his role unaffected. His mother had to pick up more and more of the family workload.

With her husband suffering from what can only be described as nervous stress, the decision for Smith was easy: she had to go. Having weathered the storm, it came down to a choice of career or family. These matters are still extremely private and painful to Smith, and it has left a deep scar for both her and the rest of the family. This is summed up by a story she told me tearfully, some distance after the event, but still deeply emotional for her.

Throughout the difficult period, her sister Sara would look after her in London and would cook for her after work.

I can remember one evening when they said, 'Come and watch the telly.' So we sat down and watched John Sergeant chairing some game show. He opened the programme by saying, 'This is the show where we get under pressure and a bit hot and sweaty, like Jacqui Smith's husband.' There was an awful lot of that, so I stopped listening to the radio because if you listened to anything that is a comedy, or any sort of panel show, the topic of reference was Jacqui Smith's husband. You would constantly hear about it.

Smith made up her mind to go. Part of the problem was also that she couldn't talk to her husband about it. She tried not to discuss it with him because he was having trouble coping with everything himself. But that Friday, late in April, she went to London to talk to Gordon Brown. Smith told the Prime Minister: 'I can't do the job you want me to do, because every time I try to talk about crime, immigration and so on, I end up talking about me, porn, where I live, et cetera. It's putting too much pressure on the family.' Her husband went with her and Brown was very kind to both of them.

Brown, in fact, persuaded Smith not to resign at that particular point. But by the following Wednesday, Smith had thought further and told Brown she had to go. Brown asked her to delay until he was ready to carry out his planned reshuffle, to which she agreed. Liberated in her own mind, now that her future was decided, she spent an enjoyable five weeks in the Home Office, with only a few people knowing she was leaving at the reshuffle. It proved a huge relief to Smith – a massive burden from her shoulders – knowing she had only five weeks to get on with the things she wanted to do. It was cathartic, as she thought, 'You f***ers can say whatever you like, I know I'm going!'

In some ways the timing could not have been worse for the government, as a particularly bad set of May local election results had been met by a series of resignations aimed at getting rid of

Brown. James Purnell went, and so did Hazel Blears with her 'Rock the Boat' badge. Smith's resignation became slightly entangled, although through talkative friends it actually leaked out a day early that she was going. It forced her into a series of interviews to ensure it was understood that she was not leaving Brown's government because she did not support the Prime Minister.

Brown appears to have treated Smith differently from other women ministers. He had a reputation for treating women badly, as others such as Caroline Flint, Hazel Blears and Kitty Ussher would privately confirm. But Brown had worked hard to persuade Smith not to resign. He told her, and with some justification, that if she resigned, 'you will always be remembered for this'. Looking back now, Smith does have regrets. She did not want to resign; she loved being a minister. She knew she would have lost her seat a year later and little or nothing could have stopped that. She believes she would have lost her seat even without the scandal over her expenses. But her resignation means that expenses and porn films are what she is now remembered for, just as Brown said they would be. She could have had another year to influence things and make a difference.

The internet and new media had a big impact on Smith. Although she wasn't on Twitter, people reported to her the vile things that were said. From time to time she would Google herself and what popped up was horrible – and indelible. 'Even when you don't read it at the time, it remains. Some of it informs newspaper and broader media comment and then it becomes a problem.'

On four occasions after she left as Home Secretary, she mustered the energy to go to the Press Complaints Commission (PCC) for clarifications or apologies and did get partial victories. But it took such a huge effort each time she did not have the time or energy to challenge all the stories (as she hadn't when Home Secretary) that were in circulation and repeated, it seemed to her, endlessly. This failure to chase them all down meant it affected her ability to get redress from the PCC for stories that appeared later, as the defence of the newspapers involved was that 'x newspaper' or 'x broadcaster' had already reported the same story and it hadn't been challenged.

Now she wishes she had taken the time and effort to challenge and clear up at least the worst of those errors – for example, that although the London flat she shared belonged to her sister it was, she insists, her proper home. She felt that there were a lot of examples of things that were inaccurate and detrimental to her side of the story, but her problem was that she was so debilitated that she simply did not have the time or energy to fight them all and sort them out. In addition, when Home Secretary, she did not feel she should be focusing her energy on her personal problems. Yet it was clearly the case that the more she allowed the 'inaccurate stories' about her to pile up, the harder it became emotionally to do her job as Home Secretary.

Of course, she thought all the way along, until Lyon's report came out, that the evidence it contained would completely vindicate her. Smith still believes to this day that the Standards Commissioner's report 'robbed me of my reputation unreasonably'. At the beginning, the bar was that Smith had to have spent more nights in London than in Redditch for it to fulfil her designation as her first home. She proved that she had. However, Lyon felt that 'gravitational pull' was also an important criterion. He had a fair point.

Logically, many MPs will spend a majority of their week in London when Parliament is sitting. Even so, if they merely rent a flat there, or even just a room in one, whilst maintaining a proper household elsewhere ('the place where the photo albums' are kept, as it has been described), the public would understand the latter to be their main home.

In Smith's defence, this was something she had tested with the Parliamentary Fees Office because she herself was unsure. With her family based full-time in Redditch, should that be considered her main home? She asked the Fees Office the criteria for a change of residence and was informed that the primary residence was the place where a Member of Parliament spent the most time. As a government minister, she spent more time in London than in Redditch. Indeed, until 2004, ministers had to choose London as their main home, there was no choice. She was therefore advised that she was within the rules to claim London as her main home and her family home in Redditch as her second one.

This is why she still feels cheated by Lyon's decision to find against her. At the time she said she was 'gutted' and that the findings were 'so unfair'. Time has, if anything, made her more bitter about the decision. The expressions she uses today to describe the decision and her reaction to it range from 'gobsmacked' to far more colourful terms. The intensity of feeling stems mainly from Lyon's decision, which cut to the heart of her as a person and questioned her honesty. 'I just thought it was terrible because everyone would think I was a big liar and a sleazebag and I wasn't. I had to talk to my mum and dad, and I thought, "They will think I have done something wrong, and I haven't." It was horrible, really horrible.'

Smith was even more shocked when the findings were published, because she had seen the body of the report, without its conclusions, beforehand and it had looked fair. It properly explained the situation regarding the London home, which was not just a room in the back of a flat. It laid out the number of nights that she spent in each, and showed that over that four-year period she had spent more nights in London than Redditch. It demonstrated that some of the things that Mrs Taplin said in her original letter were inaccurate.

The day before it was published, Smith's husband picked up a copy of the complete report, including conclusions. To Smith's astonishment and bitter disappointment, despite explaining Smith's situation and agreeing with her on key points of fact, Lyon upheld the complaints against her, concluding that she had wrongly designated London as her primary home and recommended that she apologise to the House of Commons. Though the report acknowledged that she had followed advice from officials, Lyon also wrote that she 'clearly did not treat her claims with the care expected of all those who look for reimbursement from the public purse'.

She sat and cried her heart out. No longer Home Secretary, soon to lose her seat and labelled an expenses cheat, she took to her bed worried, afraid of what her friends and family would think of her. It was official for all to see, she had broken the rules.

The Standards and Privileges Committee, which considered the report and was tasked with handing down consequent punishment, was lenient. Although it upheld the conclusions, it didn't suspend Smith as it later did David Laws, for example. It didn't ask for any money to be repaid, but it did ask for an apology in the House. As embarrassing as this was, it was in fact as little as they could ask as punishment.

Smith apologised unreservedly for the pornographic films, but was less profuse about the second home. Michael White of *The Guardian* had contacted Smith to remind her of how to make an apology that wasn't an apology, as Michael Mates MP once had over the case of Asil Nadir. She now thinks she was more apologetic than she felt and wishes she had been less so.

THE AFTERMATH

Smith spent the year following resignation rattling around on the back benches, but she felt pretty low for the entire time. It is easy to assume that because a Cabinet minister has been through many political ordeals, they are battle-hardened by the experience so that further troubles just bounce off a thick skin. In fact, this is not always the case.

In the strictly political crises discussed elsewhere in this book, such as those which affected Osborne, Cable and Hunt, all that was at stake was their careers. Although still hugely pressurised, it is much easier to cope with these stresses and pressures. But the moment a crisis impinges on the personal, with personal reputation at stake, it becomes harder to bear – even if you don't believe you have done anything wrong. Perhaps only Huhne, whose predicament was intensely personal, is an exception to this rule. Because she was a woman, Smith's personal circumstances and arrangements were also slightly different to others in this book.

She had to make an attempt to hold her seat knowing it was pretty hopeless, but also knowing that it would get in the way of job offers. Although many told her to step aside, Smith was burning to take people on and tell her side of the story, which would perhaps also serve as some form of public penance. She had to tell her constituents her story – but unfortunately, few were listening.

The campaign was demoralising, although her constituents were polite to her on the whole. There was a campaign locally collecting signatures in shopping centres against her, like the one Julie Kirkbride faced in Bromsgrove after her own expenses scandal. Smith's sons had to walk past the campaigners every day on the way to school. They didn't get many signatures but they did generate a lot of publicity. The media narrative about the campaign in Redditch became entrenched: she was going to lose because of the expenses. In the end, she lost by 6,000 votes.

Smith's particular political storm went on for a long time – indeed, for a period few could bear. It seems likely it lasted as long as it did because it happened in two phases; the first part was survivable despite it relating to her expenses. The second phase was always going to be difficult to survive when laid on top of the first, but Smith's resilience was remarkable. She took some huge emotional hits but hung on much longer than could have been expected.

Since losing her seat and political career in 2010, Smith hasn't found it easy to get the lucrative work that the newspapers like to tell us ex-Cabinet ministers move on to.

It is quite difficult, actually. Not just for me, but all former Labour MPs, because there is a combination of politicians not being very popular – the currency of former MPs is pretty low, the currency of former Labour MPs is reduced by the government having changed. And for me as well, anyone who Googled me would think, 'Why should we take the risk with her?' No, I have not been overrun by job offers.

She was earning less than an ordinary MP up until late 2013 and there was surprisingly little demand for someone who has been Home Secretary – although things have improved more recently. She still gets comments on Twitter (now she is a user) and the odd strange look in the supermarket. 'I sometimes think, "Are they looking at me and thinking, 'He's the one' or 'She's the one'?"' she says.

Unlike other Home Secretaries she has not been asked to go to the House of Lords (nor, incidentally, has Charles Clarke). Despite supporting Smith, Brown nominated others before her and it left her slightly disappointed. She is less bothered about it now, because she's found herself perfectly happy without it and feels quite liberated without having to toe a line. Would she accept if asked? Probably, yes. However, she knows she will not experience the buzz of being at the top table of politics ever again. Even the Labour Party does not seem interested in what Jacqui Smith has to offer it.

Despite this, Smith feels that in some way she has benefited from the crisis and got through it. She had had a successful school life, university life, career, ministerial career. Nothing bad had happened to her in her life up until that point. Having got through such a difficult time has made her a stronger person. That's not to say it was not a terrible ordeal or that it was not extremely difficult to recover from. But the Jacqui Smith of today is a very different person to the Jacqui Smith of five years ago. Her guard is now completely down because she does not have anything further to hide. She knows that she and her family went through a harrowing experience and she lost her career, but she could have lost so much more.

CHAPTER 8

BACKBENCHERS
FEEL THE PRESSURE

High-profile frontbenchers and members of the government are not the only people at risk of finding themselves at the centre of a political storm. There are many ordinary candidates and MPs for whom there is no protection from a good controversy or even the whiff of wrongdoing in office. The cases of Stewart Jackson and Nadhim Zahawi are two such examples.

Jackson and Zahawi were caught up in the ongoing expenses scandal, which saw five Members of Parliament and two peers go to prison. When the revelations about the MPs' expenses system were revealed in 2009, it appeared that a scandalised public was ready to take revenge on a whole class of hypocrites and liars. It was open season on all politicians, and the media's desire for embarrassing stories about pretty much any MP had become a frenzy. If the intensity of the scandal has now abated somewhat in the intervening years, the degree of public and media cynicism has not, and what they spend their taxpayer-funded expenses on remains a 'third rail' matter for MPs.

⋄⋄⋄⋄

STEWART JACKSON: STREET FIGHTER

"My wife was sitting there watching Newsnight and it was like something from a Bugs Bunny cartoon. Her eyes popped out on stalks. I just couldn't believe I was on the front page of the Daily Telegraph, *a whole page about my claims and a picture of our house, everything. When you're not in that firestorm you just can't appreciate how stressful that is."*

– Stewart Jackson

Stewart Jackson has never been one to mince his words or to step back from a fight. He doesn't go looking for controversy or fights, but he does pride himself on being on the ordinary-working-man wing of the Conservative Party. He believes in saying it as he sees it, even if occasionally he calls it wrong.

Having first been elected to Parliament as the MP for Peterborough in 2005, from 2007 to 2009 he had received very positive reports in his local press for low expenses claims. In 2007, when travel expenses claims were made public, his were the lowest of the seven MPs in the Peterborough area. In October of the same year, Jackson was named, alongside Shailesh Vara as one of the two particularly thrifty MPs in Cambridgeshire by the *Peterborough Evening Telegraph*. Jackson had claimed £120,589 and North West Cambridgeshire MP Vara claimed £112,588. Both were below the average claimed by the country's 646 MPs, which was then more than £130,000 per person.

As late as March 2009, there was no indication that Jackson's expenses claims were going to prove a problem, as his claims were again revealed to be the lowest of any MP in the local area. Jackson told his local newspaper at the time:

> Most people in my constituency seem to feel I'm doing a reasonably good job and am very accessible, with a website, a report published twice a year and regular surgeries. I always wanted to have my family home in my constituency rather than a temporary base. The expenses are fair and straightforward and I am very sorry other MPs have rather besmirched their reputation by their treatment of expenses.

Within six weeks the MPs' expenses scandal uncovered by the *Daily Telegraph* had engulfed Jackson, along with several other MPs, to the extent that he was fighting for his political survival. It was to be one of the biggest political storms in recent history and many careers were to pay a heavy price. That Jackson survived when many longer-serving and more experienced politicians fell gives a fascinating insight into the entire episode.

The MPs' expenses scandal had deep roots. It dated back to the passing of the Freedom of Information (FOI) Act 2000, which came into force on 1 January 2005, allowing members of the public to request the disclosure of information from public bodies. A number of early requests went in from journalists for details of the expenses claimed by specific MPs to be released.

The requests sparked concern among the House of Commons authorities on a number of issues, ranging from privacy to security, and so, after great deliberation, they were passed to the Information Commissioner, who collated three journalists' requests and ordered the release of part of the information requested in June 2007. Commons authorities objected to the Commissioner's instruction almost immediately, as MPs had, in May 2007, voted in favour of the Freedom of Information (Amendment) Bill, which sought to exempt MPs from the 2000 FOI Act. However, the Bill had fallen because peers in the House of Lords were unwilling to sponsor it.

In February 2008, after a referral to an information tribunal, the Commons authorities agreed to release information on fourteen MPs, only for the decision to be appealed against, delaying the release of information again. Harriet Harman, on behalf of the then Labour government, used a three-line government whip to try to force through a motion exempting itemised details of MPs' expenses from being disclosed under the Freedom of Information Act. With the public in uproar and opposition parties certain to vote against the proposal, it was dropped and it was announced all MPs' expenses would be published in July 2009.

But the official disclosure became somewhat redundant when the information was leaked to the media. A former SAS officer, Major John Wick, the owner of a London-based risk management company, became a middle-man for a whistleblower who wanted to bring the information into the public domain. The whistleblower had obtained a hard drive which contained every receipt, every claim and every piece of correspondence between MPs and Fees Office staff – said to be a huge 4 million separate pieces of information – from the previous four years.

Whilst there was undoubtedly a public interest in the information being published, the motives of the whistleblower were probably less altruistic than claimed. The information was hawked around Fleet Street's finest and offers were invited for the exclusive rights. *The Sun* and *The Times* turned the opportunity down but the *Telegraph* paid £110,000 for the information, down from an asking price of over £150,000.

The *Telegraph* knew it was on to a good thing in terms of news and scandal value, not least because a host of similar MPs' expenses stories had already provided great copy for the newspapers. Derek Conway, Ed Balls and Yvette Cooper, Caroline Spelman, Sir Nicholas and Lady Winterton, Jacqui Smith, Tony McNulty and Eric Pickles had all struggled to cope with the media onslaught that their expenses claims prompted. It was to cost some of these MPs both their political career and their reputation.

But when the *Telegraph* began its series of articles on 8 May 2009, it could not have fully appreciated the impact it would have. It caused outrage and widespread anger among the public against MPs, and a collapse of confidence in politics and politicians. The result was a large number of resignations, sackings, de-selections and retirement announcements, together with contrite public apologies from MPs and the substantial repayment of expenses to the tune of thousands, and sometimes tens of thousands, of pounds each. Several members of both the House of Commons and the Lords were prosecuted and sentenced to terms of imprisonment. The scandal also created enormous pressure for political reform; the parliament elected in 2005 became known as the 'Rotten Parliament'.

The *Daily Telegraph* began with the expenses of the governing Labour Party on 8 May 2009 and sent shockwaves through Westminster. Over the following weeks the same process was followed: an email was sent to the account of the relevant MP with the allegations in the morning and a 5 p.m. deadline was given for any statement or response. If there was no response, the allegation would be published anyway. No MP was safe from the forensic inspection of their expenses. Westminster soon became zombie-like, as politicians waited expectantly for their reputations to be trashed. It was not unusual for MPs to shed tears as they spoke of their predicament.

It was into this extraordinarily charged environment that Stewart Jackson was pitched on 11 May 2009. He received an email from the *Daily Telegraph*'s Gordon Rayner that morning, asking for a 5 p.m. response. At first, Jackson didn't think there was much to the story; with his previous good record of low claims and many other bigger fish on the line, a few hundred pounds was surely unlikely to cause a big media splash.

As Jackson and his wife sat watching television that evening, they could not believe their eyes:

> My wife was sitting there watching *Newsnight* and it was like something from a Bugs Bunny cartoon. Her eyes popped out on stalks. I just couldn't believe I was on the front page of the *Daily Telegraph*, a whole page about my claims and a picture of our house, everything. When you're not in that firestorm you just can't appreciate how stressful that is.

In its 12 May edition, the *Telegraph* published an article entitled 'MPs' expenses: Stewart Jackson admits claim for pool work was "excessive"'. The article revealed that Jackson, then a shadow minister at the Department for Communities and Local Government (DCLG), had claimed more than £66,000 for his family home, including hundreds of pounds on refurbishing his swimming pool. Having switched his second home allowance to the £470,000 property in his constituency of Peterborough when he bought it in November 2005, the article explained, Jackson had 'billed the taxpayer for more than £11,000 in professional fees and costs incurred during the move. He went on to claim thousands more in new furniture, carpets and appliances for the new house.' Jackson's case was then featured in articles on scandalous Tory expense claims across the national newspapers, including *The Guardian*, *The Express* and *The Independent*, who headed their article 'Expenses scandal – it just gets worse'.

Jackson had previously rented a £168,000 terraced house in the west of the city for about £475 per month. However, he had wanted to put down solid roots in the constituency for some time and he finally took the plunge to buy. After moving into a larger local house he claimed for interest charges on its mortgage of between £1,500 and £1,700 per month. Under the existing rules (in the Green Book) there was nothing illegal or wrong in this.

Jackson's response to the *Telegraph* piece was to explain his circumstances as fully as he could to try to draw the sting. He said:

> The expenses I have claimed under the Additional Costs Allowance since being elected to Parliament in May 2005 have been criticised in the report in the *Daily Telegraph*. Before I was elected to Parliament, I had rented in Peterborough. I lived in rented digs (one bedroom in a shared house with my wife and child).

After my election in 2005, I naturally decided to purchase a permanent home in Peterborough in order to establish a firm base in the community, by way of a family home there, to better serve my constituents. The costs mentioned in the *Daily Telegraph* relate to setting up that home. They were exceptional and one-off costs, in the main, incurred at the time of purchase in 2005 – they were outside my control and paid directly to the respective professionals; and were within the rules and agreed by the Fees Office at the House of Commons. The vast bulk of claims in the 2005–8 period have been for mortgage and utility bills.

He added:

The pool came with the house and I needed to know how to run it. Once I was shown that one time, there were no more claims. I now take care of the pool through my own means. However, I accept in hindsight that this claim could be construed as inappropriate and I therefore apologise and I will make arrangements to repay this sum.

Whilst his statement was controlled and, where necessary, contrite, privately Jackson was disgusted with the *Telegraph*, feeling what it had done was 'morally repugnant'. He believed that this was not just an attack on him personally but an attempt to traduce and attack MPs as a class. He also felt that many of the so-called 'saints' were people who, because of their family circumstances or wealth or both, did not need to claim. The *Telegraph* was picking on the people, in general, who couldn't do an MP's job if they did not claim expenses.

However, if Jackson and others in his position had known that claims such as the one for his swimming pool, even if they were within the rules and agreed by the Parliamentary Fees Office, would be made public, they would not have made them. Jackson believes that many MPs got badly stung for going along with the rules as they were at the time, but draws a distinction between these MPs and the criminal ones – those who were falsifying invoices, claiming mortgages that had already been paid off, and misappropriating equipment: 'There was a tiny sub-category of MPs who were actually criminal and most of them, apart from Margaret Moran, have gone to prison.'

Despite Jackson's statement, the local paper published a number of highly critical letters from members of the public and his local political opponents. Jackson believes that many of these letter-writers were in fact political rivals using the opportunity to bash the enemy. Whilst there were letters of support, it must have been difficult to open the letters page of the local paper for several weeks. Here is a typical letter from the *Peterborough Evening Telegraph*, although the writer was a constituent of neighbouring MP Shailesh Vara:

All this tells me is that the speed at which these MPs like Stewart Jackson, promise to repay the monies taken, proves that they must have known that these claims were inherently immoral in the first place.

I find it amazing that now they have all been caught that MPs now say that it's the system that is wrong. They didn't exactly rush to correct it whilst they were busily exploiting it AND us.

– Alfio Restaino Stanground

Like many caught in the eye of the storm, Jackson felt it was difficult to get his side of the story out into the public domain in a
way that would get a reasonable hearing. The public was in no
mood to listen to explanations or excuses – they wanted retribution. So Jackson immediately supported Cameron's crackdown on
Conservative MPs' expenses, and his ultimatum to repay frivolous
claims or be expelled from the party. He had, after all, already
repaid the £304.10 for the swimming pool and was sure the rest
of his claims were completely above board. The Conservative
Party was going to put all MPs' claims through its own scrutiny
committee for good measure. Having been hassled relentlessly for
several days and feeling nobody was listening to his side of the
story, Jackson decided that he would answer no further questions
about his expenses claims and would instead leave it to the scrutiny committee.

Yet he was desperate from the beginning of his crisis not to be
defined forever as

> the guy who was so out of touch and uncaring because he claimed
> for swimming pool maintenance. I wanted to explain that I didn't
> have inherited wealth, that I was not a grandee, that I was a normal
> working guy – everything I'd earned I had worked for. It was impor-
> tant to me to get it out there.

He therefore used his 14 May 'Westminster Life' column in the
local paper to fight back and put on record that second home
allowances existed to allow ordinary people to become MPs.
He wrote:

I have never, ever profited from any claims made to run the constituency home. As a family, we wanted to commit to the city and have a proper family home we could use for constituency events, charity fundraisers, meetings and entertaining. And give my daughter a bedroom of her own. If there was no help to pay the bills for a second home in the constituency, individuals like me, with no trust funds, private income or successful business to support them, would not be able to enter politics.

Jackson was a fighter and was not prepared to let his political career simply evaporate before his eyes. In an angry interview on BBC Radio Cambridgeshire, he insisted the criticism was unjust:

My wife and I have suffered vilification and abuse for the whole of the week on this issue. I have done nothing criminal or illegal and what I did was within the rules. I am not a thief or a liar. I am being penalised for an error of judgement. But the cost of the swimming pool represents just 0.4 per cent of the amount claimed for the whole three years (from 2005 to 2008). The claim was within the rules, I have apologised and I will be paying it back. It does not mean people have the right to be abusive or vulgar.

It was typical Jackson, always prepared to speak up and say his piece. Many MPs would have gone to ground – as indeed many did – or perhaps taken a less confrontational approach, but Jackson felt there was an injustice in penalising people for following the rules. In his endeavours he had the backing of his local association (whose chairman, Matthew Dalton, worked for Jackson as a researcher), which put out a very supportive statement that ensured people in Peterborough knew Jackson was not about to resign and would be fighting the next election. Indeed, Jackson took the decision to tough it out and made sure that he went about his normal business of attending church and doing the shopping. People would have their opportunity at an election to unseat him but until then he would not 'hide away and be hunted'. Jackson was keen to get Peterborough to think about his performance as a campaigning and hardworking local MP. He wanted to be judged on his record, on the things he achieved and the people he had helped, not his swimming pool. He wanted to make local people think beyond the hysteria of the expenses scandal and instead think about him as a person, as their local champion.

For all of Jackson's resolve, he faced a battle. Before May was out, he had an independent candidate standing against him, a local bus driver and former Labour supporter called John Swallow, specifically campaigning on the issue of his expenses, Even by mid-June, things had not settled down. A group of protestors marched on Jackson's house with the intention of swimming in his pool. About thirty people walked through the city to the MP's home one Saturday afternoon, some dressed in swimming costumes. On arrival, they were greeted by local press, along with four police officers. Protest organiser Phil Jeffery, from the West Town area of Peterborough, told the local press: 'The idea has come from the extent of the whole MPs' expenses row. In essence, it was our protest against Stewart Jackson and his claims.' Predictably, Jackson responded angrily, telling reporters: 'Police resources should be used to fight crime, rather than this sort of foolish, juvenile act. This was an unnecessary waste of police time.'

The whole saga gained another new lease of life when the Conservative Party's own scrutiny panel reported at the end of June. Jackson was one of forty-one Conservative MPs required to pay back further money out of the party's almost 200 MPs. This time, he was required to pay back £97 – the second lowest charge of all the MPs involved. He again used the opportunity to make the point that his expense claims had all been 'honest and above board'. He was holding a firm line against a fierce national media onslaught.

Jackson's consistently robust stance made him more of a target for the newspapers, and the national newspapers in particular. Here was an MP in the middle of one of the biggest expenses scandals and he did not even appear particularly contrite. Unfortunately for Jackson, he had written to Christopher Kelly in April as part of the consultation into MPs' expenses and allowances, defending the need to continue the second home allowance. When the *Daily Mail* found out in August, it took him to task for it suggesting he wanted to excuse his claims for security gates and swimming pools, but Jackson was unrepentant about it: 'My point was, if you don't want Parliament to be for wealthy people or cranks or people supported by trade unions, then you shouldn't get rid of second home allowances.'

Jackson did not let his crisis affect his robust political style. By December, with things having eased somewhat he was using his local newspaper column to attack the 'whingers and moaners' in his own constituency, suggesting that who bashed the local authority in Peterborough 'for almost everything that goes wrong' were mainly Labour Party supporters rather than members of the public with genuine complaints or concerns. The column was picked up nationally by the *Daily Telegraph* and conflated with the reports about his issues over expenses claims. Jackson now suggests it was part and parcel of the *Telegraph*'s 'dishonest' agenda, by taking his comments out of context and adding in expenses. He says:

> It was obviously in the public interest to reveal people who were thieving from the taxpayer. None of us would disagree with that, but when you get down to who bought a Pot Noodle or a Peperami or a dog bowl, then it got to barrel scraping – deeply unpleasant and a little insidious.

In February 2010 Jackson was told by Sir Thomas Legg's independent panel, which had been appointed to review all second-home expenses claims, that he was in the clear and had nothing further to pay back. It was a victory of sorts for Jackson, as he could now put the whole episode to the electorate in a few months' time knowing his expenses had been audited. But it had come at great cost to him personally in terms of reputation and, although there was a positive side to the controversy, as it stopped him being complacent about re-election, it cast a shadow over his general election campaign.

Jackson had battled it out locally and nationally over his £304 expenses claim for swimming pool maintenance for a year before the election. In the event, he held his seat in Peterborough, although his share of the vote declined slightly. The 'expenses' candidate, John Swallow, gained just 406 votes. But Jackson admits that he was expecting to have a bigger majority and his battle over expenses did have an impact.

But for the whole of that year he had had to deal with huge pressure, and the strain showed. He had suffered a number of low points as a succession of newspaper articles struck at his character; he developed a siege mentality and his brothers and parents were very concerned about him. He became slightly resentful at times that colleagues did not ring him to offer their advice and support and began to question 'whether he had any friends out there'.

Although he thinks it a selfish way to look at events, when in need, the little acts of kindness do count. However, he kept the faith that people would understand and eventually see through the fact that, as he puts it, 'the media often deal with caricature and can be spiteful. What they report, and the way they present it, is not necessarily the truth.'

His lowest point came early in the crisis, when he was thrown out of someone's house. He had received an angry email from a couple who lived nearby and when out for a pint of milk and some bread at the local shop, he thought he would pop by and chat to them. He says:

I knocked on the door and started to talk to the wife and it was awkward but she wasn't rude. She invited me in and I was explaining my statement when the husband came down from upstairs and was borderline abusive. He opened the door and he didn't quite physically throw me out but he said, 'I don't want you in my house, get out.' I think that was probably the low point – I reproached myself a bit for having put myself in that position of being humiliated but that's just my style. I like to try and talk to people and put my point of view, and if they don't agree that's fine.

The other thing that has stuck with Jackson is the one-sided nature of the reporting when the expenses were published. There wasn't any proper analysis or even an opportunity to explain anything. His local BBC radio station took the opportunity to spend part of the morning reading out things Jackson had claimed for such as a Walnut Whip, a Snickers bar and a prawn sandwich. It was making fun of his claims, hoping to embarrass him – except they weren't his claims. They were claims for his interns. As his office budget didn't allow him to pay a salary to the interns, Jackson gave them cash himself to pay for their lunch and travel, and later used the receipts to claim the money back.

As ever, Jackson decided to confront the matter head on. He rang the radio station personally and reproached it for saying that he, Jackson, expected the public to buy his Snickers, his Walnut Whip and his prawn sandwich. 'I told them, "You've got it wrong, you're making fun and trying to humiliate me and I'm not going to talk to you for six months" – and I didn't.'

THE AFTERMATH

Whilst Jackson won his Peterborough seat relatively comfortably in 2010 and 'wiped the slate clean over expenses', being readopted unanimously to fight the 2015 general election, he has continued to be dogged by negative, sometimes unfair, stories in the press.

True to form, he has continued to take on all comers in the same robust manner.

He took legal action against the *Daily Telegraph* to force an apology for its story headlined 'MPs cling on to profits from second-home sales' in October 2012, in which the paper accused Jackson of selling his second home and keeping the profit made at the taxpayer's expense. To his great delight, in December 2012, Jackson received an apology plus legal costs from the *Telegraph*. As he puts it, the newspaper 'hadn't done its homework properly and foolishly assumed they could print that someone had sold a property that they were still living in – our family home – and get away with it'.

The *Daily Telegraph*'s statement said:

Contrary to our report, Mr Jackson has not sold his relevant home, in which he and his family have lived in his constituency since 2005. We apologise for this error. He has asked us to make clear that the current value is the same as he paid in 2005, that the IPSA demand, which he is challenging, is based on a notional increase since 2010 and that he has made no profit, whether notional or otherwise, on the property to date.

The *Telegraph* story emanated from a dispute that a number of MPs were then having with the Independent Parliamentary Standards Authority (IPSA), set up after the expenses debacle. In May 2013, IPSA announced it was suing Jackson after he refused to pay the £54,000 he was alleged to have made in capital gains on his publicly funded second home. The unprecedented legal case was launched after twenty-eight other MPs agreed to repay almost £500,000 they were alleged to have made in profits after months of behind-the-scenes wrangling involving party whips and lawyers.

Jackson, a diligent and effective member of the House of Commons public accounts committee, said IPSA's legal proceedings were heavy-handed and disproportionate and were clearly intended to bully him into submission. It is believed he tried to settle the outstanding dispute by offering IPSA £10,000, with a further offer of mediation and the appointment of an independent surveyor to adjudicate on the dispute before High Court proceedings began. He explained his position in a statement on his website:

> The essence of the dispute is my challenge of the valuations of 2010 and 2012. IPSA are seeking a cash sum on a so-called capital gain 'profit' on my family home, in which I live and have not sold. The money which IPSA is demanding retrospectively is more than the total amount I received when I was claiming mortgage interest and the property is now valued at less than we purchased it for in 2005.
>
> Their assumption is that the value of my property rose by almost 20 per cent over two years whilst house prices fell by 3 per cent in my constituency in the same period. At my own expense, I have paid for an accurate recent expert valuation and I have made a reasonable offer to IPSA to settle the matter and reduce the legal costs which will have to be met by the taxpayer. My valuation recognises the need for proper recompense to be paid to the taxpayer to reflect their support for my housing costs between 2010 and 2012, in order to fulfil my duties as both a London-based legislator and a constituency MP.

IPSA have negotiated with seventy other MPs in a secretive and arbitrary manner but in respect of my case, regrettably, they have refused to negotiate. I am merely seeking fair play and consistency and will pursue legal action to receive it.

The dispute caused a huge rift between Jackson and *The Sun*, as, in an editorial titled 'Snoutrageous', it accused Jackson of 'money-grabbing' and advised his constituents to vote him out of office in 2015: 'Taxpayers will inevitably end up forking out for a lengthy legal process – to get money back from a man who is supposed to represent their interests,' the paper said. Jackson's response was typically robust as he tweeted: 'I see I've been attacked by *The Sun* for having the temerity to seek legal redress. Police-bribing, phone-hacking scumbags.'

Jackson now regrets he took to social media to hit back against *The Sun* because he believes it obscured the key message: 'that right was on my side, that an unfairness had befallen me'. Instead, the debate moved on to the language he had used in his tweet. The subsequent exchange between Tom Newton Dunn, *The Sun*'s political editor, and Jackson showed how far apart they were. Newton Dunn suggested that Jackson might express sympathy and regret for having smeared the 400 people who worked for *The Sun* who were not phone-hacking, police-bribing scum.

As it turned out, Jackson was correct in his valuation of his property and IPSA was wrong. An independent evaluation on his Broadway house in Peterborough showed that the value had fallen by £15,000 between 2010 and 2012, so Jackson has no money to pay. It is believed that IPSA has spent £25,000 on legal fees from the taxpayer's purse in its pursuit of Jackson.

Whilst Jackson continues to stand up for himself and what he believes to be right, the continuing saga has left its scars. He says:

> I think it [the expenses scandal] has made me much more cynical and defensive about dealing with the media, all media, particularly newspapers. I think it's made me value my constituents because they are the people who judge you on results, they judge you in a fair and balanced way, most of them – and people aren't daft. I think they can filter out stuff that's unfair or vicious or unpleasant.

He now looks back on his brush with expenses with the view that what doesn't kill you makes you stronger. 'I count myself lucky,' he says, 'to a certain extent at least. I know colleagues in the 2005–10 parliament who were broken by the expenses scandal … who lost their self-respect. Their self-worth was wrecked and their health was damaged. I feel that I've been quite lucky to have been re-elected and to have weathered the storm.'

NADHIM ZAHAWI:
<u>SHUTTING THE STABLE DOOR</u>

"It dents your confidence, absolutely it does. It hurts deeply and for those weeks you worry for your family, you worry for your kids, you worry how it affects them. There are nights where you just can't sleep because you are just thinking and worrying, anxious for yourself and your family. It's horrific."

– Nadhim Zahawi

◇◇◇◇

In the wake of the MPs' expenses scandal, the 2010 general election was supposed to clean out the stables once and for all. Instead, the stories have continued to run and run. This is partly due to public and media appetite for damning stories about hypocritical MPs, but also partly because MPs of all parties continue to make stupid mistakes.

Nadhim Zahawi's election as the MP for the safe seat of Stratford-upon-Avon was a huge coup for the Conservative Party. He was an Iraqi Kurd, born in Baghdad, whose father had come to the UK as an immigrant fleeing from Saddam Hussein with £50 in his pocket. He had the most modest of roots, but he went on to become a successful entrepreneur, co-founding and building his company, YouGov, into a hugely successful public company operating in many countries around the world. His drive and determination created hundreds of jobs and wealth for the UK. He was exactly the type of self-made man the Conservative Party adores, but with the added attraction of arriving as a foreign immigrant.

In the autumn of 2013, everything was going well for Zahawi; he had a job as an MP that he loved, he was doing well in Parliament, having just taken a position on the Conservative Party's policy board, he was thought to be favoured by David Cameron, his business interests were good, he was a wealthy man to the point of being a multi-millionaire and he had a happy and settled family life. Things were almost perfect. In politics, however, perfection rarely lasts for long and so it turned out for Zahawi as he was suddenly thrust into the media spotlight seemingly from nowhere. Zahawi's life moved from happiness to horror in just a few days.

❖❖❖

When life is good, perhaps paying attention to the detail becomes a bit of a chore, or perhaps one can be lulled into a false sense of security. But signs were developing during September 2013 that Nadhim Zahawi's expenses were attracting interest. His local paper, the *Stratford Herald*, published a story about him claiming over £170,000 in expenses in the year 2012–13, the 130th highest out of 650 MPs.

The paper wrote:

> Zahawi spent the majority of the money, £145,469, on five members of staff, but he spent over £30,000 more on his team than the previous year … The Conservative MP claimed £12,294 in office costs, around £5,400 less than the previous year. He also claimed £3,323 on travel, £500 less than last year, and £9,148 on accommodation, over £2,000 more than last year.

The *Herald* reported that Zahawi's expenses were at least £15,000 higher than those of neighbouring MPs, although he spent less on personal expenses such as office and accommodation costs than both:

> Stratford's MP claimed more on expenses than both neighbouring Conservatives, Chris White, (Warwick & Leamington), and Jeremy Wright, (Kenilworth & Southam). Chris White claimed £155,074, which put him 313rd in the table, whilst Jeremy Wright claimed £144,142, placing him 420th. All three MPs also received a basic salary of £65,738.

Whilst this report was not particularly negative, it should have served as a warning that nothing should be taken for granted where expenses are concerned. Many MPs had come a cropper even when following the rules religiously. The intense media attention should have made Zahawi take a closer interest in his own expenses and may have enabled him to pick up what would later turn out to be an ongoing error. It didn't – he continued to outsource their management to his staff, something he regrets in hindsight: 'I should have checked things properly, I blame myself.'

It wasn't until Friday 1 November that things got a lot worse. An email dropped into Zahawi's inbox from the *Sunday Mirror* political correspondent, Tom McTague, closely followed by a phone call to his office. Zahawi had finished top of a league table of hundreds of MPs claiming for their energy bills and the newspaper wanted an explanation before going to print.

Taken aback, Zahawi immediately asked his parliamentary researcher to look into why his claims for energy were so comparatively high. The researcher suggested that IPSA had put £2,000 from the previous year's bill into the current year, so it was abnormally high.

On Sunday 3 November, the *Sunday Mirror* went to press with their piece, in which Zahawi, described as David Cameron's 'close friend', topped a league table for high energy bills, having claimed £5,822 to heat his second home in his constituency. The *Sunday Mirror* reported that locals were stunned to discover taxpayers were actually paying to heat his £1 million mansion, whilst locals in Stratford-upon-Avon struggled to make ends meet.

The tone of criticism was summarised by a Mrs Irena Strach, who said: 'I'm appalled – this man does not have a clue what is going on. People here are struggling to survive and heating just two rooms and here we are paying to heat his entire mansion. It's ludicrous.' Just for good measure, local Labour councillor Jeff Kenner said:

> This is shocking. There are many people in this constituency who are having to decide between heating and eating. They have been badly hit by Tory policies. And here Nadhim Zahawi is claiming almost £500 a month – nearly £6,000 a year – to heat his home. It just shows how out of touch he is with his constituents and the rest of Britain. And it's coming from taxpayers' money. It's outrageous. The constituency is nowhere near as wealthy as people might think and many people here are struggling to pay their fuel bills.

The *Sunday Mirror*'s report claimed that some 340 MPs, including ministers, used the parliamentary expenses system to recoup the cost of heating their second home. Bills costing more than £1,000 were submitted by forty-one MPs, whilst seventy-eight made claims for £500 in the twelve months to March 2013. These figures suggested that Zahawi's claims, even allowing for an IPSA error, were extremely high. He was very concerned by this, given that he didn't spend much time in his constituency home as he was in London from Monday to Thursday each week, and asked his researcher to look further into the detail of his energy bills. Zahawi suggested his researcher should drive out to his house on the Monday morning and take a look at the meter in the stable block.

Meanwhile, Zahawi had written a piece for a local paper, the *Stratford Observer*, defending his claims, which appeared the same day. He suggested that he had done nothing wrong in filing his expenses claims, explaining that MPs had to live at two locations and that a mistake had been made in the in-year calculation by IPSA. Even so, he said, 'I readily admit that these are still high, but they do reflect the costs of many people in rural areas who rely only on kerosene and electricity.'

After inspecting the meter, Zahawi's researcher texted him: 'Call me urgently.' Zahawi was in a Select Committee so had to wait until it was over before calling, only to hear the news that the meter in the stable was ticking even though the house was empty. There was clearly a problem.

Zahawi then wrote an exclusive for the *Stratford Herald*, 'explaining' his £170,000 expenses claims. The story was similar to his other local article, but tried to lay out more elements of an MP's life and how expenses support it. However, it got the local paper thinking and a reporter came back to him with further questions, in particular, whether the stables were separate from the house. The local paper knew the layout of the house, its grounds and stables, and was in a position to ask more detailed questions than the nationals.

As a result, Zahawi double-checked whether the stables could be the cause of the high bills. His office had already contacted E.ON to see what the problem might be, but the local paper seemed to be on to something. It emerged that part of Zahawi's claim for energy bills was to supply electricity to a horse-riding school stable on the 31-acre estate and a yard manager's mobile home. Even if Zahawi had the plausible defence that he had only moved into the property in the past eighteen months and was still finding out about all its nooks and crannies, it was certainly excruciatingly embarrassing and arguably slightly incompetent.

After a very short deliberation with his team, Zahawi decided that, no matter how awful and embarrassing, it was imperative that they put out a statement 'coming clean' about the mistake. The only issue was timing. The phone was ringing off the hook, with both members of the public and the media asking questions. His office was under severe pressure. Whilst Zahawi's constituents were largely generous, others across the country were generally abusive, whether by email, letter or phone. One of the more dedicated members of the public sent Zahawi a jumper to wear should he get cold at home.

Zahawi and his team decided to issue a statement on Saturday night, so that the story might blow itself out quickly on the Sunday. He used social media to tweet an apology and a blog to communicate his contrition more fully. He said he was 'mortified' by the mistake of including claims for electricity used by the stable yard of his second home and pledged to repay any money that had been wrongly claimed immediately:

I have been looking into this matter further and can confirm that all claims for heating fuel relate purely to my second home. However, I have made a mistake with my electricity claims. On investigation I have discovered that electricity for a mobile home located in the stable yard, and electricity for the stables themselves, was linked to my house. Whilst a meter was installed in the stable yard, I have only been receiving one bill; it was wrong to assume I was

receiving two and have not checked this sooner. I am mortified by
this mistake and apologise unreservedly for it. I will obviously be
paying back any money that was wrongly claimed immediately.

Zahawi decided to leave the statement at that and do no further
interviews, despite numerous phone calls. He also decided that he
should not wait and quibble about which part of the energy bill
was for the stables and which for the house, better to pay the lot
and stop any further questions. He said publicly in a statement a
few days later that he would pay back £4,875.87 – the full amount
of his electricity claim for the past two years. As a wealthy man he
had no need to claim any expenses, but had been advised by the
Chief Whip that if he didn't claim he would make the expenses
claims of less well-off colleagues in nearby constituencies look
much worse.

It seems that across the political spectrum MPs have learned
not to gloat about the other side's misfortunes when it comes to
expenses. There was little activity from the Labour Party nationally.
Indeed, Labour MP Valerie Vaz, appearing on the regional political
programme, contacted Zahawi and asked if there was anything he
wanted her to explain to viewers. Former Labour Foreign Secretary
Jack Straw also put his arm around him and said, 'Listen, you're a
great guy, don't worry, it will blow over.'

On his own side, support came from the top. George Osborne
himself, it is believed, put out the word within Conservative ranks
that 'we've all got to support Nadhim'. These messages of support
from across the political spectrum meant a lot to Zahawi because he
could not expect the wider public to be anything like as generous.

Remembrance Sunday was a blaze of publicity for Zahawi and he could not hide away. He had unavoidable duties to perform and knew the interest in him would be extremely high. He had to attend a church service in the nearby market town of Shipston and then parade through the town as part of the commemoration. Although his constituents had been mostly sympathetic by post or on the phone, he was nonetheless very apprehensive about the reaction he would get from local people when he appeared in person. He had received a huge dollop of abuse from elsewhere.

Not for the first time, Zahawi was getting a considerable amount of racist abuse. 'Go back to your own country' and 'we offered you safe haven and this is how you repay us' were themes. He describes some of it as 'really nasty racist stuff' and felt that he was not in a position to report it to the police because he was an MP caught up in an embarrassing expenses scandal. It would have looked like carping or an attempt to distract attention from his own difficult situation. The police were called, however, by the local pub landlord when an envelope was delivered with a letter making racist threats.

Unfortunately for Zahawi, his children were teenagers and could see the type of response he was getting from members of the public. 'That was the hardest thing, especially for the kids. You have to explain that people are not like that normally or they're probably just angry and being silly.' His children were teased and mocked about their father at school, whilst Zahawi's staff were labelled 'immoral' for working for him.

But there was a silver lining amidst the abuse. Zahawi arrived at Shipston with his apology being broadcast on the radio as the headline every hour and people were gathering in the market town for the parade. He was worried that someone would throw rotten tomatoes at him, or that a photographer would try to get a good picture of him getting pelted with eggs.

As these worries were flickering through his thoughts, a serious-looking lady broke from the crowd and made a beeline for him with her husband in tow. Zahawi braced himself for trouble, expecting at least a mouthful of abuse with all the townsfolk in earshot. Just as she reached him she thrust out her hand and shook Zahawi's vigorously. 'You don't know me,' she said, 'but I wrote to you about my son. You helped him, he's serving in Germany and I think you're a brilliant MP, and I don't care about your energy bills.'

Suddenly, Zahawi was completely at ease. He thought,

Thank God I'm at home, thank God I'm in my constituency, that there are decent people and it's not the same as every time I open my Twitter feed and there's this tirade of abuse. The swearing, calling me all sorts of names, stuff saying 'we know where he lives, let's burn down his house and stables'. It meant a lot to me at a low point.

However, it did not stop someone deliberately letting the horses out of the stables, although the irony was that the horses were not his.

Zahawi noticed that once he had accidentally got himself into the firing line, his whole life suddenly became fair game. First it was other expenses, such as claiming 31p for paperclips, 53p to buy a hole-punch, 63p for ballpoint pens and 89p for a stapler, according to the *Daily Mirror*. Of course, it was part of a stationery order for his office and it is doubtful whether Zahawi would ever have even seen the order.

Unluckily, there was also the embarrassment in mid-November of Zahawi being dropped as chairman of a local Citizens Advice Bureau meeting to promote their report into the ethics of giving pre-pay meters to the vulnerable. In late November, another part of the Trinity Mirror Group, the *Birmingham Mail* and *Coventry Telegraph*, reported that Zahawi had 'used a firm in a tax haven to buy his £1 million home'. The papers reported that 'Conservative MP Mr Zahawi – an adviser to David Cameron – used the company in low-tax Gibraltar as a lender to buy an estate and riding stables now worth £1 million in Upper Tysoe, near Stratford-upon-Avon, in 2011.'

It was meant to sound and look bad, particularly as the recent Budget had set out plans to tackle the avoidance of stamp duty, although the papers admitted that 'using offshore companies is commonplace and not unlawful. There is no suggestion that Mr Zahawi or his wife avoided any taxes by financing their purchase with a mortgage from the Gibraltar-based company.'

Zahawi said in response:

> I did pay stamp duty on my property in Tysoe and have always paid stamp duty on my property purchases. I fully support the 2012 Budget and all Budgets of this government. I purchased my property in Tysoe with a mortgage from a Gibraltar company. This fact and the details involved are fully declared on the Land Registry and to suggest it is in any way hidden would be factually incorrect. Equally, to suggest that in any way I am using offshore to reduce my tax burden is entirely incorrect.

Whilst Zahawi accepted that most of what happened with the media was to be expected, there were two things that intensely annoyed him. First, he suspected that the *Coventry Telegraph* and a local councillor were working together, as the newspaper suggested that the questions were coming to them from him in emails. He suspected that there was an unsavoury element to what was now happening and he took legal advice and sent appropriate letters via his lawyers, which stopped any further insinuations about his house purchase in their tracks.

Second, the regional BBC politics programme, *Sunday Politics West Midlands*, leaked Zahawi's standard sign-off, 'warm regards', something he always used. The programme reproduced one of the responses Zahawi had sent to them, mocking his 'warm regards' sign-off. He felt that it was a cheap shot unworthy of a serious political programme.

But more seriously, perhaps, teams from the *Daily Mail* and *Daily Mirror* were now combing over other elements of Zahawi's affairs. They were 'going through my whole life and looking at everything', he recalls. Questions were constantly being fired into his office, ranging from 'Why does your wife own a property in her maiden name in London and not her married name?' to 'In the 1980s you rented a flat on Fulham Road: how much rent were you paying?' and many others. They delved into his expenses over twelve years as a Wandsworth councillor. Every deal at YouGov, and indeed almost every business deal he had done, came under scrutiny, as all public information and public records were trawled through.

The mistaken claim for energy expenses coloured his other political work. In mid-December 2013, the *Daily Mirror* reported that Zahawi's proposals to stop child benefit and child tax credits after two children had caused 'fury'. The plans, which Zahawi wanted to see applied to babies born after 2015, would have seen three-child families earning less than £30,000 losing £2,725 a year in tax credits, according to *The Mirror*. Families earning up to £50,000, who cannot claim tax credits, would have lost £696. It led to 10 Downing Street distancing itself from Zahawi's proposals: 'This is not government policy and is not supported by the PM.'

Zahawi acknowledges that journalists were doing a job: 'I completely understand it. They were thinking, "Well, if he made a mistake on this, what other mistakes has he made?"' His response was to try to answer all the questions in full, and where he thought they were crossing a line and were heading in a direction which was wholly untrue, he would be firm in his response.

Zahawi says the impact of being at the centre of the storm is that

> everything stops. It's literally the hardest thing, trying to focus on doing your job as a Member of Parliament because you're being bombarded with questions. For two and a half weeks everything stopped. I'd have to dig around for the answers and not get them wrong because if you get them wrong then that's a story in itself.

Most of the questions and stories eventually went nowhere, but it made Zahawi's family think about his life as a politician. His wife took it particularly hard. Going home to his wife, he says, she would often look at him despairingly; she said nothing, but her stare clearly asked, 'Why are you doing this job?' She worried that her family and friends might think badly of her husband. What is more, the family now seemed to have no privacy, and he – and, by extension, they – faced constant criticism.

But Zahawi has a simple explanation for his and his family's ability to survive the ordeal: 'You weather it because everyone around you is absolutely rowing in the same direction: my chairman, my association, my agent, my staff team, my wife, the kids, all saying, "This is clearly unjust, the level of abuse you're getting is wrong." But I never want to go through it again.'

THE AFTERMATH

Whilst the pressure was very intense over a two and a half-week period, Zahawi never contemplated resignation, despite calls for him to go from the general public and despite the abuse he received online. Although he 'hated every moment of it', he still regarded it as an enormous privilege to serve as a Member of Parliament and never lost sight of that fact. His view about politics is that there are more important things in life than accumulating wealth.

He found the acts of kindness from his constituents in the middle of the onslaught of bad news, as at Shipston parade, both reassuring and uplifting. He believes he has learned three important lessons from his own crisis. Firstly, if you make a mistake, come clean and have no hesitation in doing so; people will see you are trying to do the right thing and to make amends. Secondly, try to be with your constituents, as their generosity of spirit will help you along and most will know you by what you have tried to do for them. Finally, whatever you are involved in, whether a hobby business or ordering paperclips, it's up to you to keep an eye on it.

Whilst it was his constituency, staff and family that sustained him through the worst, perhaps another clue to his survival is offered by one of the passing conversations that took place in Portcullis House at Westminster after it all blew over. He walked past Simon Walters, the experienced political editor at the *Mail on Sunday*, who said to him: 'You've survived it, many people wouldn't have.' Why, Zahawi asked him, did he think that was? 'Because people think you're a nice guy and it was that which helped you through: you've got friends in this place. People know you do your bit for your party but you're not overly tribal.'

Zahawi doesn't blame the media or anyone else for what he went through; in many ways he regarded himself as fair game. Nonetheless, the crisis has left a deep impression and a scar. Even now, when you Google 'Zahawi', the top key word is 'expenses'.

CHAPTER 9

WILLIAM HAGUE'S
FOUR-YEAR ORDEAL

"I would not have got through those four years in the party leadership without resilience. It was the night shift, somebody had to do it, but it was dark and nobody knew how long it would be before dawn. In fact it was another decade before there was a real prospect of us winning another general election."

– William Hague

W illiam Hague is one of the most gifted politicians of his generation and regarded by many as an outstanding Foreign Secretary, yet his four years as Leader of Her Majesty's Opposition between 1997 and 2001 tested him to the limit, both personally and politically. The experience left him a changed man.

Indeed, it was a change colleagues noticed. One former Cabinet colleague, who was close to Hague during that period, tells the story of how he was a rather ambitious, engaging and approach-able colleague pre-1997. After his four years as leader, he noticed a change in Hague, much more distant and lacking 'a connection' even with close colleagues. When this colleague fell into his own media storm, despite their long friendship, Hague never picked up the phone or wrote to sympathise or commiserate. When they met, after the crisis had passed, Hague apologised and made the excuse that he was not good at dealing with such highly charged emotional issues.

That's not to suggest that Hague's not friendly – his affability and strong intelligence are well known at Westminster. These qualities make him popular in the Conservative Party, across Parliament and to some extent with the wider public. However, when Hague became Conservative Party leader he was still only thirty-six and his election followed eighteen continuous years of Conservative Party rule under Margaret Thatcher and John Major. He inherited an exhausted and fractious party seemingly determined to pull itself apart and one that had lost any real understanding of what the electorate's primary concerns were, banging on relentlessly about Europe. The country had had enough of the Conservative Party in all shapes and forms.

In another key respect Hague was deeply unfortunate, as much of the country had fallen for the broad, inoffensive smile of Tony Blair, probably one of the best communicators ever to reside in 10 Downing Street. Blair arrived on 1 May 1997 with the huge goodwill of the British people, who were grateful to him partly for ousting a tired and distrusted Tory government, but mostly for providing a confident and optimistic view of Britain that was far from Labour's traditional socialism and much more in tune with aspirant middle-class families. The media fell in love with Tony Blair and he was to enjoy a honeymoon and popularity in office that few could match.

Hague, like Neil Kinnock some ten years earlier, was about to endure four years of unceasing media hostility whilst overseeing

a party that was probably unleadable. He was to suffer the sting-
ing emotional pain and constant disappointments that a string
of political misfortunes, mistakes and misjudgements bring. The
smiling, thrusting, ambitious man who took the Tory crown in
1997 surrendered it a mere four years later downcast, exhausted and
emotionally remote.

William Hague became Leader of the Opposition after beating
Ken Clarke in June of 1997 and was immediately faced with what
could legitimately be described as the most difficult job in politics.

John Howard, then Prime Minister of Australia, once said that
the first year in opposition is terrible, but the years that follow
are worse. It was an accurate description, especially in Hague's
case. The party was down to less than half its previous strength,
something that might be hard for people to imagine – even those
MPs who arrived at Parliament in 2010. One hundred and sixty-
five Conservative MPs were sitting on the opposition's side of
the House in 1997, facing more than 400 Labour opponents on the
government side, and unable to even fill their benches. For Hague
as leader it was a dispiriting spectacle and demonstrated graphically
the size of the task he had undertaken.

William Hague claims he did not particularly want to do the
job of opposition leader. He had assumed that he would support
Michael Portillo if the election was lost and John Major had
stepped aside. But Portillo memorably lost his seat and wasn't even
in Parliament to run as a candidate for the leadership. Hague was

reluctant to step up, but he was convinced that it would be very difficult to hold the Conservative Party together on the issue of Europe and therefore only someone of a Eurosceptic disposition could do the job.

In other words, the party could not be led successfully by any of the candidates who were running. Ken Clarke had many qualities – he was popular with the public, affable, stood no nonsense and had a breadth of experience that was admired by many, including Hague. The trouble was, he was a Europhile. Most of the other candidates on Hague's wing of the party were unlikely to beat Clarke in a leadership contest, but Hague felt there was some hope for the highly experienced and able Michael Howard. In talks, he agreed that he could support Howard as leader.

Their agreement lasted for a little short of twelve hours. When Hague went back to his supporters, who were assembling to rally to his cause, their response was markedly negative. Whilst they were prepared to support him as a bloc, they would splinter in different directions if Howard were the preferred candidate. Howard could not have beaten Clarke in these circumstances and any pact was therefore a doomed enterprise. Hague decided the only solution was to step up to the plate to keep his wing of the party unified. He was not certain of winning and felt he was merely rolling the dice and taking one of life's chances. But despite his initial reluctance, Hague was a young man with intense ambition who believed he could make the Conservative Party electable again.

Michael Howard, only a few years later, would go on to do a good job as Leader of the Opposition, but by then he had slightly reinvented himself and was therefore viewed differently – at least by his party. In 1997, his run saw him finish at the bottom of the poll. The first two ballots were topped by Clarke, but as Howard, Lilley and Redwood dropped out, the majority of their supporters opted for Hague and he topped the third and decisive poll by ninety to seventy-two votes. Hague had won the leadership of the Conservative Party at the tender age of thirty-six – but what was he going to do with his victory?

The task was a huge one: to rebuild the Conservative Party, which had been shattered by an election defeat of enormous proportions. Hague knew it would probably take at least two parliaments for a Conservative Party to get back into government, simply from the mathematics of losing so heavily in 1997.

He decided that he needed to get halfway by the likely 2001 general election, and tried to develop a more modern Conservative Party, getting back in touch with the public who had rejected them through a 'Listening to Britain' campaign. He was also influenced by the 'Compassionate Conservatism' espoused by the then Governor of Texas, George W. Bush.

His promotion to Leader of the Opposition meant Hague was suddenly much higher profile. He had risen from the role of Secretary of State for Wales between 1995 and 1997, a low-ranking Cabinet position but one that would have significant profile in the principality itself. Outside of Wales, Westminster and his constituency in North Yorkshire, few people knew who he was. Suddenly there was intense interest from the media about his background, personality, friends, family and anything else positive or negative (although mainly the latter) that they could write and talk about. Hague found the sudden press attention and intrusion 'an intellectual shock'.

It's knowing that virtually every morning when you wake up, what they're talking about on the radio is what you're doing. You get that to some extent as the Foreign Secretary or as Chancellor of the Exchequer, but as Leader of the Opposition I was really thrust into that world for the first time.

Never having held one of the senior offices of state, this was a big step up for Hague – a leap into the unknown. But he was fortunate in being surrounded by resilient people, particularly his family, for whom this was not the first such readjustment. Hague had been a prodigy as a sixteen-year-old, catching the national headlines with a precocious speech at the Conservative Party conference in 1977 in front of the then Prime Minister Margaret Thatcher. His family had received an early baptism into Hague's world of politics; they could cope.

But it was more difficult for his fiancée, Ffion. The couple were recently engaged and had been looking forward to a quieter life – which would not now transpire. However, Hague describes Ffion as 'a very strong, resilient person'. She too was able to cope with the new-found attention even if she didn't particularly like it.

Hague's private office would also have to be full of robust people and, as it turned out, it would be – but first he had to reinvent that office from scratch. The Conservative Party had been in government for eighteen years; nobody could remember what you did in opposition. Tony Blair's team, when they left the Leader of the Opposition's offices in the House of Commons, had taken literally everything with them. There were just empty shelves, no phones: there was simply nothing there.

Hague had to start again from the ground up, whilst thousands of letters immediately started pouring in. There was no office structure of any kind, not even a single member of staff. Over the following six months Hague built his team and ended up with what he describes as 'a superb team of people. You only have to look at what they've done with their lives subsequently.' Hague is referring to Sebastian Coe, his chief of staff and personal aide; Tina Stowell, now Baroness Stowell of Beeston, who ran his office and was deputy chief of staff; Danny Finkelstein as head of policy; and a certain George Osborne as political secretary and speech writer.

These Hague appointments went on to run the Olympic Games, sit on the government front bench in the House of Lords, serve as associate editor of *The Times* and rise to Chancellor of the Exchequer. Hague had enormous faith in his team and they became very close, which was just as well, as they went through many difficult times and got through them only by good humour and companionship.

In the circumstances of the crushing Conservative election defeat and New Labour's seeming invincibility, the Leader of the Opposition needed not only his team's resilience and 'bounceback-ability' but also the creativity to win enough small victories so that people had some hope. Hague was concerned to keep the Conservative torch burning even if at times the flame was extremely dim.

In this respect, his team found that Prime Minister's Questions and parliamentary debates were useful, since Hague could – against the supposedly insuperable Tony Blair – score some points right from the beginning. After a few months some of these points became really quite important, which helped create a feeling, however small, that there might be a way back and therefore morale did not completely collapse in the party. It was essential that Prime Minister Blair, from his incredibly powerful position, did not have it all his own way and that there was some belief on the Conservative benches that they could make a difference and get back into government one day.

The team spirit and Hague's in particular were kept high when preparing for PMQs. The rehearsal process, led by Osborne and Finkelstein, was generally agreed to be 'hilarious as well as very creative and fascinating'. Laughter was to prove a great tonic for Hague through some hard years and it was partly down to this that, despite the many disappointments and problems, Hague never stopped enjoying the challenge of being the Leader of the Opposition on a day-to-day basis.

> I had those people around me and James Arbuthnot, the Chief Whip, and of course Ffion with all the support she gave as my new wife, which meant that life was OK actually. Life was more often amusing than it was depressing; we had an 'esprit de corps'. Without that camaraderie it would have been very hard to get through a difficult four years.

It was perhaps the camaraderie, however, that led Hague into his first main bump in the road as leader, which many still remember today and which even Cecil Parkinson, whom Hague had appointed as Party Chairman, described as 'juvenile' at the time. Along with his chief of staff, Seb Coe, and the then local MP, Hague visited Thorpe Park and the trio were pictured taking a ride on a log flume wearing baseball caps emblazoned with the word 'HAGUE'. The media reacted badly and for many it became a permanent image of his leadership. Analysing Hague's early performance, the BBC reported:

> For many people, the enduring image – unfairly or not – of William Hague's first 100 days as Conservative leader is that of him wearing a baseball cap on a visit to a theme park. The publicity stunt was an attempt to project a more youthful image for the party but it saw him mercilessly pilloried in the press. Simon Heffer in the *Daily Mail* said the new Conservative leader 'looked like a child molester on a day release scheme'.

It could not be described as the end of Hague's honeymoon period as party leader, because there hadn't been one. He'd had sniping from the old guard and European squabbles from the start. At the end of Hague's first hundred days as Leader of the Opposition, the *Sunday Times* declared in its editorial: 'Hague needs to re-establish his authority and end the sniping.' But for Hague, the focus on the theme park ride is a rewriting of history. He doesn't remember it as a crisis or a real difficulty at the time – it only became a difficulty as other things went wrong and the press then referred back to the pictures and images to poke fun.

Baseball caps were one thing, but there were plenty of other highly personal remarks about Hague, his sexuality, his marriage and his looks, in addition to the political criticism. Hague has been dogged by gay rumours and smears since his days at Oxford. In 1995, Shaun Woodward, who went on to become a Conservative MP before defecting to Labour, was reported to have told colleagues that Hague could not be a Conservative leader because he had a gay past. In 1997, Hague described the rumours of homosexuality as 'water off a duck's back' and said his friends knew them to be ridiculous. Even so, he had to endure suggestions that his engagement to Ffion in 1997 was somehow a contrivance, and even after the wedding he was repeatedly asked about his sexuality. Richard Madeley felt it was fair game on ITV's *This Morning* in 1998 and asked about the rumours.

Despite the personal nature of the remarks about him (the then Labour Party MP Tony Banks called him a foetus), Hague's instinct was to put up a mental barrier, refusing to let it bother him. He ignored the media as much as possible: 'I never read the worst or the best written about me. The experience [of being opposition leader] made me quite indifferent to personal praise or criticism, or polls.' When the attacks were impossible to ignore, Hague's approach was to adjust his mindset, forcing himself not to be bothered, to cope with the unrelenting nature of the personalised criticism.

Due to the scale of the criticism, Hague found himself cutting his emotions off to a quite remarkable degree during his time as Leader of the Opposition, something that has endured to the present day. It was remarked upon quite early during Hague's leadership, naturally as a criticism of his leadership style. His response was robust: 'If you want somebody emotional sitting here, then I'm the wrong person.' His froideur led to unfavourable comparisons with Tony Blair, who had captured the nation's affections with his 'Diana, Queen of Hearts' tribute after the Princess of Wales's untimely death.

Hague is as unrepentant today as he was then:

They want you to be 'normal', but you'll always be criticised for not being 'normal' in some way. But I'm way past that now: if you want somebody normal you've got the wrong person. Obviously I'm not normal: nobody normal takes on being the Leader of the Opposition, or becomes an MP in their twenties or writes history books in their spare time. All these things I've done. I don't pretend to be normal any more.

This attitude is not simply a bit of the characteristic Yorkshireman spilling out. Rather, Hague has thought through his tactics for functioning on an emotional level within the mad world in which he has to exist and remain sane. With a bloody-minded obstinacy he has trained his mind not to care about acceptance or conformity, and to ignore completely other people's views of 'normal'. The less he worries about being normal, the less the criticisms get through his armour.

In the face of this mental agility, the criticism of the Tory leader for what music he'd listen to, what sport he was interested in, or how much alcohol he might drink (in 2000 he agreed he claimed to have drunk fourteen pints in one day), became utterly irrelevant, however much the journalists might have wished it otherwise. This is what allowed William Hague to survive in politics after the hammering he took and then come back and prosper later on.

Yet a coping mechanism such as the one Hague employed only goes so far. One can only speculate, but it is likely Hague employed this method of dealing with events and criticism because he felt them so deeply – they were after all relentless for four years. But as we know from the likes of Jeremy Hunt and Charles Clarke, criticism that strikes at you professionally is more easily dealt with than that which strikes at you personally – such as Andrew Mitchell and Jacqui Smith. When the criticism turned more personal after 2010, as Foreign Secretary Hague displayed a much more emotional response than one would have suspected.

Despite the many obstacles in their path, the Conservatives did make limited progress at various stages in his leadership. By the time of the 2001 general election, the party was in a better tactical position, despite the huge failure at the polls. The party was more united, it had won local elections, it had won the European elections, and most of the severe back-biting in the party had stopped. The party's full-scale nervous breakdown over Europe appeared to be receding.

But these limited successes tended to provide brief interludes in a series of crisis points for Hague in getting to that 2001 election. In the most serious, at the end of 1998, the Leader of Her Majesty's Opposition was in danger of losing control of the Conservative Party opposition in the House of Lords.

The roots of the crisis lay in the new Prime Minister Tony Blair's proposal to remove the hereditary element in the House of Lords. Robert Cranborne, Hague's leader of the Conservatives in the House of Commons, negotiated a pact with the government to retain a small number (later set at ninety-two) of hereditary peers for the interim period, and he believed strongly that the Conservatives should do a deal to let Tony Blair's version of Lords reform go through in return for the maintenance of these ninety-two. After several discussions in shadow Cabinet, it was decided that the party should reject the legislation outright. Cranborne, however, continued negotiations directly with 10 Downing Street behind his party leader's back.

Having failed to get the shadow Cabinet to agree, he came to a secret agreement with Blair and agreed to a government amendment that, for the sake of form, was formally proposed in the Lords by Lord Weatherill, convenor of the crossbench peers. However, Cranborne gave his party's approval without consulting its leader, William Hague, who knew nothing of it.

A big and public bust-up between Hague and Cranborne ensued in front of the Conservative members of the House of Lords. Conservative peers found it quite distressing to see the leader in their House openly arguing with the leader of the party. It then emerged that Cranborne had called a meeting to discuss his agreement with No. 10 in the Moses Room in the House of Lords – a large, grand committee room. Hague got wind of what was going on rather late in the day and moved to put a stop to it.

He decided to gatecrash the afternoon meeting and walked in as Cranborne was explaining what he had organised and agreed. A two-hour debate then ensued, where it became apparent to all that Cranborne had circumvented both the leader of the party and the shadow Cabinet. Cranborne later accepted his error and bad behaviour, saying that he had 'rushed in, like an ill-trained spaniel'. Hague had no choice but to sack him, and appointed Tom Strathclyde, who would go on to serve for nearly fifteen years as Conservative leader in the House of Lords.

Today, Hague acknowledges the seriousness of the situation, describing it as 'a great crisis'. The deal was intended to undermine Hague's authority as party leader and it very nearly succeeded. Had the agreement gone through it could have been a terminal moment for his authority as leader. But he was quick to reassert his authority, and his dismissal of Cranborne was universally supported by the party in the House of Commons.

Nonetheless, the dispute was a particularly difficult episode and came alongside a host of other problems, when things were difficult enough and the poll ratings continually poor. The combination of problems, frustrations and disappointments left Hague thinking about the future, wondering whether his leadership should end sooner rather than later: 'In early 1999, I decided it might be better for the party if I stood down in the middle of that year if we weren't improving by then.' If things did not get better in the next few months he was going to resign after the local and European elections.

He was absolutely serious. The media had made the party a laughing stock, not least at the 1998 Conservative Party conference in Bournemouth. Referring to Monty Python's 'Dead Parrot' sketch, *The Sun* carried a front page that read 'This party is no more ... it has ceased to be ... this is an ex-party. Cause of death: suicide.' Although *The Sun* had long since switched its allegiance, it was still a massive blow to morale and signalled open season on the Conservative Party. The media was reflecting the ongoing bickering over Europe, the continuing lack of discipline in the party – as Cranborne had demonstrated – and the failure to get a grip. Hague was in serious trouble.

The *Sun* headline reverberated around the party and for Hague it was 'one of many difficult press moments', but his attitude throughout all press difficulties was something akin to Dunkirk spirit. Though things were terrible, 'we just had to find our way through it, we had to be resilient. I don't know how to describe it better than that.' Hague and his team often knew that things couldn't get much worse. The constant hope for a change of luck or a turning of the corner kept them going.

Even though *The Sun* ran a more encouraging front page closer to the election – 'The parrot is squawking again' – the change of luck never arrived. *The Sun* still backed Labour in 2001 despite becoming slightly more favourable to Hague personally. Hague's stoicism allowed him to take both the good and the bad news without over-reacting, which helped him to cope in difficult political situations – but the next disaster was never far away and it always knocked any forward momentum quickly into reverse.

One such disaster was the leaking of a speech to be given by Peter Lilley, former Cabinet minister and Hague's deputy as party leader. Lilley had proposed to acknowledge the limits of Thatcherism in this speech. When extracts were leaked, headlines such as 'Tories – We're Abandoning Thatcherism' quickly erupted onto the front pages. It caused a major row in shadow Cabinet and Central Office, and Hague's usual serenity was said to be 'at full stretch'. Danny Finkelstein recalled later that the episode 'genuinely rocked Hague's leadership' and Hague himself told Lilley that his speech 'nearly led to the end of my leadership'.

Hague was at his lowest ebb. He recalls: 'I really wondered if I could keep it together at all. I wondered if there would be an open division in the party, or if I would have to stand down as leader.' Having thought at the end of 1998 that he may resign if he didn't turn the tide by mid-1999, by the spring it looked like he might lose control and be forced to resign. Fortunately, a brief upturn in fortunes came with over 1,000 seats gained in local elections (on 33 per cent turnout of the vote) and an outright win in the European elections – the Conservatives' first national election win since 1992.

These election results saved Hague's leadership: had there been little improvement in these important elections, he maintains he would have gone soon afterwards because the quiet tests he had set himself in January and February would not have been passed. In the event, the results were good, or at least a real improvement, and in the case of the European elections were a big step forward. It was only at this point, two years into his leadership and half-way through the parliament, that Hague thought that whatever happened he would now lead the party into the general election.

His private decision to stay and fight on didn't end the party's problems; there were some extremely tense times in shadow Cabinet in the year before the 2001 election. These tensions were partly about policy – for example, the issue of taxation became very vexed – but there were also some poor dynamics and difficult relationships between shadow ministers that needed careful managing. There were few major stand-up rows, but some of Hague's shadow ministers just couldn't get along. Ironically, things were by no means as bad as the bitter hostility that Hague's nemesis, Tony Blair, faced from his Chancellor, Gordon Brown. But there were certainly times when relations were considerably strained.

Extraordinarily, tempers were raised about things such as staffing decisions, such as who got which and how many people. However, there was general agreement on the strategy for the election and nobody rocked the boat during the campaign. The media contin-ued giving the Conservatives poor publicity throughout Hague's leadership period. His team did try to improve relationships with editors and he would meet with people such as David Yelland and Trevor Kavanagh, the editor and political editor of *The Sun*. But there was no chance of reconciliation: *The Sun*, along with virtually all the rest of the Murdoch stable of newspapers, was still backing the Labour Party. Hague went through the motions of meetings as party leader with the proprietors and editors, but not to any notable effect in terms of changing their editorial stance.

But then, he was not really expecting editors to change course. His efforts were about getting a fairer hearing, and to a limited extent it worked. Hague has never been one to complain about the press.

> We have an incredibly vigorous press in this country. It's like a sailor complaining about the sea. This is what we live on, what we ride on. I think it's very important when you're in a difficult situation not to be self-pitying about it. We'd all volunteered for it, me and my shadow Cabinet colleagues. There are worse situations to be in in life; there are people who come to our constituency surgeries every week who are in worse situations.

Hague's leadership continued to be rocked by troubles. For example, Shaun Woodward defected to Labour in summer 1999, catching Hague by surprise. The impact on Hague, however, was minimal, trivial even. It would not even feature in his list of fifty terrible blows, which he says he could compile from the period. His energy was focused on the big battles, not things like defections. Hague generally was able to wear a veneer of good humour and kept an ability to look for the silver lining on every cloud. It bordered on self-delusion but made him almost indestructible when dealing with the difficult news that kept flooding in.

One particularly heavy blow was the Romsey by-election which the Conservatives lost in May 2000, though the pain was at least somewhat mitigated by the party's 38 per cent share of the vote in the local elections on the same day. Hague treated it as sort of a game of good news, bad news. He felt that after his first year, there was always progress to set alongside the continuing very serious problems, which, alongside his performances in Parliament and successful party conferences, kept his team going. 'Since we had all these things going on, it didn't feel like every day was terrible, we almost had to have that black humour of "it is so terrible, we are just going to be cheery about it and get on with it"', he says.

Hague would not allow panic to take over either himself or his office and positively discouraged people rushing around in difficult situations saying, 'Isn't this terrible?' Such people would not be in his office for very long. Hague wanted to know 'warts and all' what was going on. Worry, anxiety and panic worked against rational behaviour and deployment of the necessary information. When it did happen and people began to flap, Hague's modus operandi was to tell everybody to leave and reassemble in an hour, when he expected them to be calm. When calm, they would decide quietly what to do. Hague says now,

I would not have got through those four years in the party leadership without resilience. It was the night shift, somebody had to do it, but it was dark and nobody knew how long it would be before dawn. In fact it was another decade before there was a real prospect of us winning another general election.

On Thursday 7 June 2001, the Conservative Party suffered its second successive landslide general election defeat at the hands of Tony Blair. After four years of Hague's leadership, the Conservatives had barely made any electoral progress, with a net gain of just a single seat. In the early hours of the next day, a dejected Hague announced to the cameras that he was standing down as Tory leader, surrendering the office he had dreamed about since his teenage years.

Hague felt strongly that the Conservatives' failure to make any meaningful progress from its historic low meant there was 'no doubt' that a change of leadership was necessary. Perhaps he had simply had enough. Either way, having sailed against a surging tide of public and media opinion for four years and having been battered by a succession of storms and crises, often at the hands of his party colleagues, Hague decided that he wanted to take control for once, hence his decision to stand down immediately.

Today he doesn't even acknowledge any wounds that result from his experience – nothing he carries with him from the period, as Jacqui Smith or Andrew Mitchell do for example. He does not see himself in those terms, as the sort of person who gets wounded. He has no self-pity about what has happened to him and gets up in the morning with no bitterness. He hadn't regretted a day of being leader, and nor had he regretted giving it up. His experience as party leader made him realise that the two were not incompatible.

THE AFTERMATH

The rigours of being Leader of the Opposition, and of a deeply unpopular, unfashionable and deeply fractious party, had been useful training for Hague, as he was still to face what was probably the biggest crisis of his political life. Shortly after becoming Foreign Secretary in 2010, completing his political comeback after years of self-imposed near exile following his resignation as party leader, Hague became embroiled in an extraordinarily intense and much more personal crisis revolving around his relationship with Christopher Myers, a family friend of long standing, then aged twenty-five and employed as Hague's special adviser. Having based much of his political career on avoiding personal emotion, and having been hardened by his ordeal as party leader and Leader of the Opposition, suddenly Hague was at his most personally vulnerable.

On Sunday 22 August 2010, not long after Hague had become Foreign Secretary, the *Mail on Sunday* published an article with the title 'Another Hague Special Adviser', pointing out that Hague now had three special advisers when his Labour predecessors each had just two, despite the coalition government's pledge to cut the number and cost of so-called 'Spads'. The *Mail* named Myers as Hague's new adviser, featuring a picture of the two from the previous year strolling along London's Embankment together in a relaxed manner. The *Mail on Sunday* wrote that Hague and Myers' 'friendship' was evident from the picture and quoted a 'Tory source' who said that: 'Chris is incredibly bright and great fun and he and William get on well.' The article went on to emphasise Myers' unusual background for the role, having not worked at Conservative party headquarters, and detailed how Hague had been able to 'land him a job at the Foreign Office because special advisers are hand-picked'.

The initial reaction to the story in the press centred less on relations between Hague and Myers, and more on light-hearted derision of Hague's dress sense, with the picture of the Foreign Secretary wearing jeans, a T-shirt, Nike trainers and wraparound sunglasses, and above all a baseball cap, reminding hacks of the notorious Thorpe Park photographs during his time as Leader of the Opposition, which were described earlier in this chapter. In its editorial, the *Mail on Sunday* recommended that Hague 'for the sake of the dignity of his office ... consign ... his boy-band outfit to the charity shop.'

A follow-up story the next day in the *Daily Mail* again focused on Hague's choice of casual clothes. Under the title of 'Memo to the Foreign Secretary (Age 49): Leave baseball caps to the teen-agers', the article claimed that Hague had been dressed 'like an American tourist on his first trip to Europe'. However, the article also remarked on Hague's 'companion', Myers, saying 'the two joked as they walked along London's Victoria Embankment' and mentioning that Hague's decision to appoint Mr Myers had 'raised eyebrows' in Whitehall. An article in that day's edition of the London *Evening Standard* also mentioned Myers, dragging up negative comments he had made about David Cameron in 2005.

The following day, the political blog 'Guido Fawkes' revealed that it had asked a number of questions under the Freedom of Information Act about Myers' appointment, remarking that it

'[S]eems odd that young Christopher Myers (25) should go from driving William Hague (49) around his constituency during elections, where according to *The Mirror*, "although he never worked at Tory HQ in London ... they became close during campaigns"'. By the following Sunday, a week after the *Mail on Sunday*'s initial article, the blog featured another post under the title of 'Flashback: Hague's gay special adviser'. The post referred to Hague's decision, when Secretary of State for Wales, to appoint a young, openly gay man called Barnaby Towns to be his special adviser, despite Towns having no experience of policy in relation to Wales. The post remarked that Towns had 'certain similarities' to Myers, and rounded off by saying 'To instead hire an inexperienced, poorly qualified young man over and above more qualified candidates does raise the question: what special talent, unseen by the rest of us, does Mr Myers possess? The existence of the government car pool rather makes Mr Myer's experience as Hague's driver during the election campaign redundant...'

Fawkes' probing questions led to a swirl of rumours and suggestions on the internet and Twitter that Myers and Hague were having a gay relationship. The insinuations grew in intensity, reaching a fever pitch on Tuesday 31 August when Fawkes revealed that Hague and Myers had shared a hotel bedroom for at least one night during the general election campaign, with one anonymous witness apparently telling the blog that 'the room sharing couple's body language at breakfast was eye opening'.

To try and stem the tide of rumours, the Foreign Office issued a short but firm statement insisting that Hague and Myers' relationship was professional and warning that anyone making allegations to the contrary was putting themselves at risk of legal action for libel. The statement failed, resulting in Hague and his wife Ffion being forced to issue a deeply personal statement of their own in response to the rumours. They affirmed that they were happily married and discussed their desire to start a family, but also confided their difficulties in doing so, including many miscarriages. It was incredibly risky to put something so personal on public display and, although most were sympathetic, some, usually unnamed, Tories were not and provided a host of unhelpful quotes to the newspapers.

The issue burnt brightly for over two weeks, which would have been a distraction for most politicians dealing with enormous pressure. But Hague insists that during the storm he did not spend very many minutes away from all the duties of the Foreign Secretary, maintaining a determined focus on his Cabinet work. As we have seen, Liam Fox took a similar view of how to deal with events, but failed to make the press back off and ultimately found that the media attention made it impossible for him to do his job. Conversely, Hague's categorical denial of the rumours and deeply personal statement, supported by his wife, may have created the firewall that was needed to protect their privacy.

With '100 per cent backing' from 10 Downing Street throughout and Andy Coulson (then No. 10's Director of Communications) heavily involved, Hague's highly personal statement pulled the rug from under the media and the political bloggers who were driving the rumours. They now faced the challenge of producing hard evidence that Hague was gay and that his denials were false. Not only did they face the implicit threat of legal action if their innuendo and suggestions tipped over into clear allegations without the evidence to back them up, but the mainstream media in particular now had to weigh up whether they wished to be seen to be intruding on the private grief of a couple who had lost children and seemed unable to have the family they wanted. Amidst a surge of sympathy for the Hagues both among the public and at Westminster, although tittle-tattle continued on the internet, the story was more or less killed.

The *Mail on Sunday*'s photograph of Myers and Hague strolling along Victoria Embankment together which gave fuel to the rumours must have been deeply embarrassing, as must the following speculation about Hague's marriage and sexuality. The media and the public were fascinated by Hague's relationship with his special adviser because it was rumoured to be a gay relationship at the heart of a new coalition government. As we also saw with Liam Fox, there's nothing that causes a media frenzy like the suggestion, implicit or otherwise, that a Cabinet minister might be gay.

The Myers episode is still a raw nerve for Hague. The rumours and the media coverage caused enormous pain in the Hague household at the time. The difference with this issue was that it was highly personal and struck directly at his character. Whilst it is possible to block out political difficulties, whether peddled by the media or political opposition, highly personal accusations that affect the way your wife and family might perceive you are not. There can be no doubt that Hague and his wife were extremely distressed and distraught by the allegations and smears. The highly emotional statement reflects the deeply personal reaction of a couple who felt terribly wronged but was also very unusual for Hague. This type of emotionally charged statement was everything that he had avoided in the past – but it was the difference between a strictly political and a personal storm.

But he was able to turn the tables on his detractors when he needed to. It wasn't long before Hague was able to tweet (and he writes his tweets himself) his thanks for his followers' supportive comments and that he was 'enjoying his work'. He went further and tweeted, 'What was said about me was a big lie which I hope has been nailed.'

Having been able to move on from the crisis, Hague has remained in the post of Foreign Secretary up to the time of this book's publication. He has clearly learned lessons from the everyday crises he has faced and taken these into his leadership of the Foreign Office. His aim is clarity: as his blunt statement over the Myers allegations showed, clear, decisive action is his preferred method. In the Foreign Office, he seeks to pursue a clear strategy, with a clear line on where the country is heading, where the organisation is heading and what policies are being pursued.

He likens it to a ship that knows where it is going and 'can take a big wave hitting it'. This may be a reaction to his time as Leader of the Opposition, when the sheer volume of waves buffeting him made it difficult to decide where the ship should even be heading, let alone whether it could get into port in the end. That was 'much more difficult psychologically' for Hague than what he is doing now.

Hague still has no such thing as a typical day, which must be what keeps him motivated in the job. It's not unusual for him to do five countries in five different continents in a few days. It is an around-the-clock, on-call, 365-days-a-year, 24-hours-a-day existence. He works closely with the Prime Minister and attends a lot of the internal meetings at No. 10. When they are in the country, Cameron, Hague and Osborne meet most days. It's a tough schedule and doesn't allow much time for his family.

'I'm not complaining,' says Hague. 'It goes with the territory at such a busy period but for anybody who is interested in a work–life balance, this is not the job for them. You're never away from the work and you get used to that, you get used to anything and we don't complain.'

Fortunately for Hague, he came through his many trials, and has gone on to have the most enjoyable and fulfilling time in his twenty-three years in Parliament. He now feels he's achieving the most he has done in his political career. Hague may not be normal, and some may find his lack of emotion somewhat cold and even rather strange. But his drive, coupled with his rational approach and affability have carried him through the darkest of times.

CHAPTER 10

CONCLUSION

We have seen in this book how politicians' problems can escalate very rapidly into full-blown crises that can bring down the careers of even the high-flying, self-confident and well-connected. Resignations and sackings are not just an opportunity for parties to land blows on and create weaknesses in the ranks of the others (or indeed, rival camps within parties to strike at each other); even in this age of apparent disinterest and cynicism towards politics in Britain, the downfall of a politician or the revelation of wrongdoing is invariably an 'event' and a story with elements of sensationalism, public outrage, personal drama and salacious details to varying degrees.

It is no surprise that the public, fed by an ever eager media, continue to lap up political scandals. Once a scandal or a crisis really starts to build, there is a rapacious demand on the part of the media collectively to move the story on and get the latest scoop. With political parties quick to want a scalp, the way the media and political parties often appear to swarm around a scandal or crisis-hit politician comes to resemble a pack hunt.

As we saw vividly in the cases of Andrew Mitchell and Liam Fox in particular, the pack hunt effect often does not allow politicians who are the subject of allegations or hit by crisis a fair hearing at the crucial time. Newspapers of the right and left are often even less inclined to present a fair and balanced account if the politician is of the opposite leaning. It remains to be seen if the widespread reservations, and even remorse, felt by many in politics and the media over the way Andrew Mitchell was hounded out of his job on the basis of what appear to have been trumped up allegations and fabricated evidence leads to a softening of such behaviour, or whether the Leveson reforms on the ethics of the press have a dampening effect on the aggression and intensity with which the media pursues politicians in trouble and delves into all aspects of their working and private lives. Of course, anything that reduced the vigour of the free press would be a concern in and of itself, and we should assume that for the foreseeable future politicians who find themselves in the eye of the storm will still find themselves fighting against the odds in the battle to save their job, career, or reputation.

So what, if any, lessons can be learned from the experiences described in this book about how to survive a political scandal or crisis? Lesson one is surely to prepare the ground. Whilst many would be tempted to say that the best advice would be to avoid getting into situations giving rise to scandals or crises in the first place, as we have seen in the foregoing chapters, sometimes scandals are simply not foreseeable, for example, those that happen as a result of the actions of others or the publication of private conversations or supposedly private expense claims. Politicians, like everyone else, are bound to make mistakes from time to time in what they say or how they behave and in terms of their judgement about how this might be perceived. Individual scandals can appear from nowhere, but in general they are a foreseeable hazard in political lives and it would be very sensible for politicians to try to put themselves in as strong a position as possible in advance.

As we have seen, a major part of this is securing the support of others. The support and backing of the party leadership is particularly crucial. The clear messages of support from No. 10 and their respective party leaderships enabled Jeremy Hunt and Vince Cable to get through their ordeals when they might otherwise have been forced out. Cable benefitted from his strong standing in his own party and the public, which amounted to a rival powerbase to Nick Clegg. David Cameron's clear statement that he would stand by Hunt, and to protect him from a further investigation over potential breaches of the Ministerial Code, arguably helped put Hunt's detractors off from going in for the kill entirely. Hunt's enemies were unable to force his sacking or resignation, and without a smoking gun or a new angle they were left with no way of moving the story on. Jacqui Smith also received the strong backing, and personal support, of the then Prime Minister Gordon Brown, to the extent that even once she had decided to resign due to the effect on her family, Brown persuaded her to delay her departure.

Nonetheless, even if the Prime Minister and No. 10 backs a politician, their minds can always be changed if the person becomes too much of a liability or a sacrificial lamb is required, as Charles Clarke ultimately found to his cost. The trigger for such a change of heart could be if the person in the eye of the storm suffers a disastrous appearance in the Commons or begins to haemorrhage support on the backbenches or from the party's activists and voters. A good rapport with political colleagues and a strong reputation among activists, constituents and the general public can be huge assets when trouble strikes.

Jeremy Hunt's proactive decision to build up support and relations among backbenchers left him with reserves of political capital that he was able to draw down when he needed it: at a crucial point, Hunt received strong backing from his own side and lived to fight another day. Vince Cable's particularly strong following among Lib Dem activists and supporters, and indeed the wider electorate, was a major factor in the calculations about how to deal with the scandal surrounding him. Nadhim Zahawi also found that good relations built up with colleagues and constituents provided a source of solace and moral support in getting through difficult times.

By contrast, the cases of Andrew Mitchell, Chris Huhne and Charles Clarke all provide examples of the dangers of failing to prepare the ground. Mitchell, in contrast to Hunt, believes that his frequent travels in his International Development portfolio had left him unfamiliar to the new generation of MPs. In addition, the clear-out of the Whips' Office that he had overseen on becoming Chief Whip left a legacy of bitterness and resentment among those sacked, many of whom were experienced insiders who would know how and when to strike.

Huhne, also, had created enemies. In his case, he believes he was perhaps foolish to have made such a powerful enemy as a newspaper group. In Clarke's case, he had failed to deal with a weakness in a key relationship – that with his permanent secretary – until it was too late. He had also grown to accept the relentless hostility from those in the Labour Party close to Gordon Brown as a fact of political life, and arguably did too little to strengthen his own position within Labour ranks and the eyes of the public to defend himself against the Brownites' scheming.

Lesson two would appear to be obvious, but as we have seen, is often not followed in practice. If a politician fails to focus on dealing with a potential scandal in its infancy, it can have huge consequences down the line. The resignation of Liam Fox is the clearest example of this. Whilst Fox believes he could have dealt with any of the allegations made against him individually, by not acting early and decisively, the allegations snowballed and Fox found himself under siege.

In his interview with me, Chris Huhne rightly pointed out that politicians shouldn't always seek to fight back against every attack and allegation, and that some are better left ignored, as to publicly rebut them may give the allegations and those making them the oxygen of publicity and provoke interest in stories that would otherwise have faded away. Whilst what to do is ultimately a matter of judgement, the key point is that it is a judgement that the politician has to make. To try to put their head in the sand or ignore the matter entirely without giving it proper consideration is very unwise. Misjudgements at the start, such as Charles Clarke's initial assessment that the Foreign National Prisoners issue was of interest only to the politically-interested people working in the 'Westminster bubble', can return to haunt politicians later on.

If they act early, particularly powerful and well-connected politicians, or those whose scandals maybe so bad as to cause damage to their parties or destabilise entire governments, may be able to rely on their personal clout or that of their party machine respectively to keep rumours or allegations out of the media, at least for a time. In addition, lawyers are now seeking to use the post-Leveson legal and regulatory landscape to intimidate newspapers into not running damaging stories. But the rise of political bloggers such as Guido Fawkes, outside of the traditional press sector, offers a new route for allegations and rumours to incubate and gather momentum. Once a scandal does break, the experiences recounted in this book point to lessons three and four – the need for a strategy and to mobilise allies.

The need for a politician under pressure to come up with a strategy to get themselves out of trouble highlights one of the great ironies of political crises and scandals. Whilst a politician's judgement and decision-making will never be more important than at these times, several of this book's subjects have reported how the pressure and intrusion destroyed their capacity to make rational decisions. What lesson three really suggests is the need for a politician to get someone trusted to advise them at every stage in times of trouble. Andrew Mitchell has vividly recalled how he felt he needed someone to decide the strategy and tell him what to do. Liam Fox recalled playing this role for others, even if he didn't have anyone to play the role for him. The Mitchell and Fox cases also provide a warning to politicians that they should not necessarily assume that the interests of Downing Street and the party leadership will coincide with their own. A politician should ideally find an experienced and trusted strategist who is acting unequivocally in their interests.

Lesson four highlights the need to mobilise allies. We have seen how Jeremy Hunt mobilised his allies in Parliament ahead of potentially perilous appearances in the House of Commons. Vince Cable, too, canvassed support from his supporters in the Liberal Democrat parliamentary party. Stewart Jackson was able to rely on the support of his local Conservative association for a clear statement that they were standing by him and re-adopting him as their candidate. By contrast, we have seen how Liam Fox apparently went abroad as Defence Secretary without leaving a point of contact in charge of his growing crisis. Charles Clarke made little attempt to reach out to backbenchers, leaving him at the mercy of the briefing campaign against him conducted by Gordon Brown's supporters.

If, despite initial efforts, a scandal has really caught the imagination of the opposition, the media, and possibly the public, and the story is really starting to move quickly, with new revelations coming out or new questions or angles of inquiry opening up, lesson five suggests the need to try and stop the momentum by getting a full statement of defence, with all of the relevant facts from the person's point of view, into the public domain. This should help to put a cap on where stories can go. Responsible commentators will take note, and if the statement of the facts in the politician's defence appears robust, it will give them cause to ponder whether the allegations against them are fair or really have weight, and also to consider the possibility of libel action should they repeat or publish false allegations. At the very least, a statement of the facts should help psychologically to show that the politician is fighting, that there are two sides to the issue, and put some of the onus back on those making the attacks to prove their case. Crucially, it might help the under-fire politician get more of a fair hearing for their defence.

Lesson five is that how politicians conduct themselves throughout their time at centre of the storm is hugely important. The importance of this was made most forcefully by Chris Huhne. Even though Huhne suffered the most dramatic and serious fall of all of the subjects of this book, what is remarkable about his case is that he survived for so long, and could, but for a procedural decision from a judge, have got away with it entirely. With his calm and supremely confident demeanour, and his almost abnormal ability to compartmentalise his personal issues and focus on his job as a government minister, Huhne certainly had much of Westminster convinced that he would survive the trouble he found himself in.

In a slightly different context, Charles Clarke, too, spoke of the paramount importance for a senior government minister to maintain public confidence in their handling of matters at times of crisis. In a more local context, despite being caught up in the great expenses scandal of 2009, Stewart Jackson made it his business to be out and about doing normal things in his constituency – and to be seen doing so.

Lesson six is the importance of character and resolve. Andrew Mitchell appears to have been crippled by the thought that people would wish to make false allegations against him, whilst Chris Huhne, who knew full well that he had committed a criminal offence that could result in him going to jail, was made of sterner stuff and, in the political arena at least, was able to brazen out the allegations against him. Although the merits of each are very different, Huhne, Jeremy Hunt and Stewart Jackson all gained resolve and determination from their belief that, ultimately, they were in the right. Vince Cable and Nadhim Zahawi recall having their resolve bolstered by their families and colleagues.

Ultimately, a politician's ability to withstand the pressure will, to a large extent, depend on the type of scandal or crisis. Some may simply not be survivable. A few months before this book's publication, the Immigration Minister, Mark Harper, resigned after learning that the cleaner he employed was an illegal immigrant. Harper resigned even before the scandal broke, making the judgement that the media and the general public would not accept the apparent hypocrisy of a minister breaking the rules that they were directly responsible for. Similarly, Jacqui Smith was almost certain to lose her marginal seat once the expenses claim for the pornographic films was revealed and she was censured by the Standards Commissioner. It was simply a matter of time before her political career was brought to a halt.

What brought forward Smith's fall was when the crisis started to affect the health and wellbeing of her loved ones. The political then truly became personal. In Andrew Mitchell's case, the destruction of his reputation in political and media circles left him unable to find any sanctuary in his personal life, hastening his departure. Although they would be loath to admit it, the pressure that Liam Fox and William Hague were under got under their skins to the extent that it hastened their decisions to resign as Defence Secretary and Leader of the Opposition respectively.

With the exception of Chris Huhne, one wonders whether the other subjects of this book would have been able to ride out the storm if the crisis they found themselves in stemmed from their family or personal relations, or if the pressure began to seriously affect the welfare of their families. Crises with a particularly personal resonance seem to wear down even the most thick-skinned of politicians in the end.

Finding oneself in the eye of the storm is an occupational hazard of politics. For greater or lesser periods of time, those who do will nearly always find that the crises or scandal overwhelms their capacity to do anything else in their working life. Some will see no way through the torrent of headlines or allegations other than by giving in. Whilst some undoubtedly deserve to be forced out, it would be a pity if the careers of hard-working and dedicated politicians who may have made less serious mistakes continue to be ended by the failure to learn the lessons of how to handle a media crisis.

INDEX

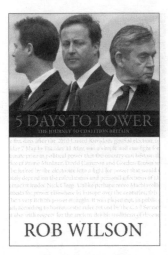

Also available from Biteback Publishing

THE 'TOO DIFFICULT' BOX

THE BIG ISSUES POLITITIANS CAN'T CRACK

CHARLES CLARKE

How do you solve a problem like...
Banking? Drug regulation? Nuclear disarmament?
Prostitution? Pensions?

It's no secret that a myriad of long-term problems facing our society are not effectively dealt with by our current system of government; indeed, many are simply set aside and disappear completely from the short-term political agenda. Why? Because they are 'too difficult' to solve.

Former Home Secretary Charles Clarke argues, along with a cast of heavy hitters from the worlds of politics, academia and public service, that although change is difficult, it is sorely needed, and in some cases, time is not on our side.

352pp hardback, £25

Available from all good bookshops
www.bitebackpublishing.com

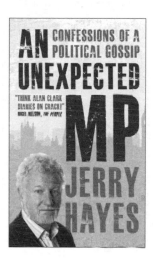

BC	8/14